D1566804

A GOOD START.

C. H. Spurgeon

A GOOD START

A BOOK FOR

YOUNG MEN AND WOMEN

BY

C. H. SPURGEON

WITH A PREFATORY NOTE BY

SIR GEORGE WILLIAMS,

Founder and President of the Young Men's Christian Association

Soli Deo Gloria Publications
...for instruction in righteousness...

Soli Deo Gloria Publications
P.O. Box 451, Morgan, PA 15064
(412) 221-1901/FAX 221-1902

*

A Good Start was first published in 1898
in London by Passmore and Alabaster.
This Soli Deo Gloria reprint is 1995.

*

ISBN 1-57358-008-2

PREFATORY NOTE.

THIS book is intended especially for those who are in the Spring-time of life. It is at this character-forming period that the faithful warning, the wise counsel, and the sympathetic admonition are particularly valuable.

Many young men and young women fail in life from the want of a friendly guiding word at the outset of their career; while many, now occupying good and honorable positions, owe and attribute their success to the timely counsel, at the start, of some friend practically interested in their welfare.

Mr. SPURGEON was emphatically the friend of the young. During the course of his marvellous and God-honoured ministry, his supreme aim was to lead them to Christ, and to encourage and stimulate them in their aspirations after true nobility. Now that his voice is hushed, his powerful pen still speaks; and in this book, with persuasive earnestness, and characteristic force, he shows those who are standing upon the threshold how to make

"A GOOD START."

It is impossible to over-estimate the importance of the start we make in the journey of life, since it necessarily affects and largely determines all that follows.

By personal experience I can bear my unqualified testimony to the wisdom and sagacity of my friend C. H. SPURGEON's teaching. No life can be truly successful unless lived on the lines of Christian principles. The first step must be the surrender of the heart to Christ, and the whole of life's journey must be lived, as it may, in conscious fellowship with Him. It is in this way we form true conceptions of life and duty, and are enabled to give practical embodiment to God's idea concerning us.

I wish for this book a large and growing circulation, and pray that it may be used by God in helping thcusands of young men and young women, not only to make a good start, but also in the upbuilding of a useful, a righteous and God-glorifying life.

George Williams

George Williams

CONTENTS.

———◆———

Contents.

A YOUNG MAN IN CHRIST.

HE is a very different person from a Christian who is only called so because he happens to dwell in a Christian nation, for, unfortunately, the Christianity of Christian nations is something like the gold which is spread over many of our household ornaments—very thin indeed. A little Christian gold leaf goes a very long way, and makes things look respectable, but the gilded articles are not solid gold. National Christianity is no more the real thing than a gilded farthing is a golden coin of the realm. It is a lamentable fact that many who are called Christians, because they belong to a Christian nation, are a grievous dishonour to the name of Christ. The heathen, judging of Christianity by them, have often been heard to say, "We had better·remain as we are than become as drunken, or swear as profanely, or act as viciously as these so-called Christian people do." Our missionaries have found this to be a terrible impediment to the success of their work. I have nothing to do now with merely nominal Christianity. Do what you like with it. Use it as a football if you will.

Neither do I at all identify a man in Christ with one who is profoundly conversant with all the externals of the Christian religion, and who gives himself up devotedly to them, but never looks into the centre—into the heart and kernel—of the matter. It has been well said that, when a man possesses nothing

but the externals of religion, he is generally a great
bigot for them, because he has nothing else; while a
man who has passed beyond the externals into the
very soul and essence of our holy faith, can allow a
thousand differences of opinion in his fellow Christians
as to outward forms, without feeling that these diver-
gencies constitute any barrier whatever to the heartiest
fellowship. No, a man may go as far as ever he
pleases in the observance of religious rites, and become
a stickler for even the tithing of the mint, and the
anise, and the cumin of ceremonials, and sacraments, and the like, and yet, for all that, he may not
be "a man in Christ."

I am also bound to confess that there are members
of evangelical churches, not devotees of ceremonialism,
but advocates for the barest simplicity of worship,
who make a very high profession of being real
Christians, and talk a great deal about vital godliness,
who, nevertheless, are not men in Christ. The church
of Christ has been plagued by hypocrites from the
first day even until now. There was a Judas among
the apostles themselves. Are you surprised at this?
I confess I am not. Because Christianity is in itself
so valuable, therefore there are many worthless imita-
tions. Men counterfeit a sovereign because it is
worth having; if it ever should become worthless the
trade of the counterfeiter would be gone: and it is
because the possession of true godliness is so valuable
a thing that there are so many who pretend to have
it who know nothing about it. I distrust full often
those who are so loud in their professions. I know
that the cart which rings the loudest bell when it goes
through the street only carries dust; but I never hear

a bell rung when they are carrying diamonds or bullion through the city. The best actions which are wrought in this world are for the most part done in secret by those who desire no eye to observe them except the eye of the Almighty God. But some, under the pretence of doing that, are rather standing up for themselves than for Christ, and are not quite so anxious to cry, " Behold the Lamb of God," as to say, "Come, see my zeal for the Lord of hosts! Admire me, and see what a wonderful honour I am to the religion of Jesus Christ." Now I give up these religious pretenders to the world's utmost scorn. I have nothing to say in their defence, but very much by way of disgust at their untruthfulness. I am now going to speak about men who are *really in Christ*— who have Christ in their heart of hearts, and are *in Christ* themselves.

A man in Christ *is* a man, and, being a man, he is, therefore, imperfect. I have heard a great deal of talk of perfect men, but I believe that a little examination with the microscope, or even without it, would have discovered a great many flaws in them, and probably more in those who thought themselves perfect than in others who have honestly confessed their imperfections. There is not a Christian man whose entire life might be read instead of the Bible his life would need notes, ,additions, and corrections ere it would exactly correspond with the perfect law of the Lord. Ask him, " May I learn Christian principles entirely from your conduct ? " and he would say, " I wish I could answer ' Yes.' I am striving to make my conduct so, but I am afraid that, though I try to copy my Master, stroke by stroke, yet I have failed in some respects to reproduce the full spirit of the grand original. I wish you could read me, and see the spirit of the New Testament in every little as well as in every great transaction of my life. But," he will add, "I make mistakes, and, what is more, I am sometimes off my guard, and allow the old nature that remaineth in me to come to the front. I am not what I ought to be, nor what I want to be, nor, blessed be God, what I shall be. You may, I trust, see something of Christ in me," he will say, "but yet I am a man ; and, being in this body, I am compassed with infirmities." Ought not you who may not happen to be Christians to recollect this when you are judging Christian men ? Be fair ! Be honest ! If a man receives not the gospel himself, at least let him treat those who do receive it with the candour which he would desire to be exercised towards himself. A man in Christ is a man ; do not expect him to be an angel.

When I say that a man in Christ *is* a man, I mean that, if he be truly in Christ, he is therefore manly. There has got abroad a notion, somehow, that if you become a Christian, you must sink your manliness and turn milksop. It is supposed that you allow your liberty to be curtailed by a set of negations which you have not the courage to break through, though you would if you dared You must not do this, and you must not do the other : you are to take out your backbone and become molluscous ; you are to be sweet as honey towards everybody, and every atom of spirit is to be evaporated from you. You are to ask leave of ministers and church authorities to breathe, and to become a sort of living martyr, who lives a wretched life in the hope of dying in the odour of sanctity. I do not believe in such Christianity at all. The Christian man, it seems to me, is the noblest style of man ; the freest, bravest, most heroic, and most fearless of men. If he is what he should be, he is, in the best sense of the word, a man all over, from the crown of his head to the sole of his foot.

He is such a man because he has realized his own personal responsibility to God. He knows that to his own Master he stands or falls,—that he shall have to give an account in the day of judgment for his thoughts, his words, his acts, and therefore he does not pin himself to any man's sleeve, be he priest, or minister, or whatever he may be called. He thinks for himself, takes the Bible and reads for himself, and comes to God in Christ Jesus personally, and on his own account. He is not content to do business with underlings, but goes to the Head of the great firm.

Being accustomed also to endeavour to do that which is right at all times, if he be a man in Christ, he is bold. I have heard a story of a man who was so continually in debt, and was so frequently arrested for it, that one day, catching his sleeve on a palisade, he turned round, and begged to be let alone this time. There are many people who go about the world much in that style. They know that they have done wrong, and that they are doing wrong, and therefore "conscience doth make cowards" of them. But when the conscience has been quieted, and the heart knows itself to be set upon integrity and established in the right, the Christian man is not afraid to go anywhere.

Moreover, a man in Christ is accustomed to wait upon his Lord and Master to know what he should

2

do, and he recognizes Christ's law as being his sole
rule ; and for this reason he is the freest man under
heaven, because he does not recognize the slavish
rules which make most men tremble lest they should
lose caste, or forfeit the favour of the society in which
they move. He obeys the laws of his country because
Christ has commanded him so to do, and all things
that are right and true are happy bonds to him which
he does not wish to break ; but, as for the foolish
customs and frivolous conventionalities which fashion
ordains, he delights to put his foot through them and
trample them under his feet, for he saith, " I am Thy
servant, O Lord : Thou hast loosed my bonds."
When he has anything to say, he looks at it to see
whether his Master would approve ; and as to whether
the world would approve or not, it does not enter into
his mind to consider. He has passed beyond that.
He knows the liberty wherewith Christ makes us free.
When we become the servants of Christ we cease to
be the servants of men. When Christ's yoke is upon
you, then are you free to do the right, whoever may
forbid. From that time forth you would not speak the
thing that is not true to win the acclamation of a
nation, nor suppress the truth though the universe
itself should frown. A man in Christ bowing the
knee before the King Himself, is too high-minded to
pay obeisance to error or to sin, though robed in all
the pomp of power : he stands up for the right and
for the true, and if the heavens should fall he would
be found erect.

A man in Christ is manly because he is trustful in
Providence. If he be what I mean by a man in
Christ, he believes that whatever happens here below

is ordered and arranged by his great Lord and
Master ; so that when anything occurs which sur-
prises, and, perhaps, perplexes him for the moment,
he feels that it is still not an accident nor an un-
foreseen calamity beyond the Divine control. He
believes that his Lord has a bit in the mouth of the
tempest and reins up the storm. He is sure that
Jesus, as King of kings, sits in the cabinets of princes,
and rules all the affairs of mankind. Therefore he is
not afraid of evil tidings, his heart is fixed, trusting in
the Lord. If he live as a Christian should live, when
others are seized with sudden panic he can wait, for
he knows that there is no panic in Heaven, and that
all things are rightly arranged and ordered by the
powers above ; and committing his present case into
the hand of his Lord Jesus, he both patiently waits
and quietly hopes. He is thus enabled to become
master of the situation, for he is cool and calm when
others are confused. He is a match for any man in
the hour of perplexity, for he has flung his burden off
his shoulder and left it with his Lord ; and now he
can go forward with a clear and placid mind to do his
business, or to leave it undone, as the peril of the
moment demands. A Christian man, because he
trusts in the God of providence, quits himself like
a man, and is not afraid.

And he is manly because, being a Christian, he
does not wince when he is opposed, for he expects
opposition. That man who, being in Christ, never
meets with any opposition, must either be very
happily circumstanced, or he must somewhat conceal
his religion ; for from the first day until now it has
been found that those who will live godly in Christ

Jesus must suffer persecution. The man in Christ, being a true man, does not fret about that. If a joke is passed off at his expense, he knows that it breaks no bones. There is a little laughter over a story, more witty than true, and perhaps a sneer or two caused by a very nasty sarcasm ; but he bargained for that, he discounted that matter, when he became a Christian. Nay, he has by degrees become so accustomed to it that if it pleases other people it does not annoy him. And, now and then, when a sting does go rather near the heart, he is accustomed to sing to himself very quietly—

> " If on my face, for Thy dear name,
>   Shame and reproach shall be,
>   I'll hail reproach and welcome shame,
>   For Thou'lt remember me."

And so he gets to be a man all round ; and it frequently happens that, as he pursues the even tenor of his way, those who at first despised him come to respect him. Men trust him, and finding him upright, they honour him, yea, and honour him for his fidelity to his convictions ; for even with those who care not for Christianity, there is a something which makes them reverence the man who is truly what he professes to be. We have seen it so in others, and may each one of us live long enough to experience it in our own persons. Let but the Christian live on and live well, and he will live down opposition ; or, if the opposition live, he will live above it and flourish all the more.

I have said that a man in Christ is truly a man, and I will give one more meaning to my words. *He is a man in this sense, that he is human ; or, lengthen out that last syllable, and it gives a better meaning—he is humane.* Of all who live, the man in Christ is the most human, or really humane man. In this he follows the Lord Christ Himself. Ah, what a man He was! There is not one whom you could not point to and say, " *That* is an Englishman," or " *That* is a German," or " *That* is a Jew," or " *That* is a philosopher," or " *That* is a clergyman," or something or other special and distinguishing ; but of Jesus of Nazareth, as a human being, you could never say more than that He was *a Man*—the noblest, purest specimen of man who ever adorned this world. A Man belonging to all nations, to all ranks, and to all times. Do you not notice in His life how everything that had to do with man lay near His heart. I take it that He was more completely a man than John the Baptist, although there are many who consider that type of manhood to be the very highest. John the Baptist came neither eating nor drinking, but Jesus came both eating and drinking ; and though the ribald throng said, " He is a drunken Man and a wine-bibber," yet He was all the more a perfect Man, because He was a Man among men. He dwelt not in the wilderness, but among the people ; he did not eat locusts and wild honey, but went to a marriage, and ate bread at the tables of those who invited Him. He entered into all that men did except their sins. He was in all things to man a true brother and friend. He was not merely a preacher, but He became a Physician and healed bodily sicknesses. The Christian man should always be the helper of everything which promotes the health and welfare of the people. Christ was not only the bread from Heaven, but the Giver of

the bread of this life to the poor and needy. He fed
thousands of the fainting with loaves and fishes. If
all other hands be fast closed, the hand of the
Christian man should always be open to relieve
human necessity. Being a man, the believer is a
brother to all men—rich and poor, sick or healthy—
and he should seek their good in every possible way,
aiming still at the highest good—namely, the saving
of their souls.

The man in Christ, also, is in the best sense human,
in that he lives in a real world and not in an ideal
castle of sanctity. He has found out how to spiritualise
the secular. He elevates the things of a man till they
become the things of God. You know it is very easy
to secularise the spiritual : there are many who have
desecrated the pulpit, and brought it down to the
lowest conceivable level ; but there are others who
have elevated the carpenter's bench, and made it holiness unto the Lord. The man in Christ does exactly
that. He does not draw a line and say, " So far
my life in Christ goes, but no further. My religion is
a thing for Sundays, but not for the Stock Exchange.
' Do unto others as you would that they should do
unto you,' is a golden rule for the domestic circle, but
it will not do for our market at all, we could not get a
living on any such principle." No, he considers that
no religion can be true which unfits a man for a lawful
calling. His religion is part and parcel of himself.
He does not carry it *with* him, but it is *in* him. It has
come to be himself. A man in Christ makes up his
accounts as sacredly as he reads his Bible. He does
not pray upon his knees alone, but in all places he
speaks with God. His service of God is not confined

to his closet and his pew ; but, diligent in business, he is still fervent in spirit, serving the Lord. All that Christians do ought to be done as unto the Lord— whether ye eat or drink, or whatsoever ye do. If there be anything in this world that you cannot do to the glory of God you must not do it at all ; but all things that ye do, if ye be Christian men, are to be done in the spirit of faith, in the presence of God, unto the glory of God Most High. Such is the man in Christ Jesus.

This also is his mark as a man, and humane—that he does not seek his own. Of course, going into the world, he does not tell a lie and say, " I am not going to try and make money. I shall not aim at doing business." He *is* going to do that, and he would be a great fool for going upon 'Change at all if he had no such object. Does he become a broker with the design of *losing* his capital? Nobody would believe him if he said so. But he goes to his office with this determination : " I am not going to rob another to enrich myself. It shall not be said of one single grain of gold that I add to my heap that I wrung it from the widow or the orphan, or that I gained it by driving a man hard who needed it more than I, or that I wrested it from one who, whether he needed it or not, had a better right to it than I." The doctrine of the worlding in Horace, " Get money, fairly if thou canst, but by all means get it," is no Christian doctrine : it is worthy of heathenism in its worst form. The man in Christ, though active, earnest, intelligent, and by no means a simpleton (if you think he is, deal with him and see), yet is so far a fool in some men's esteem that when he sweareth to his own hurt he changeth not ;

and when he seeth a fine opportunity, at which some
would leap, he standeth back and says, "So do not I,
because of the fear of the Lord." He cannot and he
will not bring a curse upon himself by an unjust
action, and this, it seems to me, makes him all the
more truly a man, though it manifests one of the
characteristics of his being a man in Christ Jesus.

Young men, to you I would honestly say that I
should be ashamed to speak of a religion that would
make you soft, cowardly, effeminate, spiritless, so that
you would be mere naturals in business, having no
souls of your own, the prey of every designing knave.
Young men, I have tried the faith of Jesus Christ, and
I have found it give me "pluck"—that is an old
Saxon word, but it is exactly what I mean. It puts
soul into a man, firmness, resolution, courage. If he
is in the habit of talking with his own conscience, and
his Bible, and his God, he can look the whole universe
in the face—ay, and a universe of devils, too—and
never feel the slightest fear. Why should he? Is not
the Eternal on the Christian man's side? Is not the
risen and reigning Christ on his side? Is not the
blessed Spirit his friend? Yes, the angels of God, and
providence, and time, and eternity, and all the forces
that exist, are his allies, save only those of death and
hell, and these his Lord has conquered and trampled
under foot. I would that every young man were
enlisted in the army of Christ right early, for none
make such good soldiers as those who begin while yet
they are young.

A YOUNG MAN IN CHRIST.

II. SOME ADVANTAGES.

FIRST, he has this advantage, that the greatest burden of this mortal life is off his shoulders. He is less weighted in the race of life than the common run of men, for the main load of life is sin—the consciousness of having broken the law of God—the consciousness that all is not right—and this is gone from him. A man in Christ has confessed his sin to his Lord, and there is a promise that he that confesseth and forsaketh his sin shall find mercy. He has looked to Jesus, the great sin-bearer, and he has seen his sin transferred to the great Substitute, and put away ; and now, being justified by faith, he has peace with God through Jesus Christ his Lord. That great load has gone. Oh, when a man sits quietly down in his chamber, in the watches of the night, and begins to think over his past life, it will make him tremble, unless he is able to see Christ on the cross putting away sin, and unless he knows by the assuring witness of the Holy Spirit that his transgressions were thus put away. Then the nightmare of a half-awakened conscience is gone. The dreadful burden from the spirit is lifted, and he is another man—a man with this grand advantage that, whatever burdens he has to bear, the intolerable weight of sin is gone, for ever gone.

Better still, he has this further advantage—that all

his major matters are perfectly safe. He goes into business, and knows that he may lose a fortune with the turn of the market. But his best capital is settled upon him for ever. Perhaps, week after week, everything goes against him, but he is like Little Faith, of whom John Bunyan says that the thieves robbed him of all his spending money, but they could not find his jewels, for they were hidden away where none could reach them. So the Christian man feels, " I may lose everything I possess of worldly sub-stance, but I shall never lose my God ; and while I possess my God and my hope, I can still ' take arms against a sea of troubles, and, by opposing, end them.' " I heard of one who walked down the Borough, with unpardonable carelessness, carrying a considerable sum of money in his coat pocket. As he stopped to look in a window, a thief stole his handkerchief from that very pocket. He was not at all distressed about that loss when he reached home, for, thrusting his hand to the bottom of his pocket, he found that the parcel which contained his money was all right, and he said, " I have not lost the money. I care little for the handkerchief ! " In fact, he seemed so rejoiced that his money was safe, that he forgot the other loss. And so a man in Christ considers all that he has on earth to be inconsiderable compared with the treasure of salvation which he knows to be secure in the keeping of his Redeemer. His sorrow at pre-sent losses is swallowed up in the joy that his eternal interests are safe.

As for his minor burdens, here is another point of advantage to a Christian man, for by faith he leaves them with his God, and expects that good will come of them. He believes that any evil which happens to him is robbed of its sting, and made to benefit him. He bears the ills of life, not with patience merely, but with acquiescence in the will which appointed them, because he has this promise, "All things work together for good to them that love God, to them who are the called according to His purpose." So the great load of sin is gone, and now the little loads are transformed, and the great future is all secure. Is not such a man placed at a wonderful advantage in the race of life?

Besides all this, the fear of death is removed from him. Is there anything more desirable than to have the dread of the grave, and of that "something after death," effectually taken away? This body loves not death, nor is it right that it should, for the law of self-preservation is stamped upon us, and a natural fear of the mortal stroke hangs over us, lest in some evil hour we should be tempted to suicide. But, still, the Christian frequently looks forward to the time of his departure with intense expectancy and joy, and he awaits the inevitable hour with perfect peace; for he knows that his Redeemer liveth, and that though the worms devour his body, yet in the latter day he shall in his flesh behold his God; and so he looks serenely forward to the awful article of death. Is he not placed at an advantage compared with all the rest of mankind?

Let me say, also, of the man in Christ that he has other advantages. First, in the troubles of life he has always a Friend. You know how it is in business: if you have a good substantial friend at your back you feel very much confidence. Many a young man

starting in life would have made a failure of it if he
had not had a wise and wealthy friend to support him.
Sometimes he slips out of the Exchange or out of the
warehouse and consults this friend, and he feels that
his advice is worth anything to him.   Now, a man in
Christ has a Friend.   It is his own living, loving Lord,
who condescends to speak with him, and to hear his
griefs, and to render him assistance.   Many a Christian man here knows what it is to seek that Friend
and to speak with Him.   Would not your heart have
broken sometimes if it had not been that you could
pour your sorrows into that fraternal bosom, and tell
them to One who, having been tempted in all points
like as you are, is able to meet your cares?

It is a great thing to a man, too, in the voyage of
life, to have a good chart; and that the Christian man
has.   He has the Bible, to tell him exactly what to do
under all circumstances.   You say to me, " Nay, not
so ; that Book gives general principles, but not specific
directions."   But these general principles are appli-
cable under all circumstances.   And then I claim that
the Bible does more than supply principles, for its
words are often as peculiarly appropriate to the individual case as if it alone had been in the writer's
eye.   I have often met with texts which seemed
written for that very hour, and which met my case to
the very letter.   Every believer knows that this has
occurred to himself.   After all, the general principle
of the Bible—namely, always to do the right—is the
best chart a man can have.   When ambassadors meet
in the council chamber, the man who baffles all the
rest with his policy is he who has no policy at all
except that of speaking the truth.   He puzzles rivals,

and they suspect him of some deep-laid scheme. All over the world, the man whom nobody can match or defeat is the man who has no policy but that of believing that a straight line is the shortest distance between any two places, which straight line he means to follow, leaving the zigzag and the serpentine to those who prefer them. The Word of God makes the simplest mind wise and discreet because it sets forth the path of right and truth.

Moreover, remember that a Christian man has a mighty Spirit dwelling within him. Every Christian has had a miracle wrought upon him, nature has been outdone by a Divine work. The Holy Ghost has come to dwell in the believer, and He, in addition to enlightening him as to his way, arouses him that he may follow it. He chides him when he goes astray, and inspires him with ardour and zeal to press forward in his life-work. Our own spirits flag and falter, but the Divine Spirit is free from all imperfections, and where He dwells there is a power, a light, and a joy unknown to all the world besides.

A man in Christ has also the high privilege of being under the special care of God. He and his brethren are like an army marching through a foreign country, having at its back *a good basis of supplies.* Many a commander has been beaten because he has advanced too far and forgotten the necessity of a commissariat ; but the Christian knows that it is written, "My God shall supply all your needs according to His riches in glory by Christ Jesus." His firm conviction is that "they that wait upon the Lord shall not want any good thing," and, then being free from care, he has in his bosom a well-spring of content.

Moreover, he has a constant communication with head-quarters where his stores are laid up, for prayer telegraphs to Heaven, and the promise is, "Before they call I will answer, and while they are yet speaking I will hear."

A man in Christ is a man upon an extraordinary vantage ground. The world cannot understand him, nor can it withstand him ; he lives in it and yet lives above it : he glides through it, not without trial, for "in the world ye shall have tribulation," but certainly without defeat, for Christ has said, "Be of good cheer : I have overcome the world." If I did not look for immortality, but expected to die like a dog, I would wish to be a Christian. If there were no hereafter, if there were no Heaven or hell, if I only had to meet the sorrows and the strifes and the cares and burdens of this mortal life, I would ask Thee, great Master, Jesus, to let me enlist beneath Thy banner ; for Thou giveth peace and rest to all who come beneath Thy sway.

A man in Christ ; how came he to be there ? It began this way,—he became uneasy at finding himself where he was ; he had many pleasures, but they palled ; he used to enjoy many sweets, but suddenly they cloyed upon his appetite. The world grew stale ; the sere and yellow leaf was on all its trees, its flowers were faded, and its lights burned low. The man began to look about him ; upward and downward, within, around, things looked as he did not like to see them ; he became thoughtful, and the more he thought the more unrestful was his heart. Dare you all think ? I know some men who dare not. If they were set to think for two hours about their own condition they would almost as soon be flogged. Well, that is how it came about. The man considered himself and his ways, and, as he considered, he discovered that he was without God, without Christ, and without hope. He knew that he must die; he trembled as to what must be his destiny, and a voice within him warned him to expect the worst. The good Spirit was sobering him, and this was the beginning of a blessed change.

Then there came across his path the good news that Jesus Christ was able to save him, and to save him at once; that He could blot out all his past sins, and ransom him from the present power of evil. Only one thing must be done, Christ must be trusted; and he did trust Him. It took him some time to see that this simple trust in Jesus could do such wonders, but he did at last see it, and he trusted Jesus Christ for everything, and found sin pardoned and conquered, too. He had always trusted himself before, but now he gave himself up to be saved by the merit of the Redeemer's blood, and by the power of the Holy Spirit. Then he became indeed " a man in Christ."

What further happened to him when he was saved ? A new life was given him. A miracle was wrought upon him : a life that he had never before possessed was bestowed upon him, which elevated him as much above other men as other men are elevated above the beasts that perish. He was body and soul before, but the Spirit of God came upon him, and gave him a spirit—a third and higher principle which lifted him up into a spiritual region in which he lived as a spiritual man. He found himself altogether changed from his former self: the things he loved before he hated now, and the things he hated before he loved now. He could see what he never saw before, and what seemed very attractive to him once had lost all its attractiveness. He would not have known his former self if he had met him in the street. In fact, his old self and he fell out once for all, and they have never made up the quarrel, and never will. He is a new creature in Christ Jesus; old things have passed away, behold all things have become new.

Since he has received that life he has entered farther into Christ, for he has consecrated himself to Christ. If he be a man in Christ of the type I mean, he has given himself up, and all that he has, to serve his Saviour. Some Christians remind me of the little boys who go to bathe: all frightened and shivering they enter the water just a little—up to their ankles they wade, and shiver again; but the man who is really in Christ is like the practised swimmer, who plunges into the stream head first and finds waters to swim in. He never shivers. It braces him: he rejoices in it. And see how at home he is in the river of grace. It has become his element. Now for him "to live is Christ." He has devoted himself, his substance, and all that he has to the glory of God. This is the man who understands the happiness of religion in a manner far beyond the conception of the half-and-half professor, who has only religion enough to make him miserable.

An American gentleman said to a friend, " I wish you would come down to my garden and taste my apples." He asked him about a dozen times, but the friend never did come, and at last the fruit-grower said,

" I suppose you think my apples are good for nothing, and so you won't come and taste them." "Well, to tell you the truth," said the friend, "I have tasted them. As I went along the road I picked up one that fell over the wall, and I never tasted anything so sour in all my life ; and I do not particularly wish to have any more of your fruit." "Oh," said the owner of the garden, " I thought it must be so. Why, don't you know, those apples round the outside are for the special benefit of the boys. I went fifty miles to select the sourest sorts to plant all round the orchard, so that the boys might give them up as not worth stealing ; but if you come inside you will find that we grow a very different quality there ; sweet as honey." Now, you will find that on the outskirts of religion, there are a number of " *Thou shalt nots,*" and "*Thou shalts,*" and convictions and terrors and alarms, but these are only the bitter fruits with which this wondrous Eden is guarded from thievish hypocrites. If you can pass by the exterior bitters, and give yourself right up to Christ and live for Him, your peace shall be like a river, and your righteousness like the waves of the sea ; and you shall find that the fruits of " this apple tree among the trees of the wood " are the most luscious that can be enjoyed this side our eternal home.

I commend to all who are men in Christ the fullest consecration to His service ; and may this lead to your being in Christ in the sense of being enthusiastic for Him. The flower and crown of true religion is enthusiasm. Until the name of Jesus stirs our blood, as the blast of the clarion stirs the soldier in the day of battle—till we feel that for Jesus we could die—

3

till we "count all things but loss that we may win Christ and be found in Him"—till we grow so enthusiastic that we wish all others to know what we know, and to feel what we feel, and to enjoy what we enjoy—till we become so intense that our religion becomes aggressive, and seeks to conquer the world, we have not known the full elevating power of the gospel of Jesus Christ.

RUTH'S FAITH AND REWARD.

MANY young converts deserve encouragement because they have left all their old associates. Ruth, no doubt, had many friends in her native country, but she tore herself away to cling to Naomi and her God. Perhaps she parted from a mother and a father; if they were alive she certainly left them to go to the Israelites' country. Possibly she bade adieu to brothers and sisters, certainly she quitted old friends and neighbours; for she resolved to go with Naomi, and share her lot. She said, "Intreat me not to leave thee, or to return from following after thee: for whither thou goest, I will go: and where thou lodgest, I will lodge: thy people shall be my people, and thy God my God: where thou diest, will I die, and there will I be buried: the Lord do so to me, and more also, if ought but death part thee and me."

The young convert is an emigrant from the world; and has become, for Christ's sake, an alien. Possibly he had many companions, friends who made him merry after their fashion, men of fascinating manners, who could easily provoke his laughter, and make the hours dance by; but, because he found in them no savour of Christ, he has forsaken them, and for Christ's sake they have forsaken him. Among his old associates he has become as a speckled bird, and they are all against him. You may, perhaps, have

seen a canary which has flown from its home, where
it enjoyed the fondness of its mistress : you have seen
it out among the sparrows.   They pursue it as though
they would tear it into pieces, and they give it no
rest anywhere.   Just so the young convert, being no
longer of the same feather as his comrades, is the
subject of their persecution.   He endures trials of
cruel mockings, and these are as hot irons to the soul.
He is now to them a hypocrite, and a fanatic ; they
honour him with ridiculous names by which they
express their scorn.   In their hearts they crown him
with a fool's cap, and write him down as both idiot
and knave.   He will need to exhibit years of holy
living before they will be forced into respect for him ;
and all this because he is quitting their Moab to join
with Israel.   Why should he leave them?   Has he
grown better than they?   Does he pretend to be a
saint?   Can he not drink with them as he once did ?
He is a protest against their excesses, and men don't
care for such protests.   Can he not sing a jolly song,
as they do?   Forsooth, he has turned saint ; and
what is a saint but a hypocrite ?   He is a deal too
precise and Puritanical, and is not to be endured in
their free society.   According to the grade in life, this
opposition takes one form or another, but in no case
does Moab admire the Ruth who deserts her idols to
worship the God of Israel.   It is not natural that the
prince of darkness should care to lose his subjects, or
that the men of the world should love those who
shame them.

   When Ruth had quitted her former connections, it
was wise and kind for Boaz to address her in the words
of comfort which I will again quote : "The Lord

recompense thy work, and a full reward be given thee of the Lord God of Israel, under whose wings thou art come to trust."

Next, Ruth, having left her old companions, had come amongst strangers. She was not yet at home in the land of Israel, but confessed herself "a stranger." She knew Naomi, but in the whole town of Bethlehem she knew no one else. When she came into the harvest-field the neighbours were there gleaning, but they were no neighbours of hers: no glance of sympathy fell upon her from them; perhaps they looked at her with cold curiosity. They may have thought, "What business has this Moabitess to come here to take away a part of the gleaning which belongs to the poor of Israel?" I know that such feelings do arise among country people when a stranger from another parish comes gleaning in the field. Ruth was a foreigner, and, of course, in their eyes an intruder. She felt herself to be alone, though under the wings of Israel's God. Boaz very properly felt that she should not think that courtesy and kindness had died out of Israel; and he made a point, though he was by far her superior in station, to go to her and speak 'a word of encouragement to her.

The new convert is like Ruth in another respect: he is very lowly, in his own eyes. Ruth said to Boaz, "Why have I found grace in thine eyes, that thou shouldest take knowledge of me, seeing I am a stranger?" She said again, "Let me find favour in thy sight, my lord; for that thou hast comforted me, and for that thou hast spoken friendly unto thine handmaid, though I be not like unto one of thine handmaidens." She had little self-esteem, and there-

fore she won the esteem of others. She felt herself
to be a very inconsiderable person, to whom any
kindness was a great favour; and so do young
converts, if they are real and true. We meet with a
certain class of them who are rather pert and forward,
as the fashion of the day is in certain quarters; and
then we do not think so much of them as they do of
themselves; but the genuine ones, who are truly
renewed, and who really hold out, and continue to
the end, are always humble, and frequently very
trembling, timid, and diffident. They feel that they
are not worthy to be put among the children, and
they come to the Lord's table with holy wonder. I
remember when I first went to the house of God as a
Christian youth, who had lately come to know the
Lord, that I looked with veneration on every officer
and member of the church. I thought them all, if
not quite angels, yet very nearly as good; at any
rate, I had no disposition to criticise them, for I felt
myself to be so undeserving.

The young convert is like Ruth because he has
come to trust under the wings of Jehovah, the God of
Israel. Herein is a beautiful metaphor. You know
that the wing of a strong bird especially, and of any
bird relatively, is strong. It makes a kind of arch,
and from the outer side you have the architectural
idea of strength. Under the wings, even of so feeble
a creature as a hen, there is a complete and perfect
refuge for her little chicks, judging from without.
And then the inside of the wing is lined with soft
feathers for the comfort of the young. The interior
of the wing is arranged as though it would prevent
any friction from the strength of the wing to the

weakness of the little bird. I do not know of a more
snug place than under the wing-feathers of the hen.
Have you never thought of this? Would not the
Lord have us in time of trouble come and cower
down under the great wing of His omnipotent love,
just as the chicks do under the mother? Here is the
Scripture—" He shall cover thee with His feathers,
and under His wings shalt thou trust : His truth shall
be thy shield and buckler." What a warm defence!
When I have seen the little birds put their heads out
from under the feathers of their mother's breast, it
has looked like the perfection of happiness ; and
when they have chirped their little notes, they have
seemed to tell how warm and safe they were, though
there may have been a rough wind blowing around
the hen. They could not be happier than they are.
If they run a little way, they are soon back again to
the wing, for it is house and home to them ; it is
their shield and succour, defence and delight. This
is what our young converts have done : they have
come, not to trust themselves, but to trust in Jesus.
They have come to find a righteousness in Christ,—
ay, to find everything in Him, and so they are trusting, trusting under the wings of God. Is not this
what you are doing ?

There is no rest, no peace, no calm, no perfect quiet,
like that of giving up all care, because you cast your
care on God ; renouncing all fear, because your only
fear is a fear of offending God. Oh, the bliss of
knowing that sooner may the universe be dissolved,
than the great heart that beats above you cease to be
full of tenderness and love to all those who shelter
beneath it ! Faith, however little, is a precious plant

of the Lord's right hand planting; do not trample on it, but tend it with care, and water it with love.

What is the full reward of those who come to trust under the wings of God?

I would answer that a full reward will come to us in that day when we lay down these bodies of flesh and blood, that they may sleep in Jesus, while our unclothed spirits are absent from the body but present with the Lord. In the disembodied state we shall enjoy perfect happiness of spirit; but a fuller reward will be ours when the Lord shall come a second time, and our bodies shall rise from the grave to share in the glorious reign of the descended King. Then we shall behold the face of Him we love, and shall be like Him. Then shall come the adoption—to wit, the redemption of our body; and we, as body, soul, and spirit, a trinity in unity, shall be for ever with Father, Son, and Holy Ghost, our triune God. This unspeakable bliss is the full reward of trusting beneath the wings of Jehovah.

But there is a present reward, and to that Boaz referred. There is in this world a present recompense for the godly, notwithstanding the fact that many are the afflictions of the righteous. Years ago a brother minister printed a book, "How to Make the Best of Both Worlds," which contained much wisdom; but at the same time many of us objected to the title, as dividing the pursuit of the believer, and putting the two worlds too much on a level. Assuredly, it would be wrong for any godly man to make it his object in life to make the best of both worlds in the way in which the title is likely to suggest. This present world must be subordinate to the world to come, and is to be cheerfully sacrificed to it, if need be. Yet, be it never forgotten, if any man will live unto God he will make the best of both worlds, for godliness has the promise of the life that now is, as well as of that which is to come. Even in losing the present life for Christ's sake we are saving it, and self-denial and taking up the cross are but forms of blessedness. If we seek first the kingdom of God and His righteousness, all other things shall be added to us.

Do you ask, " How shall we be rewarded for trusting in the Lord ? " I answer, first, by the deep peace of conscience which He will grant you. Can any reward be better than this ? When a man can say, " I have sinned, but I am forgiven," is not that forgiveness an unspeakable boon ? My sins were laid on Jesus, and He took them away as my scapegoat, so that they are gone for ever, and I am consciously absolved. Is not this a glorious assurance ? Is it not worth worlds ? A calm settles down upon the heart which is under the power of the blood of sprinkling ; a voice within proclaims the peace of God, and the Holy Spirit seals that peace by His own witness ; and thus all is rest. If you were to offer all that you have to buy this peace, you could not purchase it ; but where it purchasable it were worth while to forego the dowry of a myriad worlds to win it. If you had all riches and power and honour, you could not reach the price of the pearl of peace. The revenues of kingdoms could not purchase so much as a glance at this jewel. A guilty conscience is the undying worm of hell ; the torture of remorse is the fire that never can be quenched : he that hath that worm gnawing at his heart and that fire burning in his bosom is lost already.

On the other hand, he that trusts in God through Christ Jesus is delivered from inward hell-pangs : the burning fever of unrest is cured. He may well sing for joy of soul, for heaven is born within him, and lies in his heart like the Christ in the manger. O harps of glory, ye ring out no sweeter note than that of transgression put away by the atoning sacrifice !

What was the full reward that Ruth obtained ? I do not think that Boaz knew the full meaning of what he said. He could not foresee all that was appointed of the Lord. In the light of Ruth's history we will read the good man's blessing. This poor' stranger, Ruth, in coming to put her trust in the God of Israel, was giving up everything : yes, but she was also gaining everything. If she could have looked behind the veil which hides the future, she could not have conducted herself more to her own advantage than she did. She had no prospect of gain ; she followed Naomi, expecting poverty and obscurity ; but in doing that which was right, she found the blessing which maketh rich. She lost her Moabitish kindred, but she found a noble kinsman in Israel. She quitted the home of her fathers in the other land to find a heritage among the chosen tribes, a heritage redeemed by one who loved her. Ah ! when you come to trust in Christ, you find in the Lord Jesus Christ one who is next of kin to you, who redeems your heritage, and unites you to Himself. You thought that He was a stranger ; you were afraid to approach Him ; but He comes near to you, and you find yourself near to His heart, and one with Him for ever.

Yes, this is a fair picture of each convert's reward. Ruth found what she did not look for—she found a husband. It was exactly what was for her comfort and her joy, for she found rest in the house of her husband, and she became possessed of his large estate by virtue of her marriage union with him. When a poor sinner trusts in God he does not expect so great a boon, but, to his surprise, his heart finds a Husband, and a home, and an inheritance priceless beyond all conception ; and all this is found in Christ Jesus our Lord. Then is the soul brought into loving, living, lasting, indissoluble union with the Well-beloved, the unrivalled Lord of love. We are one with Jesus. What a glorious mystery is this !

Ruth obtained an inheritance among the chosen people of Jehovah. She could not have obtained it except through Boaz, who redeemed it for her ; but thus she came into indisputable possession of it. When a poor soul comes to God, he thinks that he is flying to Him only for a refuge, but, indeed, he is coming for much more ; he is coming for a heritage undefiled, and that fadeth not away. He becomes an heir of God, a joint-heir with Jesus Christ.

PARENTS' GOOD PRINCIPLES TO BE FOLLOWED.

"My son, keep thy father's commandment, and forsake not the law of thy mother : bind them continually upon thine heart, and tie them about thy neck. When thou goest, it shall lead thee ; when thou sleepest, it shall keep thee ; and when thou awakest, it shall talk with thee. For the commandment is a lamp ; and the law is light ; and reproofs of instruction are the way of life."—Proverbs vi. 20—23.

YOU have here the advice of King Solomon, rightly reckoned to be one of the wisest men ; and verily he must be wise indeed who could excel in wisdom the son of David, the king of Israel. It is worth while to listen to what Solomon has to say ; it must be good for the most intelligent young person to listen, and to listen carefully, to what so experienced a man as Solomon has to say to young men. But I must remind you that a greater than Solomon—the Spirit of God—inspired the Proverbs. They are not merely jewels from earthly mines, but they are also precious treasures from the heavenly hills ; so that the advice we have here is not only the counsel of a wise man, but the advice of that Incarnate Wisdom who speaks to us out of the Word of God. Would you become the sons of wisdom ? Come and sit at the feet of Solomon. Would you become spiritually wise ? Come and hear what the Spirit of God has to say by the mouth of the wise man. I want to show that true religion comes to many recommended by parental example.

Unhappily, it is not so with all. There are some who had an evil example in their childhood, and who never learnt anything that was good from their parents. I adore the sovereignty of Divine grace that there are many who are the first in their families that ever made a profession of faith in Christ. They were born and brought up in the midst of everything that was opposed to godliness; yet they are, they can themselves hardly tell you how, brought out from the world as Abraham was brought from Ur of the Chaldees. You have special cause for thankfulness; but it should be a note to be entered in your diary, that your children shall not be subjected to the same disadvantages as you yourselves suffered. Since the Lord has looked in love upon you, let your households be holiness to the Lord, and so bring up your children that they shall have every advantage that religious training can give, and every opportunity to serve the living God.

But there are many who have had the immense privilege of godly training. Now, to my mind, it seems that a father's experience is the best evidence that a young man can have of the truth of anything. My father would not say that which was false anywhere to anyone; but I am sure that he would not say it to his son; and if, after serving God for fifty years, he had found religion to be a failure, even if he had not the courage to communicate it to the whole world, I feel persuaded that he would have whispered in my ear, " My son, I have misled you. I was mistaken, and I have found it out." But when I saw the old man, the other day, he had no such information to convey to me. Our conversation was con-

cerning the faithfulness of God ; and he delights to
tell of the faithfulness of God to him and to his
father, my dear grandfather, who has now gone up
above. How often have they told me that, in a long
lifetime of testing and proving the promises, they
have found them all true, and they could say, in the
language of the hymn,—

> " 'Tis religion that can give
> Sweetest pleasures while we live ;
> 'Tis religion must supply'
> Solid comfort when we die."

As for myself, if I had found out that I was mistaken,
I should not have been so foolish as to rejoice that
my sons should follow the same way of life, and
should addict themselves with all their might to
preaching the same truth that I delight to proclaim.
Dear son, if thou hast a godly father, believe that the
religion upon which he has fixed his faith is true.
He tells thee that it is so ; he is, at any rate, a sincere
and honest witness to thee ; I beseech thee, therefore,
forsake not thy father's God.

Then I think that one of the most tender bonds
that can ever bind man or woman is the affection of a
mother. Many would, perhaps, break away from the
law of the father ; but the love of the mother, who
among us can break away from that ? So, next, a
mother's affection is the best of arguments. You
remember how she prayed for you. Among your
earliest recollections is that of her taking you between
her knees, and teaching you to say,—

> " Gentle Jesus, meek and mild,
> Look upon a little child."

Perhaps you have tried to disbelieve, but your

mother's firm faith prevents it. I have heard of one who said that he could easily have been an infidel if it had not been for his mother's life and his mother's death. Yes, these are hard arguments to get over ; and I trust that you will not get over them. You remember well her quiet patience in the house when there was much that might have ruffled her. You remember her gentleness with you when you were going a little wild. You hardly know, perhaps, how you cut her to the heart, how her nights were sleepless because her boy did not love his mother's God. I do charge you, by the love you bear her, if you have received any impressions that are good, cherish them, and cast them not aside. Or, if you have received no such impressions, yet at least let the sincerity of your mother, for whom it was impossible to have been untrue,—let the deep affection of your mother, who could not, and would not betray you into a lie,— persuade you that there is truth in this religion which now, perhaps, some of your companions are trying to teach you to deride. "My son, keep thy father's commandment, and forsake not the law of thy mother."

I think that, to any young man, or any young woman either, who has had a godly father and mother, the best way of life that they can mark out for themselves is to follow the road in which their father's and mother's principles would conduct them. Of course, we make great advances on the old folks, do we not ? The young men are wonderfully bright and intelligent, and the old people are a good deal behind them. Yes, yes ; that is the way we talk before our beards have grown. Possibly, when we have more sense, we shall not be quite so conceited of it. At any rate, I, who am not very old, and who dare not any longer call myself young, venture to say that, for myself, I desire nothing so much as to continue the traditions of my household. I wish to find no course but that which shall run parallel with that of those who have gone before me. And I think, dear friends, that you who have seen the holy and happy lives of Christian ancestors, will be wise to pause a good deal before you begin to make a deviation, either to the right or to the left, from the course of those godly ones. I do not believe that he begins life in a way which God is likely to bless, and which he himself will, in the long run, judge to be wise, who begins with the notion that he shall upset everything, that all that belonged to his godly family shall be cast to the winds. I do not seek to have heirlooms of gold or silver; but, though I die a thousand deaths, I can never give up my father's God, my grandsire's God, and *his* father's God, and *his* father's God. I must hold this to be the chief possession that I have; and I pray young men and women to think the same. Do not stain the glorious traditions of noble lives that have been handed down to you; do not disgrace your father's shield, bespatter not the escutcheons of your honoured predecessors by any sins and transgressions on your part. God help you to feel that the best way of leading a noble life will be to do as they did who trained you in God's fear!

Solomon tells us to do two things with the teachings which we have learned of our parents. First he says, " Bind them continually upon thine heart," for they are worthy of loving adherence. Show that you love

4

these things by binding them upon your heart. The
heart is the vital point ; let godliness lie there, love
the things of God. If we could take young men and
women, and make them professedly religious without
their truly loving godliness, that would be simply to
make them hypocrites, which is not what we desire.
We do not want you to' say that you believe what
you do not believe, or that you rejoice in what you
do not rejoice in. But our prayer—and, oh, that it
might be your prayer, too !—is that you may be
helped to bind these things about your heart. They
are worth living for, they are worth dying for, they
are worth more than all the world besides, the immortal principles of the Divine life which come from
the death of Christ. " Bind them continually upon
thine heart."

And then Solomon, because he would not have us
keep these things secret as if we were ashamed of
them, adds, " and tie them about thy neck," for they
are worthy of boldest display. Did you ever see my
Lord Mayor wearing his chain of office ? He is not
at all ashamed to wear it. And the sheriffs with their
brooches ; I have a lively recollection of the enormous
size to which those ornaments attain ; and they take
care to wear them, too. Now then, you who have
any love to God, tie your religion about your neck.
Do not be ashamed of it, put it on as an ornament,
wear it as the mayor does his chain. When you go
into company, never be ashamed to say that you are
a Christian ; and if there is any company where you
cannot go as a Christian, well, do not go there at all.
Say to yourself, " I will not be where I could not in-
troduce my Master ; I will not go where He could not

go with me." You will find that resolve to be a great help to you in the choice of where you will go, and where you will not go ; therefore bind it upon your heart, tie it about your neck. God help you to do this, and so to follow those godly ones who have gone before you !

I hope that I am not weak in wishing that some may be touched by affection to their parents. I have had very sorrowful sights, sometimes, in the course of my ministry. A dear father, an honest, upright, godly man, what lines of grief I saw upon his face when he came to say to me, " Oh, sir, my boy is in prison ! " I am sure that, if his boy could have seen his father's face as I saw it, it would have been worse than prison to him. I have known young men,—nice boys, too, they were,—and they have gone into situations in the city, where they have been tempted to steal, and they have yielded to the tempter, and they have lost their character. Sometimes, the deficiency has been met, and they have been rescued from a criminal's career ; but, alas, sometimes they have fallen into the hands of a wicked woman, and then woe betide them ! Occasionally, it has seemed to be sheer wantonness and wickedness that has made them act unrighteously. I wish I could let them see, not merely the misery they will bring upon themselves, but show them their mother at home when news came that John had lost his position because he had been acting dishonestly, or give them a glimpse of their father's face when the evil tidings reached him. The poor man stood aghast ; he said, " There was never a stain upon the character of any of my family before." If the earth had opened under the godly man's feet, or if the good mother could have gone down straight into the grave, they would have preferred it to the life-long tribulation which has come upon them.   Therefore, I charge you, young man, or young woman, do not kill the parents who gave you life, do not disgrace those who brought you up ; but I pray you, instead thereof, seek the God of your father, and the God of your mother, and give yourselves to the Lord Jesus Christ, and live wholly to Him.

Solomon also tells us that true religion guides us under all circumstances.   He says, in the 22nd verse, that when we are active, there is nothing like true godliness to help us : " When thou goest, it shall lead thee."   He tells us that, when we are resting, there is nothing better than this for our preservation : "When thou sleepest, it shall keep thee."   And when we are just waking, there is nothing better than this with which to delight the mind : " When thou awakest, it shall talk with thee."   I do not intend to expand those three thoughts except just to say this.   When thou art busiest, thy religion shall be thy best help. When thy hands are full of toil, and thy head is full of thought, nothing can do thee more service than to have a God to go to, a Saviour to trust in, a Heaven to look forward to.   And when thou goest to thy bed to sleep, or to be sick, thou canst have nothing better to smooth thy pillow, and to give thee rest, than to know that thou art forgiven through the precious blood of Christ, and saved in the Lord with an everlasting salvation.

WHY THE YOUNG NEED CONVERSION.

I WANT to say something to you who are unconverted. Our great anxiety is that you should
know the Lord at once ; and our reason is, that it will
prepare you for the world to come. Whatever that
world may be, full of vast mysteries, yet no man
is so prepared to launch upon the unknown sea as
the one who is reconciled to God. who believes
in the Lord Jesus Christ, who trusts Him, and rejoices
in the pardon of his sin through the great atoning
sacrifice, and experiences in his own heart the
marvellous change which has made him a new
creature in Christ Jesus

I think that is a very good reason for seeking the
Lord, that you may be prepared for eternity. I saw
an aged friend, who was eighty-six, and her faculties
failing ; she said, "I have no fear, I have no fear of
death ; I am on the Rock, I am on the Rock Christ
Jesus. I know whom I have believed, and I know
where I am going." It was delightful to hear the
aged saint speak like that ; and we are always hearing
such talk from our dear friends when they are going
home, they never seem to have any doubts. I have
known some who, while they were well, had many
doubts ; but when they came to die, they seemed to
have none at all, but were joyously confident in
Christ.

But there is another reason why we want our friends converted, and that is, that they may be prepared for this life. I do not know what kind of life you have set before yourself. Perhaps some young men hope to have lives consecrated to learning, and crowned with honour. Possibly, some have no prospect but that of working hard to earn their bread with the sweat of their brow; some have begun to lay bricks, or to drive the plane, or to wield the pen. There are all sorts of ways of mortal life; but there is no better provision and preparation for any kind of life on earth than to know the Lord, and to have a new heart and a right spirit. He that rules millions of men will do it better with the grace of God in his heart; and he that had to be a slave would be the happier in his lot for having the grace of God in his heart You that are young, you that are masters and you that are servants, true religion cannot disqualify you for playing your part here in the great drama of life; but the best preparation for that part, if it is a part that ought to be played, is to know the Lord, and feel the power of Divine grace upon your soul.

Let me just show you how this is the case. The man who lives before God, who calls God his Father, and feels the Spirit of God working within him a hatred of sin and a love of righteousness, he is the man who will be conscientious in the discharge of his duties; and, you know, that is the kind of man, and the kind of woman, too, that we want nowadays. We have so many people who want looking after; if you give them anything to do, they will do it quickly enough if you stand and look on; but the moment you turn your back, they will do it as slovenly or as slowly, and as badly as can be. They are eye-servants only. If you were to advertise for an eye-servant, I do not suppose anybody would come to you ; yet they might come in shoals, for there are plenty of them about. Well now, a truly Christian man, a man who is really converted, sees that he serves God in doing his duty to his fellow-men. "Thou God seest me," is the power that ever influences him ; and he desires to be conscientious in the discharge of his duties, whatever those duties may be. I once told the story of the servant girl who said that she hoped she was converted. Her minister asked her this question, "What evidence can you give of your conversion?" She gave this among a great many other proofs, but it was not a bad one ; she said, "Now, sir, I always sweep *under* the mats." It was a small matter, but if you carry out in daily life that principle of sweeping under the mats, that is the kind of thing we want. Many people have a little corner where they stow away all the fluff and the dust, and the room looks as if it was nicely swept, but it is not. There is a way of doing everything so that nothing is really done, but that is not the case where there is grace in the heart. Grace in the heart makes a man feel that he would wish to live wholly to God, and serve God in serving man. If you get that grace, you will have a grand preparation for life as well as for death.

The next thing is, that a man who has a new heart has imparted to him a purity which preserves him in the midst of temptation. Oh, this dreadful city of London ! I wonder that God endures the filth of it. I frequently converse with good young men, who

come up from the country to their first situation in
London, and the first week they live in London is a
revelation to them which makes their hair almost
stand on end. They see what they never dreamt of.
Well now, you young fellows who have just come to
London, give yourselves to the Lord at once, I pray
you. Yield yourselves to Jesus Christ, for another
week in London may be your damnation. Only a
week in London may have led you into acts of
impurity that shall ruin you for ever. Before you
have gone into those things, devote yourselves to
God, and to His Christ, that with pure hearts and
with right spirits you may be preserved from " the
pestilence that walketh in darkness, and the destruction that wasteth at noonday," in this terribly
wicked city. There is no hope for you young men
and young women in this great world of wickedness
unless your hearts are right towards God. If you go
in thoroughly to follow the Lamb whithersoever He
goeth, He will keep and preserve you even to the end ;
but if you do not give yourselves to the Lord, whatever good resolutions you may have formed, you are
doomed—I am sure you are—to be carried away with
the torrents of iniquity that run down our streets to-
day. Purity of heart, then, which comes from faith
in Christ, is a splendid preparation for life.

So also is truthfulness of speech. Oh, what a
wretched thing it is when people will tell lies ! Now,
the heart that is purified by the grace of God, hates
the thought of a lie. The man speaks the truth, the
whole truth, and nothing but the truth ; and he is
the man who shall pass through life unscathed, and
shall be honoured, and in the long run successful.

He may have to suffer for a time through his truthfulness; but, in the end, nothing shall clear a way for him so well as being true in thought and word and deed.

If you love the Lord with all your heart, you will also learn honesty in dealing; and that is a grand help in life. I know that the trickster does sometimes seem to succeed for a time; but what is his success? It is a success which is only another name for ruin. Oh, if all men could be made honest, how much more of happiness there would be in the world! And the way to be upright among men is to be sincere towards God, and to have the Spirit of God dwelling within you.

Again, true religion is of this value, that it comforts a man under great troubles. You do not expect many troubles, my young friend, but you will have them. You expect that you will be married, and then your troubles will be over; some say that *then* they begin. I do not endorse that statement; but I am sure that they are not over, for there is another set of trials that begin then. But you are going to get out of your apprenticeship, and then it will be all right; will it? Journeymen do not always find it so. But you do not mean always to be a journeyman; you are going to be a little master. Ask the masters whether everything is pleasant with them in these times. If you want to escape trouble altogether, you had better go up in a balloon; and then I am sure that you would be in trouble for fear of going up too high or coming down too fast. But troubles will come; and what is there that can preserve a man in the midst of trouble like feeling that things are safe in his Father's hands? If you can say, "I am His child, and all things are working together for my good. I have committed myself entirely into the hands of Him who cannot err, and will never do me an unkindness," why, you have on a breastplate which the darts of care cannot pierce, you are shod with the preparation of the gospel of peace, and you may tread on the briars of the wilderness with an unwounded foot.

True religion will also build up in you firmness of character, and that is another quality that I want to see in our young people nowadays. We have some splendid men, and some splendid women, too. I should not be afraid, if the devil himself were to preach, that he would pervert them from the faith; and if all the new heresies that can rise were to be proclaimed in their presence, they know too well what the truth is ever to be led astray. But, on the other hand, we have a number of people who are led by their ears. If I pull their ear one way, they come after me; if they happen to go somewhere else, and somebody pulls their ear the other way, they go after him. There are lots of people who never do their own thinking, but put it out, as they put out their washing; they do not think of doing it at home. Well now, these people are just like the chaff on the threshing-floor, and when the wind begins to blow, away they go. Do not be like that. Dear young sons and daughters of church-members, know the Lord. May He reveal Himself to you at once; and when you do know Him, and get a grip of the gospel, bind it to your heart, and tie it about your neck, and say, "Yes, I am going to follow in the footsteps of those I love, and especially in the footsteps of the Lord Jesus Christ.

> " ' Through floods and flames, if Jesus lead,
> I'll follow where He goes.' "

God help you to do it! But first believe in the Lord Jesus Christ; trust yourselves wholly to Him, and He will give you grace to stand fast even to the end.

A. DESIRABLE SERVICE.*

WHEN a young man starts in life he is apt to enquire of an older person in this fashion—"I should like to get into such a business, but is it a good one; you have been in it for years, how do you find it?" He seeks the advice of a friend who will tell him all about it. Some will have to warn him that their trade is decaying, and that there is nothing to be done in it. Others will say that their business is very trying, and that if they could get out of it they would; while another will answer for his work, "Well, I have found it all right. I must speak well of the bridge which has carried me over. I have been able to earn a living, and I recommend you to try it." I give my own experience, and therefore I wish to say concerning the service of the Lord that I have never regretted that I entered it. Surely, at some time or other since I put on Christ's livery and became His servant, I should have found out the evil if there had been anything wrong in the religion of Jesus. At some time or other I should have discovered that there was a mistake, and that I was under a delusion. But it has never been so. I have regretted many things which I have done, but I have never regretted that I gave my heart to Christ and became a servant of the Lord. In times of deep depression—and I have had plenty of them—I have

---

* Psalm cxvi. 16.

feared this and feared the other, but I have never had any suspicion of the goodness of my Master, the truth of His teaching, or the excellence of His service; neither have I wished to go back to the service of Satan and sin. Mark you, if we had been mindful of the country from whence we came out, we have had many an opportunity to return. All sorts of enticement have assailed me, and siren voices have often tried to lure me upon the rocks; but never, never since the day in which I enlisted in Christ's service have I said to myself, "I am sorry that I am a Christian; I am vexed that I serve the Lord." I think that I may, therefore, honestly, heartily, and experimentally recommend to you the service which I have found so good. I have been a bad enough servant, but never had a servant so lovable a Master or so blessed a service.

I would add this personal testimony: so blessed is the service of God, that I would like to die in it! When I have been unable to preach through physical pain, I have taken my pen to write, and found much joy in making books for Jesus; and when my hand has been unable to wield the pen, I have wanted to talk about my Master to somebody or other, and I have tried to do so. I remember that David Brainerd, when he was very ill, and could not preach to the Indians, was found sitting up in bed, teaching a little Indian boy his letters, that he might read the Bible; and so he said, "If I cannot serve God one way, I will another. I will never leave off this blessed service." This is my personal resolve, and verily, there is no merit in it, for my Lord's service is a delight. It is a great pleasure to have anything to

do for our great Father and Friend, and most affectionately, for your own good, I commend the service
of God to you.

To serve God is the most reasonable thing in the
world. It was He who made you : should not your
Creator have your service? It is He who supports
you in being : should not that being be spent to
His glory? If you had a cow or a dog, how long
would you keep either of them if it were of no service
to you? Suppose it were a dog, and it never fawned
upon you, but followed at everybody else's heel, and
never took notice of *you*—never acknowledged *you* as
its master at all : would you not soon tire of such a
creature? Which of you would make an engine, or
devise any piece of machinery, if you did not hope that
it would be of some service to you? Now, God has
made you, and a wonderful piece of mechanism is the
body, and a wondrous thing is the soul ; and will you
never obey Him with the body or think of Him with
the mind? This is Jehovah's own lament : " Hear, O
heavens, and give ear, O earth : for the Lord hath
spoken, I have nourished and brought up children,
and they have rebelled against Me. The ox knoweth
his owner, and the ass his master's crib : but Israel
doth not know, My people doth not consider." To
have lived to be one-and-twenty without God is a
terrible robbery ; how have you managed it? To
have lived to be thirty or forty, and never to have
paid any reverence to Him who has kept the breath
in your nostrils, without which you would have been
a loathsome carcass in the grave long ago, is a base
injustice ; how dare you continue in it? To have
lived so long, and, in addition to that, to have often

insulted God ; to have spoken against Him ; to have profaned His day ; to have neglected His Book ; to have turned your back on the Son of His love—is not this enough ? Will you not cease from such an evil course ? Why, there are some men who cannot bear five minutes' provocation, nay, nor five seconds', either. It is "a word and a blow" with them ; only the blow frequently comes first. But here is God provoked by the twenty years at a stretch—the thirty, the forty, the fifty years right on ; and yet He bears patiently with us. Is it not time that we render to Him our reasonable service ? If He has made us, if He has redeemed us, if He has preserved us in being, it is but His due that we should be His servants.

And this is the most honourable service that ever can be. Did you say, "Lord, I am Thy servant"? I see, coming like a flash of light from Heaven, a bright spirit, and my imagination realizes his presence. There he stands, a living flame. It is a seraph fresh from the throne, and what does he say ? "O Lord, I am Thy servant." Are you not glad to enter into such company as this ? When cherubim and seraphim count it their glory to be the servants of God, what man among us will think it to be a mean office ? A prince, an emperor, if he be a sinner against God, is but a scullion in the kitchen compared with the true nobleman who serves the Lord in poverty and toil. This is the highest style of service under heaven : no courtier's honour can rival it. Knights of the Garter or what else you like lose their glories in comparison with the man whom God will call servant in the day of the appearing of our Lord and Saviour Jesus Christ. You are in grand company, young friend, if you are a servant of God.

And let me note that this service is full of beneficence. If I had to engage in a trade, I should like to spend my time and strength in a pursuit which did no hurt to anybody, and did good to many. Somehow, I do not think that I should like to deal in deadly weapons—certainly not in the accursed drink. I would sooner starve than earn my bread by selling that or anything else that would debase my fellowmen, and degrade them below the level of brute beasts. It is a grand thing, I think, if a young man can follow a calling in which he may do well for himself, and be doing well to others at the same time. It is a fine thing to act as some have done who have not grown rich by grinding the faces of poor needlewomen, or by stinting the wage of the servant behind the counter, but have lifted others up with them, and as they have advanced, those in their employment have advanced also. That is a something worth living for in the lower sphere of things. But he that becomes a servant of God is doing good all along, for there is no part of the service of God which can do any harm to anybody. The service of the Lord is all goodness. It is good for yourself, and it is good for your fellow-men ; for what does God ask in His service but that we should love Him with all our heart, and that we love our neighbour as ourselves? He who does this is truly serving God by the help of His Spirit, and he is also greatly blessing men. I say, it is a most beneficent work to engage in ; and therefore it is that I commend it to you—for its reasonableness, its honourableness, and its beneficence.

5

It is the most remunerative work under heaven.
"Not always to-day," someone may say. Yet I venture
to say, "Always to-day." To serve God is remunerative *now*. How so? Certainly not in hard cash, as
misers rightly call their gold ; but in better material
A quiet conscience is better than gold ; and to know
that you are doing good is something more sweet in
life than to know that you are getting rich or famous.
Have not some of us lived long enough to know that
the greater part of the things of this world are so
much froth upon the top of the cup, far better blown
away than preserved ? The chief joy of life is to be
right with yourself, your neighbour, your God. And
he that gets right with God—what more does he
want ? He is paid for anything that he may suffer in
the cause of God by his own peace of mind. There
was a martyr once in Switzerland standing barefooted
on the fagots, and about to be burnt quick to the
death—no pleasant prospect for him. He accosted
the magistrate who was superintending his execution,
and asked him to come near him. He said, "Will
you please to lay your hand upon my heart. I am
about to die by fire. Lay your hand on my heart.
If it beats any faster than it ordinarily beats, do not
believe my religion." The magistrate, with palpitating heart himself, and all in a tremble, laid his
hand upon the martyr's bosom, and found that he
was just as calm as if he was going to his bed rather
than to the flames. That is a grand thing! To
wear in your buttonhole that little flower called
heart's-ease, and to have the jewel of contentment in
your bosom—this is heaven begun below : godliness
is great gain to him that hath it.

I think that all that we can get in this world is paltry, because we must leave it, or it must leave us, in a very short time. Young men—but in how very short a time, if you all live, will your hair be powdered with the grey of age! How short life is! How swift is time! The older we get the faster years fly. That only is worth my having which I can have for ever. That only is worth my grasping which death cannot tear out of my hand. The supreme reward of being a servant of God is hereafter; and if, young man, you should serve God and you should meet with losses here for Christ's sake, you may count these "light afflictions which are but for a moment," and think them quite unworthy to be compared with the glory that shall be revealed; for there is a resurrection of the dead; there is a judgment to come; there is a life eternal; there is a Heaven of unutterable splendour; there is a place in that Heaven for every one of us who become true servants of the living God.

I think that I hear somebody saying, "Well, I do not want to be a servant." You cannot help it, my friend; you cannot help it. You must be a servant of somebody. "Then I will serve myself," says one Pardon me, brave sir, if I whisper in your ear that if you serve yourself you will serve a fool. The man who is the servant of himself—listen to this sentence —the man who is the servant of himself is the slave of a slave; and I cannot imagine a more degrading position for a man to be in than to be the slave of a slave. You will assuredly serve somebody. You will wear fetters, too, if you serve the master that most men choose. Oh, but look at this city—this city full of free men; do the most of them know real liberty?

Look at this city full of "free-thinkers." Is there any
man that thinks in chains like the man who calls
himself a free-thinker? Is there any man so credu-
lous as the man who will not believe in the Bible?
He swallows a ton of difficulties, and yet complains
that we have swallowed an ounce of them. He has
much more need of faith of a certain sort than we
have, for scepticism has far harder problems than
faith. And look at the free-liver, what a bondage is
his life! "Who hath woe? who hath redness of
eyes" but the slave of strong drink? Who has
rottenness in the bones but the slave of his passions?
Is there any wretch that ever tugged in the Spanish
galley, or any bondsman beneath the sun, that is half
such a slave as he who will be led to-night of his lusts
like a bullock to the slaughter, going to his own
damnation, and even to the ruin of his body, while he
makes himself the victim of his own passions? If I
must be a slave, I will be a slave to Turk or savage,
but never to myself, for that were the nethermost
abyss of degradation. You. must be a servant to
somebody ; there is no getting through the world
without it, and if you are the servant to yourself, your
bondage will be terrible. "Choose you this day
whom ye will serve," for serve ye must. Every man
must get him to his task, whether he be peer or
pauper, millionaire or beggar. Kings and queens are
usually the most wearied servants of all. The higher
men climb, the more they have to serve their fellow-
men. You must serve. Oh, that you would enter
the service of your God!

There is room in it. Other places are crowded.
Hundreds of young men go from shop to shop, and

beg for the opportunity to earn a livelihood ; I
lament that in many instances they beg in vain.
Some of you wear the boots from off your feet in
trying to get something to do : how anxiously do I
desire that you may find the employment you seek !
But there is room in the service of God, and He is
willing to receive you. And let me tell you that, if
you enter His service, *it will help you in everything
that you have to do in this life.* They say that a
Christian man is a fool. Ah ! proud opposers, though
we say not the same to you, we might, perhaps, with
truth think so. I have seen many believers in Jesus
whom it would have been very dangerous to deal
with as with fools, for very soon he that dealt with
them in that fashion would have found that he made
a great mistake. They are not always fools who are
called so ; they are such sometimes who use those
names. I like a Christian man to be all the better in
every respect for being a Christian. He should be a
better servant and a better master. He should be a
better tradesman and a better artisan. Surely, there
is no poet whose minstrelsy excels that of the poet of
the sanctuary : Milton still sits alone. There is no
painter that should paint so well as he who tries to
make immortal the memorable scenes in which great
deeds were done. That which you can now do well
you might do better by becoming a servant of God.

ON OVERCOMING THE EVIL-ONE.

THERE are men who have overcome the devil,
and they have overcome him in many shapes.
There are many pictures of the devil about, but I am
afraid there are none of them accurate, for he assumes
different shapes in different places. He is a chame-
leon, always affected by the light in which he happens
to be; a Proteus, assuming every shape, so that it
may but subserve his purpose. Some young men
have overcome that blue devil which keeps men
despairing, doubting, trembling, and fearing. You
once were subject to him, you could not, you said,
believe in Christ. You were afraid you never should
be saved. You wrote bitter things against yourself.
Ah! but you have cast him out now by a simple faith
in Jesus ; for you know whom you have believed, and
you are persuaded that He is able to keep that which
you have committed unto Him. You have overcome
that devil, and though he does try to come back, and
when your business is a little troublesome, or the liver
may not be acting properly, he endeavours to insinuate himself, yet by God's grace, he shall never fasten
on the old chains again.

Then there is that dust-eating devil, of whom we
can never speak too badly—the yellow devil of the
mammon of unrighteousness, the love of gold and
silver ; the dread god of London, rolling over this
city as if it were all its own. I think I see him
as a dragon on the top of the church steeple,

chuckling at the inscription over the Royal Exchange —THE EARTH IS THE LORD'S, AND THE FULNESS THEREOF, and laughing because he knows better, for he reckons it all belongs to him ; even as of old he said to Christ, " All these things will I give Thee, if Thou wilt fall down and worship me." What tricks are done nowadays in business for the love of gold ! In fact, we know, some of us who are not business men, but who, nevertheless, are not blind, that dishonest marks and dishonest measures have become so systematic that their effect is lost, and the thing itself is almost as honest as if it were honest. It is the fact that men have become so accustomed to say that twice three make seven that their neighbours all say, " Exactly so, and we will pay you for the goods after the same reckoning," so that the thing has to square itself. But the genuine Christian, the man who is strong, and has the Word of God abiding in him, scorns all this. He hears others say, " We must live," but he replies, " Yes, but we must die." He determines that he will not throw away his soul in order to grasp wealth, and that if it be not possible to become a merchant prince without the violation of the code of honour and of Christ's law, then he will be content to be poor. O young man, if you have come to this you have overcome a wicked one indeed ! I am afraid there are some with gray heads who have hardly ventured on the fight. Alas ! for them.

Another form of the wicked one we must speak of but softly, but oh ! how hard to be overcome by the young man—I mean Madame Wanton, that fair but foul, that smiling but murderous fiend of hell, by whom so many are deluded. Solomon spake " of the strange woman," but the strong Christian in whom the Word of God abides, passes by her door, and shuts his ear to her siren song. He flees youthful lusts which war against the soul, he reserves both his body and his soul for his Lord, who has redeemed him by His precious blood.

Young man, if you are strong, and have overcome the wicked one, you have overcome, I trust, that Lucifer of pride, and it is your endeavour to walk humbly with your God! You have given up all idea of merit. You cannot boast nor exalt yourself, but you bow humbly at the foot of the cross, adoring Him who has saved you from the wrath to come.

You have given up also, I trust, young man, all subjection to the great red dragon *of fashion*, who draws with his tail even the very stars of heaven. There are some who would think it far worse to be considered unfashionable than to be thought unchristian. To be unchristian would be but such a common accusation that they might submit to it ; but to be unfashionable would be horrible indeed! Young men in London get to be affected by this. If the young men in the house are going to such-and-such an entertainment—they all read a certain class of books—if they are dissipated and sceptical, then the temptation is to chime in with them, and only the man who is strong, and hath the Word of God abiding in him, will overcome the wicked one by doing the right alone—

" Faithful among the faithless found."

Of course, certain talents are necessary for certain positions, but it is a rule without exception that every child of God may be useful in the Divine family.

God has not one single servant for whom He has not appointed a service. Now, you are strong : granted that, then this very strength which you now have will enable you to do mission-work for God, and the graces which have been wrought in you, through Christ Jesus—faith, love, courage, patience—are your fitnesses for sacred labour.

If you are to be a minister, you may need to acquire a measure of learning ; if you are to be a missionary, you will need a peculiar training, but you can get these ; God will give you strength to obtain them, and the spiritual strength will go very far to help you. Meanwhile, for other work, all the strength you require is that which you already possess. There are persons in the world who will not let us speak a word to the unconverted, because they say, and say very truly, that unconverted men are dead in sin, and therefore we are not to tell them to live, because they have no power to live. They forget that we have the power in the quickening Word and Spirit of God, and that as we speak the Word for God, power goes with it. Now, there is among us too much of this forget-fulness of the fact, that we actually have power from on high. In prayer we are always praying for the outpouring of the Holy Spirit, which is very proper ; but, remember we have the Holy Spirit—the Spirit *is* here. He is not always manifest, but He is given to His church to abide in every one of His people, and if we would but believe in His presence we should feel it more. They who preach most successfully will tell you that one cause of it is that they *expect* to be successful. They do not preach hoping that one or two may be saved, but *knowing* that they will be, because the Word of God is the power of God unto salvation. They believe in the Holy Ghost, and they who do so see the Holy Ghost, but they who only waveringly hope in the Holy Ghost, discern Him not : according to their faith so is it unto them. Believe, my brother, that you have within you, as a believer, the power which is necessary for reforming that house of business of yours, which is now so godless, into a house of prayer. Believe it, and begin to work like those who do believe it. Believe that those who pass you in the morning, my young artisan friend, may be and shall be converted by you and by God if you speak to them out of your heart. Go up to them as one who knows that God is working with him ; they will be awed by your manner, and if they reject your message they will feel it go hard with their con-sciences.

If the young man enquires for tools and weapons with which to serve his Master, " The Word of God abideth in you." Now, if you desire to teach others, you have not to ask what the lesson shall be, for it abides in you. Do you want a text that will impress the careless ? What impressed you ? You cannot have a better. You desire to speak a word in season from the Word of God which shall be likely to comfort the disconsolate. What has comforted your own soul ? You cannot have a better guide. You have within your own experience a tutor that cannot fail you, and you have also an encouragement that cannot be taken from you. The Word of God within you will well up like a spring : and truth and grace will pour forth from you in rivers. I have heard our Lord likened to a man carrying a water-pot, and as he carried it upon his shoulder, the water fell dropping, dropping, dropping, so that everyone could track the water-bearer. So should all His people be, carrying such a fulness of grace that everyone should know where they have been by that which they have left behind. He who hath lain in the beds of spices will perfume the air through which he walks. One who, like Asher, has dipped his foot in oil, will leave his footprints behind him. When the living and incorruptible seed remains within, the Divine instincts of the new nature will guide you to the wisest methods of activity. You will do the right thing under the inward impulse rather than the written law, and your personal salvation will be your prime qualification for seeking out others of your Master's flock.

"You have overcome the wicked one." The man who has once given Satan a slap in the face need not be afraid of men. If you have often stood foot to foot with a violent temptation, and, after wrestling have overcome it, you can laugh to scorn all the puny adversaries who assail you. It will breed manliness within the young man, and make him a truly muscular Christian, to have been practised in inward conflicts. *You* have overcome Satan by the power of grace—*you;* why, then there is hope that in the Sunday-school class which you have to teach, in the hearts of those boys and girls, Satan may again be conquered. There is hope for that drunken man you have been talking with lately ; why should not he overcome the wicked one? You were once weak enough, but grace has made you strong : what grace has done for you it can do for another. "After I was saved myself," said one, "I never despaired of any other." So should the fact that you have been enabled to achieve a conquest in a very terrible strife, comfort you with regard to all other cases. Go into the back slums—they are not far off ; penetrate the dark lanes and alleys. You have overcome the wicked one ; you cannot meet with anything worse than him whom you have already vanquished. Let the majesty of grace in your souls be to you a solace and a stimulus, and never say anything is too hard for you to do who have already met Apollyon face to face and put him to the rout.

In the French wars, certain young men, unhappily, found their names written down in the conscription, and were marched to the wars. Now, in a war from which none of us desire to escape, I hope there are young men whose names are written down—heavenly conscripts—who are summoned more fully than ever before in their lives, to go forth to the battle of the Lord of Hosts. I invite every young man who is already converted to God, to dedicate himself to the Lord Jesus Christ. It is not a matter that I can talk you into, nor indeed would I try it, but I would ask you to sit still a moment, and consider with your-selves thus : " I am a believer in Christ ; I have been lately to the sacramental table ; I profess to have been chosen of God, to have been redeemed with precious blood, to have been separated from the rest of mankind, to be destined for an immortality most brilliant : am I living as becometh a redeemed one ? " Passing your hand over your brow thoughtfully, you will come to the conclusion, probably, " I am not ; I am serving God, I trust, in a way, but not with all my heart, and soul, and strength, as I should. How

about my time ?   Do I devote as much of that as I
can to sacred work ?   How about my talent ?   Does
that display itself most in the Literary Association
or in the Sabbath-school ?   Are my oratorical abilities
most developed in the debating room or in preaching
at the street corner ?   Am I giving to Christ the
prime, and choice, and vigour of my life ?   If I am
not, I ought to do so ; I ought, I feel I ought, to be
altogether Christ's ; not that I should leave my business, but I must make my business Christ's business,
and so conduct it, and so to distribute of its results,
as to prove that I am Christ's steward, working in the
world for Him, and not for self."   If this night
you shall not so much vow as pray that from
this time there shall not be a drop of blood in your
body, nor a hair of your head, nor a penny in your
purse, nor a word on your tongue, nor a thought in
your heart, but what should be altogether the Lord's,
I shall be glad enough.

It will be well if you take a step further as conscripts.   You " holy work-folk "—as they used to
call those who dwelt around the cathedral at Durham,
and were exempt from all service to the baron because
they served the church — think of some particular
walk and department in which as young men you can
devote yourselves wholly to Christ.   Generalities in
religion are always to be avoided, more especially
generalities in service.   If a man waits upon you for
a situation, and you say to him, " What are you ? " if
he replies, " I am a painter, or a carpenter," you can
find him work perhaps ; but if he says, " Oh ! I can do
anything," you understand that he can do nothing.
So it is with a sort of spiritual jobbers who profess

to be able to do anything in the church, but who really do nothing.

What can you do? What is your calling? Ragged-schools? Sunday-schools? Street preaching? Tract distribution? Here is a choice for you, which do you select? Waste no time, but say, " This is my calling, and by God's grace I will give myself up to it, meaning to do it as well as any man ever did do it —if possible, better ; meaning, if I take to the ragged-school, to be a thoroughly good teacher of those little Arabs ; if I take to the Sunday-school intending to make myself as efficient in the class as ever teacher could be." It shall be no small blessing to the churches whom you represent if such a resolve be made, and if the conscripts be found of such a sort.

There are many men who ought to be employed in the Christian ministry who stand back. You need not expect that you will gain earthly wealth by it. If you have any notion of that sort, I pray you keep to your breaking of stones ; that will pay you better. If you have any idea that you will find the ministry an easy life, I entreat you to try the treadmill, for that would be an amusement compared with the life of the genuine Christian minister—in London, at least. But if you feel an intense earnestness, if you have succeeded in speaking on other subjects, and can get some attention, think whether you cannot devote yourself to the work. Ah! young man, if I cast an ambitious thought into your mind I mean it only for my Master's glory. If the Lord should say, " Separate Me Saul and Barnabas to this work," if He should call out some fine, noble young fellow, who might have given himself up, perhaps, to the pursuits of commerce, but who now will dedicate himself to the service of the Christian ministry, it would be well. Take care you keep not back whom God would have.

Then, *may there not be* some young man who will become a conscript for missionary service abroad? " I write unto you, young men, because ye are strong, and the Word of God abideth in you, and ye have overcome the wicked one." *You* are the men we want.

" Wanted, young men who are strong ; in whom the Word of God abideth, and who have overcome the wicked one." You who are weak had better stop at home in the Christian nursery a little while. You, in whom the Word of God does not as yet abide, had need to stay till you be taught what be the elements of the faith. You, who have not overcome the wicked one, had better flash your maiden swords in home fields of conflict. You are not the men who are wanted. But you who are strong enough to do and to dare for Jesus — you who are spiritually-minded enough to have overcome the monster of evil within yourselves—you are the men to fight Satan abroad, in his strongholds of heathendom, and Popery, and Mahometanism. You, the choice men of the church, you are the men whom the Missionary Society requires. Think of it before you go to sleep, and if the Lord incline you, come forward and say, " Here am I ; send me."

It is good to be zealous *always* in a good thing. We should forget the things that are behind, and press forward to that which is before. It will be a great thing when all Christian merchants do what some are doing—namely, give of their substance to the cause of

Christ in due proportion. It is a blessed thing for a young man to begin business with the rule that he will give the Lord at least his tenth. That habit of weekly storing for Christ, and then giving to Christ out of His own bag, instead of giving from your own purse, is a most blessed one. Cultivate it, you young tradesmen who have just set up in business for yourselves; and you good wives, help your husbands to do it. You young men who are clerks, and have regular incomes, make that a regular part of your weekly business, and let some share of the consecrated spoil go to the Lord's foreign field. At the same time, never let your subscriptions to this or that act as an exoneration from personal service ; give yourselves to Christ—your whole selves in the highest state of vigour, your whole selves constantly, intelligently, without admixture of sinister motives.

6

ESTHER DEFEATS HER ENEMIES.

THE Lord intended by the narrative of Esther's history to set before us a wonderful instance of His providence, that when we had viewed it with interest and pleasure, we might praise His name, and then go on to acquire the habit of observing His hand in other histories, and especially in our own lives. Well does Flavel say, that he. who observes providence will never be long without a providence to observe. The man who can walk through the world and see no God, is said upon inspired authority to be a fool ; but the wise man's eyes are in his head, he sees with an inner sight, and discovers God everywhere at work. It is his joy to perceive that the Lord is working according to His will in heaven, and earth, and in all deep places. It has been well said that the Book of Esther is a record of wonders without a miracle, and therefore, though equally revealing the glory of the Lord, it sets it forth in another fashion from that which is displayed in the overthrow of Pharaoh by miraculous power.

Let us come now to the story. There were two races, one of which God had blessed and promised to preserve, and another of which he had said that he would utterly put out the remembrance of it from under heaven. Israel was to be blessed and made a blessing, but of Amalek the Lord had sworn that " The Lord will have war with Amalek from generation to generation." These two peoples were therefore in deadly hostility, like the seed of the woman and the seed of the serpent, between whom the Lord Himself has put an enmity. Many years had rolled away ; the chosen people were in great distress, and at this far off time there still existed upon the face of the earth some relics of the race of Amalek ; among them was one descended of the royal line of Agag, whose name was Haman, and he was in supreme power at the court of Ahasuerus, the Persian monarch. Now it was God's intent that a last conflict should take place between Israel and Amalek : the conflict which began with Joshua in the desert was to be finished by Mordecai in the king's palace. This last struggle began with great disadvantage to God's people. Haman was prime minister of the far-extending empire of Persia, the favourite of a despotic monarch, who was pliant to his will. Mordecai, a Jew in the employment of the king, sat in the king's gate ; and when he saw proud Haman go to and fro, he refused to pay to him the homage which others rendered obsequiously. He would not bow his head or bend his knee to him, and this galled Haman exceedingly. It came into his mind that this Mordecai was of the seed of the Jews, and with the remembrance came the high ambition to avenge the quarrel of his race. He thought it scorn to touch one man, and resolved that in himself he would incarnate all the hate of generations, and at one blow sweep the accursed Jews, as he thought them, from off the face of the earth. He went in to the king, with whom his word was power, and told him that there was a singular people scattered up and down the Persian empire, different from all others, and opposed to the king's laws, and that it was not for the king's profit to suffer them. He asked that they might all be destroyed, and he would pay into the king's treasury an enormous sum of money to compensate for any loss of revenue by their destruction. He intended that the spoil which would be taken from the Jews should tempt their neighbours to kill them, and that the part allotted to himself should repay the amount which he advanced, thus he would make the Jews pay for their own murder. He had no sooner asked for this horrible grant than the monarch conceded it ; taking his signet ring from off his finger, he bade him do with the Jews as seemed good to him. Thus the chosen seed are in the hands of the Agagite, who thirsts to annihilate them. Only one thing stands in the way, the Lord has said, "No weapon that is formed against thee shall prosper, and every tongue that riseth against thee in judgment thou shalt condemn." We shall see what happens, and learn from it.

We shall learn from the narrative that God places His agents in fitting places for doing His work. The Lord was not taken by surprise by this plot of Haman ; He had forseen it and forestalled it. It was needful, in order to match this cunning, malicious design of Haman, that some one of Jewish race should possess great influence with the king. How was this to be effected ? Should a Jewess become Queen of Persia, the power she would possess would be useful in counteracting the enemy's design. This had been all arranged years before Haman had concocted in his wicked heart the scheme of murdering the Jews. Esther, whose sweet name signifies myrtle, had been elevated to the position of Queen of Persia by a singular course of events. It happened that Ahasuerus, at a certain drinking bout, was so far gone with wine as to forget all the proprieties of eastern life, and send for his queen, Vashti, to exhibit herself to the people and the princes. No one dreamed in those days of disobeying the tyrant's word, and therefore all stood aghast when Vashti, evidently a woman of right royal spirit, refused to degrade herself by being made a spectacle before that ribald rout of drinking princes, and refused to come. For her courage Vashti was divorced, and a new queen was sought for. We cannot commend Mordecai for putting his adopted daughter in competition for the monarch's choice; it was contrary to the law of God, and dangerous to her soul in the highest degree. It would have been better for Esther to have been the wife of the poorest man of the house of Israel than to have gone into the den of the Persian despot. The Scripture does not excuse, much less commend, the wrong doing of Esther and Mordecai in thus acting, but simply tells us how divine wisdom brought good out of evil, even as the chemist distils healing drugs from poisonous plants. The high position of Esther, though gained contrary to the wisest of laws, was overruled for the best interests of her people. Esther in the king's house was the means of defeating the malicious adversary. But Esther alone would not suffice; she is shut up in the harem, surrounded by her chamberlains and her maids of honour, but quite secluded from the outside world. A watchman is needed outside the palace to guard the people of the Lord, and to urge Esther to action when help is wanted. Mordecai, her cousin and foster-father, obtained an office which placed him at the palace gate. Where could he be better posted? He is where much of the royal business will come under his eye, and he is both quick, courageous, and unflinching : never had Israel a better sentinel than Mordecai, the son of Kish, a Benjamite—a very different man from that other son of Kish, who had suffered Amalek to escape in former times. His relationship to the queen allowed him to communicate with her through Hatach, her chamberlain, and, when Haman's evil degree was published, it was not long before intelligence of it reached her ear, and she felt the danger of which Mordecai and all her people were exposed. By singular providences did the Lord place those two most efficient instruments in their places. Mordecai would have been of little use without Esther, and Esther could have rendered no aid had it not been for Mordecai. Meanwhile, there is a conspiracy hatched against the king, which Mordecai discovers, and communicates to the highest authority, and so puts the king under obligation to him, which was a needful part of the Lord's plan.

Now whatever mischief may be brewing against the cause of God and truth, and I dare say there is very much going on at this moment, for the devil, the Jesuits, nor the atheists are long quiet, this we are sure of, the Lord knows all about it, and He has His Esther and His Mordecai ready at their posts to frustrate their designs. The Lord has His men well placed, and His ambushes hidden in their coverts, to surprise His foes. We need never be afraid but wh⸗

the Lord has forestalled His enemies, and provided against their mischief.

Every child of God is where God has placed him for some purpose, and the practical use of this first point is to lead you to inquire for what practical purpose has God placed each one of you where you now are ? You have been wishing for another position where you could do something for Jesus : do not wish anything of the kind, but serve Him were you are. If you are sitting at the King's gate there is something for you to do there, and if you were on the queen's throne, there would be something for you to do there ; do not ask to be either gate-keeper or queen, but whichever you are, serve God therein. Are you rich ? God has made you a steward, take care that you are a good steward. Are you poor ? God has thrown you into a position where you will be the better able to give a word of sympathy to poor saints. Are you doing your allotted work ? Do you live in a godly family ? God has a motive for placing you in so happy a position. Are you in an ungodly house ? You are a lamp hung up in a dark place ; mind you shine there. Esther did well, because she acted as an Esther should, and Mordecai did well, because he acted as Mordecai should. I like to think God has put each one in the right place, even as a good captain well arranges the different parts of his army, and though we do not know his plan of battle, it will be seen during the conflict that he has placed each soldier where he should be. Our wisdom is not to desire another place, nor to judge those who are in another position, but each one being redeemed with the precious blood of Jesus, should say, " Lord, what would thou have *me* to do, for here I am, and by Thy grace I am ready to do it." Forget not then the fact that God in His providence places His servants in positions where He can make use of them.

The Lord not only arranges His servants, but He restrains His enemies. I would call your attention particularly to the fact that Haman, having gained a decree for the destruction of all the Jews upon a certain day, was very anxious to have his cruel work done thoroughly, and therefore, being very superstitious, and believing in astrology, he bade his magicians cast lots that he might find a lucky day for his great undertaking. The lots were cast for the various months, but not a single fortunate day could be found till hard by the close of the year, and then the chosen day was the thirteenth of the twelfth month. On that day the magicians told their dupe that the heavens would be propitious, and the star of Haman would be in the ascendant. Truly the lot was cast into the lap, but the disposal of it was of the Lord. See ye not that there were eleven clear months left before the Jews would be put to death, and that would give Mordecai and Esther time to turn round, and if anything could be done to reverse the cruel decree they had space to do it in. Suppose that the lot had fallen on the second or third month, the swift dromedaries and camels and messengers would scarcely have been able to reach the extremity of the Persian dominions, certainly a second set of messengers to counteract the decree could not have done so, and, humanly speaking, the Jews must have been destroyed ; but oh, in that secret council

chamber where sit the sorcerers and the man who
asks counsel at the hands of the infernal powers, the
Lord Himself is present, frustrating the tokens of the
liars and making diviners mad. Vain were their
enchantments and the multitude of their sorceries ;
the astrologers, the star-gazers, and the monthly
prognosticators were all fools together, and led the
superstitious Haman to destruction. "Surely there
is no enchantment against Jacob, nor divination
against Israel." Trust ye in the Lord ye righteous,
and in patience possess your souls. Leave your
adversaries in the hands of God, for He can make
them fall into the snare which they have privily laid
for you.

Notice, attentively, that Haman selected a mode of
destroying the Jews which was wonderfully overruled
for their preservation. They were to be slain by any
of the people among whom they lived who chose to
do so, and their plunder was to reward their slayers.
Now, this was a very cunning device, for greed would
naturally incite the baser sort of men to murder the
thrifty Jews, and no doubt there were debtors who
would also be glad to see their creditors disposed
of : but see the loophole for escape which this
afforded ! If the decree had enacted that the Jews
should be slain by the soldiery of the Persian empire
it must have been done, and it is not easy to see how
they could have escaped, but, the matter being left in
private hands, the subsequent decree that they might
defend themselves, was a sufficient counteraction of
the first edict. Thus the Lord arranged that the
wisdom of Haman should turn out to be folly
after all.

In another point, also, we mark the restraining hand of God : namely, that Mordecai, though he had provoked Haman to the utmost, was not put to death at once. Haman "refrained himself." Why did he do so? Proud men are usually in a mighty tiff if they consider themselves insulted, and are ready at once to take revenge ; but Haman "refrained himself;" until that day in which his anger burned furiously, and he set up the gallows, he smothered his passion. I marvel at this ; it shows how God makes the wrath of man to praise Him, and the remainder He doth restrain. Mordecai must not die a violent death by Haman's hand. The enemies of the church of God, and of His people, can never do more than the Lord permits ; they cannot go a hair's breadth beyond the divine license, and when they are permitted to do their worst there is always some weak point about all that they do, some extreme folly which renders their fury vain. The wicked carry about them the weapons of their own destruction, and when they rage most against the Most High, the Lord of all brings out of it good for His people and glory to Himself. Judge not providence in little pieces, it is a grand mosaic, and must be seen as a whole. Say not of any one hour " This is dark," —it may be so, but that darkness will minister to the light, even as the ebon gloom of midnight makes the stars appear the more effulgent. Trust ye in the Lord for ever, for in the Lord Jehovah there is everlasting strength. His wisdom will undermine the mines of cunning, His skill will overtop the climbings of craft ; " He taketh the wise in their own craftiness, and the counsel of the froward is carried headlong."

God in His providence tries His people. God tried Mordecai ; he was a quiet old man, I have no doubt, and it must have been a daily trial to him to stand erect, or to sit in his place when that proud peer of the realm went strutting by. His fellow-servants told him that the King has commanded all men to pay homage to Haman, but he held his own, not, however, without knowing what it might cost him to be so sternly independent. Haman was an Amalekite, and the Jew would not bow before him. But what a trouble it must have been to the heart of Mordecai, when he saw the proclamation that all the Jews must die : the good man must have bitterly lamented his unhappy fate in being the innocent cause of the destruction of his nation. For even if you know you have done right, yet if you bring down trouble, and especially destruction, upon the heads of others it cuts you to the quick. You could bear martyrdom for yourself, but it is sad to see others suffer through your firmness.

PRAYER AND PROVIDENCE— ESTHER'S ACTION.

ESTHER had to be tried. Amid the glitter of the Persian court she might have grown forgetful of her God, but the sad news comes to her, "Your cousin and your nation are to be destroyed." Sorrow and dread filled her heart. There was no hope for her people, unless she would go in unto the king— that despot from whom one angry look· would be death; she must risk all, and go unbidden into his presence, and plead for her nation.· Do you wonder that she trembled? Do you marvel that she asked the prayers of the faithful? Are you surprised to see both herself and her maids of honour fasting and lamenting before God? Do not think, my prosperous friend, that the Lord has given you a high place that you may escape the trials which belong to all His people: yours is no position of ease, but one of the hottests parts of the battle. Neither the lowest and most quiet position, nor the most public and exposed condition, will enable you to escape the "much tribulation" through which the church militant must fight its way to glory. Why should we wish it? Should not the gold be tested in the crucible? Should not the strong pillar sustain great weights? When the Menai bridge was first flung across the straits the engineer did not stipulate that his tube should never be tried with great weights; on the contrary, I can imagine his saying, "Bring up your heaviest trains and load the bridge as much as ever you will, for it will bear every strain." The Lord trieth the righteous because He has made them of metal which will endure the test, and He knows that by the sustaining power of His Holy Spirit they will be held up and made more than conquerors ; therefore is it a part of the operation of providence to try the saints. Let that comfort those of you who are in trouble at this time.

The Lord's wisdom is seen in arranging the smallest events so as to produce great results. We frequently hear persons say of a pleasant or a great event, "What a providence!" while they are silent as to anything which appears less important, or has an unpleasant savour. But the place of the gorse upon the heath is as fixed as the station of a king, and the dust which is raised by a chariot-wheel is as surely steered by providence as the planet in its orbit. There is as much providence in the creeping of an aphis upon a rose leaf as in the marching of an army to ravage a continent. Everything, the most minute, as well as the most magnificent, is ordered by the Lord who has prepared His throne in the heavens, whose kingdom ruleth over all. The history before us furnishes proof of this.

We have reached the point where Esther is to go in unto the king and plead for her people. Strengthened by prayer, but doubtless trembling still, Esther entered the inner court, and the king's affection led him instantly to stretch out the golden sceptre. Being told to ask what she pleases, she invites the king to come to a banquet, and bring Haman with him. He comes, and for the second time invites her

to ask what she wills to the half of his kingdom.
Why, when the king was in so kind a spirit, did not
Esther speak? He was charmed with her beauty,
and his royal word was given to deny her nothing,
why not speak out? But no, she merely asks that
he and Haman will come to another banquet of wine
to-morrow. O, daughter of Abraham, what an
opportunity hast thou lost! Wherefore didst thou
not plead for thy people? Their very existence
hangs upon thy entreaty, and the king has said,
"What wilt thou?" and yet thou art backward!
Was it timidity? It is possible. Did she think that
Haman stood too high in the king's favour for her to
prevail? It would be hard to say. Some of us are
very unaccountable, but on that woman's unaccountable silence far more was hanging than appears at
first sight. Doubtless she longed to bring out her
secret, but the words came not. God was in it; it
was not the right time to speak, and therefore she
was led to put off her disclosure. I dare say she
regretted it, and wondered when she should be able
to come to the point, but the Lord knew best. After
that banquet Haman went out joyfully at the palace
gate, but being mortified beyond measure by
Mordecai's unbending posture, he called for his wife
and his friends, and told them that his riches and
honours availed him nothing so long as Mordecai,
the Jew, sat in the king's gate. They might have
told him, "You will destroy Mordecai and all his
people in a few months, and the man is already
fretting himself over the decree ; let him live, and be
you content to watch his miseries and gloat over his
despair!" But no, they counsel speedy revenge.

Let Mordecai be hanged on a gibbet on the top of the house, and let the gallows be set up at once, and let Haman early in the morning ask for the Jew's life, and let his insolence be punished. Go, call the workmen, and let the gallows be set up at a great height that very night. It seemed a small matter that Haman should be so enraged just at that hour, but it was a very important item in the whole transaction, for had he not been so hasty he would not have gone so early in the morning to the palace, and would not have been at hand when the king said, " Who is in the court ? "

But what has happened ? Why, that very night, when Haman was devising to hang up Mordecai, the king could not sleep. What caused the monarch's restlessness ? Why happened it on that night of all others ? Ahasuerus is master of one hundred and twenty and seven provinces, but not master of ten minutes' sleep. What shall he do ? Shall he call for soothing instruments of music, or beguile the hours with a tale that is told, or with a merry ballad of the minstrel ? No, he calls for a book. Who would have thought that this luxurious prince must listen to a reader at dead of night. " Bring a book ? " What book ? A volume perfumed with roses, musical with songs, sweet as the notes of the nightingale ? " No, bring the chronicles of the empire." Dull reading, that ! But there are one hundred and twenty seven provinces,—which volume shall the page bring from the recorder's shelves ? He chose the record of Shushan the royal city. That is the centre of the empire, and its record is lengthy, in which section shall the reader make a beginning ? He may begin

where he pleases, but ere he closes the book the
story of the discovery of a conspiracy by Mordecai
has been read in the king's hearing. Was not this a
singular accident? Singular if you like, but no
accident. Out of ten thousand other records the
reader pitches upon that one of all others. The
Jews tell us that he began at another place, but that
the book closed and fell open at the chapter upon
Mordecai. Be that as it may, this is certain, that the
Lord knew where the record was, and guided the
reader to the right page. Speaking after the manner
of men, there were a million chances against one that
the king of Persia should, in the dead of the night, be
reading the chronicle of his own kingdom, and that
he should light upon this particular part of it. But
that was not all, the king is interested, he had desired
to go to sleep, but that wish is gone, and he is in
haste to act. He says, "This man Mordecai has
done me good service, has he been rewarded?"
"No." Then cries the impulsive monarch, "He shall
be rewarded at once. Who is in the court?" It
was the most unlikely thing in the world for the
luxurious Ahasuerus to be in haste to do justice, for
he had done injustice thousands of times without
remorse, and chiefly on that day when he wantonly
signed the death warrant of that very Mordecai and
his people. For once, the king is intent on being
just, and at the door stands Haman,—but you know
the rest of the story, and how he had to lead Mordecai
in state through the streets. It seems a very small
matter whether you or I shall sleep to-night, or toss
restlessly on our beds, but God will be in our rest or
in our wakefulness ; we know not what His purpose

7

may be, but His hand will be in it, neither doth any man sleep or wake but according to the decree of the Lord.

Observe well how this matter prepared the way for the queen at the next banquet ; for when she unfolded her sorrow and told of the threatened destruction of the Jews, and pointed to that wicked Haman, the king must have been the more interested and ready to grant her request, from the fact that the man who had saved his life was a Jew, and that he had already awarded the 'highest honours to a man in every way fitted to supersede his worthless favourite. All was well, the plotter was unmasked, the gibbet ready, and he who ordered it was made to try his own arrangements.

The Lord in His providence calls His own servants to be active. This business was done, and well done, by divine providence, but those concerned had to pray about it. Mordecai and all the Jews outside in Shushan fasted, and cried unto the Lord. Unbelievers inquire, " What difference could prayer make ? " Prayer is an essential part of the providence of God, so essential, that you will always find that when God delivers His people, His people have been praying for that deliverance. They tell us that prayer does not affect the Most High, and cannot alter His purposes. We never thought it did ; but prayer is a part of the purpose and plan, and a most effective wheel in the machinery of providence. The Lord sets His people praying, and then He blesses them. Moreover, Mordecai was quite sure the Lord would deliver His people, and he expressed that confidence, but he did not therefore sit still : he stirred up Esther, and when she seemed a little slack, he put it very strongly, " If thou altogether holdest thy peace at this time, then enlargement and deliverance will arise from another place, but thou and thy father's house shall be destroyed." Nerved by this message, Esther braced herself to the effort. She did not sit still and say, " The Lord will arrange this business, there is nothing for me to do," but she both pleaded with God, and ventured her life and her all for her people's sake, and then acted very wisely and discreetly in her interviews with the king. So we rest confidently in providence, but we are not idle. We believe that God has an elect people, and therefore do we preach in the hope that we may be the means, in the hands of His Spirit, of bringing this elect people to Christ. We believe that God has appointed for His people both holiness here and heaven hereafter ; therefore do we strive against sin, and press forward to the rest which remaineth for the people of God. Faith in God's providence, instead of repressing our energies, excites us to diligence. We labour as if all depended upon us, and then fall back upon the Lord with the calm faith which knows that all depends upon Him.

Never was a man so utterly defeated as Haman, never was a project so altogether turned aside. He was taken in his own trap, and he and his sons were hanged up on the gibbet set up for Mordecai. As for the Jews, they were in this special danger, that they were to be destroyed on a certain day, and though Esther pleaded with the king for their lives, he was not able to alter his decree, though willing to do so, for it was a rule of the constitution that the law of the Medes and Persians altered not. The king might determine what he pleased, but when he had once decreed it he could not change it, the people feeling it better to submit to the worst established law than to be left utterly to every capricious whim of their master.   Now, what was to be done ?   The decree was given that the Jews might be slain, and it could not be reversed.   Here was the door of escape, —another decree was issued giving the Jews permission to defend themselves, and take the property of any who dared to attack them ; thus one decree effectually neutralized the other.   With great haste this mandate was sent all over the kingdom, and on the appointed day the Jews stood up for themselves and slew their foes.   According to their tradition nobody attempted to attack them except the Amalekites, and consequently only Amalekites were slain, and the race of Amalek was on that day swept from off the face of ·the earth.   God thus gave to the Jews a high position in the empire and we are told that many became Jews, or were proselytes to the God of Abraham, because they saw what God had done.   As I commenced by saying that God sometimes darted flashes of light through the thick darkness, you will now see what a flash this must have been.   All the people were perplexed when they found that the Hebrews might be put to death, but they must have been far more astonished when the decree came that they might defend themselves.   All the world enquired "Why is this ? " and the answer was " The living God, whom the Jews worship, has displayed His wisdom and rescued His people."   All nations were compelled to feel that there was a God in Israel, and thus the divine purpose was fully accomplished, His people were secured, and His name was glorified to the world's end.

It is clear that the divine will is accomplished, and yet men are perfectly free agents. Haman acted according to his own will, Ahasuerus did whatever he pleased, Mordecai behaved as his heart moved him, and so did Esther. We see no interference with them, no force or coercion; hence the entire sin and responsibility rest with each guilty one, yet, acting with perfect freedom, none of them acts otherwise than divine providence had foreseen. "I cannot understand it," says one. I am compelled to say the same,—I do not understand it either. I have known many who think they comprehend all things, but I fancy they had a higher opinion of themselves than truth would endorse. Certain of my brethren deny free agency, and so get out of the difficulty; others assert that there is no predestination, and so cut the knot. As I do not wish to get out of the difficulty, and have no wish to shut my eyes to any part of the truth, I believe both free agency and predestination to be facts. How they can be made to agree I do not know, or care to know; I am satisfied to know anything which God chooses to reveal to me, and equally content not to know what He does not reveal. There it is; man is a free agent in what he does, responsible for his actions, and verily guilty when he does wrong, and he will be justly punished too, and if he be lost the blame will rest with himself alone: but yet there is One who ruleth over all, who, without complicity in their sin, makes even the actions of wicked men to subserve His holy and righteous purposes. Believe these two truths and you will see them in practical agreement in daily life, though you will not be able to devise a theory for harmonising them on paper.

Wonders can be wrought without miracles. When God does a wonderful thing by suspending the laws of nature men are greatly astonished and say, "This is the finger of God," but now-a-days they say to us, "Where is your God? He never suspends His laws now!" Now, I see God in the history of Pharaoh, but I must confess I see Him quite as clearly in the history of Haman, and I think I see Him in even a grander light; for (I say it with reverence to His holy name) it is a somewhat rough method of accomplishing a purpose to stop the wheels of nature and reverse wise and admirable laws; certainly it reveals His power, but it does not so clearly display His immutability. When, however, the Lord allows everything to go on in the usual way, and gives mind and thought, ambition, and passion their full liberty, and yet achieves His purpose, it is doubly wonderful. In the miracles of Pharaoh we see the finger of God, but in the wonders of providence, without miracle, we see the hand of God. To-day, whatever the event may be, the attentive eye will as clearly see the Lord as if by miraculous power the hills had leaped from their places, or the floods had stood upright as an heap. I am sure that God is in the world, ay, and is at my own fireside, and in my chamber, and manages my affairs, and orders all things for me, and for each one of His children. We want no miracles to convince us of His working, the wonders of His providence are as great marvels as miracles themselves.

Let each child of God rejoice that we have a guardian so near the throne. Every Jew in Shushan must have felt hope when he remembered that the queen was a Jewess. To-day let us be glad that Jesus is exalted.

> " He is at the Father's side,
> The Man of love, the crucified."

How safe are all His people, for "if any man sin, we have an advocate with the Father, Jesus Christ the righteous." There is one that lieth in the bosom of God who will plead for all those who put their trust in Him. Therefore be ye not dismayed, but let your souls rest in God, and wait patiently for Him, for sooner shall heaven and earth pass away than those who trust the Lord shall perish.

THE WORD IN THE HEART.

"THE Word of God abideth in you." I labour
under the opinion that there never was a time
in which the people of God had greater need to
understand this passage than now. We have entered
upon that part of the pilgrim path which is described
by Bunyan as the Enchanted Ground : the Church
and the world appear to be alike bewitched with
folly. Half the people of God hardly know their head
from their heels at this time. They are gaping after
wonders, running after a sounding brass and a tinkling
cymbal, and waiting for yet more astounding in-
ventions. Everything seems to be in a whirligig ;
a tornado has set in, and the storm is everywhere.
Christians used to believe in Christ as their Leader,
and the Bible as their rule ; but some of them are
pleased with lords and rules such as He never knew !
Believe me, there will soon come new Messiahs. Men
are already pretending to work miracles, we shall
soon have false Christs ; and " Lo ! here," and " Lo !
there," will be heard on all sides. Anchors are up,
winds are out, and the whole fleet is getting into con-
fusion. Men in whose sanity and stability I once
believed, are being carried away with one fancy or
another, and I am driven to cry, " What next ? and
what next ? " We are only at the beginning of an era
of mingled unbelief and fanaticism. Now we shall
know who are God's elect and who are not ; for there
are spirits abroad at this hour that would, if it were

possible, deceive even the very elect ; and those who are not deceived are, nevertheless, sorely put to it. Here is the patience of the saints ; let him look to himself who is not rooted and grounded in Christ, for the hurricane is coming. The signs of the times indicate a carnival of delusions ; men have ceased to be guided by the Word, and claim to be themselves prophets. Now we shall see what we shall see. Blessed is the sheep that knows his Shepherd, and will not listen to the voice of strangers. But here is the way to be kept steadfast—" The Word of God abideth in you."

" The Word of God "—that is to say, we are to believe in the doctrines of God's Word, and these will make us strong. What vigour they infuse ! Get the Word well into you, and you will overcome the wicked one. When the devil tempted Luther, the Reformer's grand grip of justification by faith made him readily victorious. Keep you a fast hold of the doctrines of grace, and Satan will soon give over attacking you, for they are like plate-armour, through which no dart can ever force its way.

The promises of God's Word, too, what power they give ! To get a hold of a " shall " and " will " in the time of trouble is a heavenly safeguard. " My God will hear me." "I will not fail thee nor forsake thee." These are Divine holdfasts. Oh, how strong a man is for overcoming the wicked one when he has such a promise to hand ! Do not trust yourself out of a morning in the street till you have laid a promise under your tongue. I see people put respirators on in foggy weather ; they do not make them look very lovely, but I daresay they are useful. I recommend the best respirator for the pestilential atmosphere of this present evil world when I bid you fit a promise to your lips. Did not the Lord rout the tempter in the wilderness with that promise, " Man shall not live by bread alone, but by every word that proceedeth out of the mouth of God shall man live"? Get the promises of God to lodge within you, and you will be strong.

Then mind the precepts, for a precept is often a sharp weapon against Satan. Remember how the Lord Jesus Christ struck Satan a killing blow by quoting a precept—" It is written, Thou shalt worship the Lord thy God, and Him only shalt thou serve." If the precept had not been handy, wherewith would the adversary have been rebuked? Nor is a threatening at all a weak weapon. The most terrible threatenings of God's Word against sin are the best helps for Christians when they are tempted to sin :—How can I do this great wickedness, and sin against God? How should I escape if I turned away from Him who speaketh from heaven? Tell Satan the threatenings, and make him tremble. Every word of God is life to holiness and death to sin. Use the Word as your sword and shield : there is none like it.

Now notice that John not only mentions "the Word of God," but the Word of God " in you." The inspired Word must be received into a willing mind. How? The Book which lies *there* is to be pleaded *here*, in the inmost heart, by the work of the Holy Ghost upon the mind. All of *this* letter has to be translated into spirit and life. " The Word of God abideth in you "— that is, first to know it,—next to remember it and treasure it up in your heart. Following upon this, we must understand it, and learn the analogy of faith by comparing spiritual things with spiritual till we have learned the system of Divine truth, and are able to set it forth and plead for it. It is, next, to have the Word in your affections, to love it so that it is as honey or the droppings of the honeycomb to you. When this is the case, you must and shall overcome the wicked one. A man instructed in the Scriptures is like an armed knight, who when he goes among the throng inflicts many a wound, but suffers none, for he is locked up in steel.

Yes, but that is not all ; it is not the Word of God in you alone, it is "the Word of God *abideth* in you." It is always there, it cannot be removed from you. If a man gets the Bible right into him, he is all right then, because he is full, and there is no room for evil. When you have filled a measure full of wheat, you have effectually shut the chaff out. Men go after novel and false doctrines because they do not really know the truth ; for if the truth had gotten into them and filled them, they would not have room for these day-dreams. A man who truly knows the doctrines of grace is never removed from them : I have heard our opponents rave at what they call obstinacy. Once get the truth really into you, it will enter into the texture of your being, and nothing will get it out of you. It will also be your strength, by setting you watching against every evil thing. You will be on your guard if the Word abide in you, for it is written, "When thou goest it will keep thee." The Word of God will be to you a bulwark and a high tower, a castle of defence against the foe. Oh, see to it that the Word of God is in you, in your very soul, permeating your thoughts, and so operating upon your outward life, that all may know you to be a true Bible-Christian, for they perceive it in your words and deeds.

This is the sort of army that we need in the Church of God—men who are strong by feeding on God's Word. Aspire to it, and when you have reached it, then aspire unto the third degree, that you may become fathers in Israel? Up to this measure, at any rate, let us endeavour to advance, and advance at once.

THE ATTACK.

" YE are strong, and ye have overcome the wicked one." Young men who are strong must expect to be attacked. This also follows from a rule of Divine economy. Whenever God lays up stores it is because there will be need of them. When Egypt's granaries were full with the supply of seven years of plenty, one might have been sure that seven years of famine were about to come. Whenever a man is strong it is because he has stern work to do ; for as the Israelite of old never had an ounce of manna left over till the morning except that which bred worms and stank, so there never will be a Christian who has a pennyworth of grace left over from his daily requirements. If thou art weak thou shalt have no trial happen to thee but such as is common to men ; but if thou be strong, rest thou assured that trials many and heavy are awaiting thee. Every sinew in the arm of faith will have to be tested. Every single weapon given out of the armoury of God will be called for in the conflict. Christian soldiering is no piece of military pastime ; it is no proud parade ; it means hard fighting from the day of enlistment to the day of reward. The strong young man may rest assured that he has no force to spend in display, no energy which he may use in vapouring and vainglory. There is a heavy burden for the strong shoulder, and a fierce fight for the trained hand.

Why does Satan attack this class most ?   I reckon,
first, because Satan is not always sure that the babes
in grace are in grace, and therefore he does not
always attack beginners ; but when they are sufficiently
developed to make him see who and what they are,
then he arouses his wrath.   Those who have clean
escaped from him he will weary and worry to the
utmost of his power.   A friend writes to me to
enquire whether Satan knows our thoughts.   Of
course he does not, as God does.   Satan pretty
shrewdly guesses at them from our actions and our
words, and perhaps even from manifestations upon
our countenances ; but it is the Lord alone who knows
the thoughts of men immediately and by themselves.
Satan is an old hand at studying human nature : he
has been near six thousand years watching and
tempting men and women, and therefore he is full of
cunning ; but yet he is not omniscient, and therefore
it may be that he thinks such and such a person is so
little in grace that perhaps he is not in grace at all ;
so he lets him alone : but as soon as ever it is certain
that the man is of the royal seed, then the devil is at
him.   I do not know whether our Lord was ever
tempted at Nazareth, while He was yet in His
obscurity ; but the moment He was baptized, and the
Spirit of God came upon Him, He was taken into the
wilderness to be tempted of the devil.   If you become
an avowed servant of God do not think the conflict
is over : it is then that the battle begins.   You will
have to go into such a wilderness and such a conflict
as you never knew before.   Satan knows that young
men in grace can do his kingdom great harm, and
therefore he would fain slay them early in the day, as

Pharaoh wished to kill all the male children in Israel. You are strong to overthrow his kingdom, and therefore you need not marvel that he desires to overthrow you.

It is right that young men should endure hardness, for else they might become proud. It is hard to hide pride from men. Full of strength, full of courage, full of patience, full of zeal, such men are ready enough to believe the wicked one when he whispers that they are perfect ; and therefore trial is sent to keep them out of that grievous snare of the evil one. The devil is used by God as a householder might employ a black, smutty scullion to clean his pots and kettles. The devil tempts the saint, and thus the saint sees his inward depravity, and is no longer able to boast. The devil thinks he is going to destroy the man of God, but God is making the temptation work for the believer's eternal good. Far better to have Beelzebub, the god of flies, pestering you, than to become fly-blown with notions of your own excellence.

Besides, not only might this young man be a prey to pride, but he certainly would not bring the glory to God untried that he brings to Him when he overcomes temptation. Read the story of Job up to the time when he is tempted. Say you, " We have no story to read." Just so, there was nothing worthy of record, only that his flocks and herds continued to multiply, that another child was born, and so forth. There is no history to a nation when everything goes well ; and it is so with a believer. But when trial comes, and the man plays the man, and is valiant for God against the arch-enemy, I hear a voice from

8

Heaven saying, Write. Now you shall have history
—history that will glorify God. It is but right that
those who are young men in Christ should endure
conflicts that they may bring honour to their Father,
their Redeemer, and the Holy Spirit who dwells in
them.

Besides, it prepares them for future usefulness, and
here I venture to intrude the testimony of my own
experience. I often wondered, when I first came to
Christ, why I had such a hard time of it when I was
coming to the Lord, and why I was so long and so
wearied in finding the Saviour. After that, I wondered
why I experienced so many spiritual conflicts while
others were in peace. I did not know that I was
destined to preach. I did not understand in those
days that I should have to minister to hundreds, and
even thousands, of distressed spirits, storm-tossed, and
ready to perish. But it is so now with me that when
the afflicted mention their experience I can, as a
rule, reply, " I have been there " ; and so I can help
them, as one who has felt the same. It is meet, therefore, that the young men should bear the yoke in
their youth, and that while they are strong they
should gain experience, not so much for themselves
as for others, that in after days when they come to be
fathers they may be able to help the little ones of the
family. Take your tribulation kindly : yea, take it
gratefully; thank your King that He puts you in com-
mission where the thick of the battle centres around
you. You will never be a warrior if you never enter
the dust-clouds where garments are rolled in blood.
You will never become a veteran if you do not fight
through the long campaign. The man who has been

at the head of the forlorn hope is he who can tell what stern fighting means. So be it unto you : may your Captain save you from the canker of inglorious ease. You must fight in order that you may acquire the character which inspires others with confidence in you, and thus fits you to lead your comrades to the fray. Oh, that we may have here an abundance of the young men of the heavenly family who will defend the Church against worldliness and error, defend the weaker ones from the wolves that prowl around, and guard the feeble against the many deceivers that waylay the Church of God ! As you love the Lord, I charge you grow in grace and be strong, for we have need of you just now. Take hold on sword and buckler ; watch ye, and stand fast ! May the Lord teach your hands to war and your fingers to fight. In these evil days may you be as a phalanx to protect our Israel. The Canaanites, the Hivites and the Jebusites are upon us just now ; war is in all our borders : now, therefore, let each valiant man stand about the King's chariot, each man with his sword upon his thigh, because of fear in the night.

"I have written unto you young men because ye are strong " : they have overcome the wicked one. Then they must be strong ; for a man who can overcome the wicked one is no mean man of war—write him down among the first three. Wicked ones abound ; but there is one crafty being who deserves the name of *the* wicked one : he is the arch-leader of rebellion, the first of sinners, the chief of sinners, the tempter of sinners. He is the wicked one who heads assaults against the pilgrims to Zion. If any man has ever stood foot to foot with him he will never forget it : it is a fight that once fought will leave its scars, even though the victory be won.

In what sense have these young men overcome the wicked one ? They have broken right away from his power. They were once his slaves, they are not so now. They once slept beneath his roof in perfect peace : but conscience raised an uproar, and the Spirit of God troubled them, and they clean escaped his power. Once Satan never troubled them at all. Why should he ? They were good friends together. Now he tempts them and worries them, and assaults them because they have left his service, engaged themselves to a new Master, and become the enemies of him who was once their god. I speak to many who gladly own that not a bit of them now belongs to the devil, from the crown of their head to the sole of their foot ; for Christ has bought them, body, soul, and spirit, with His precious blood, and they have assented to the purchase, and feel that they are not their own, and certainly not the devil's : for they are bought with a price, and belong to Him who purchased them. The strong man armed has been turned out by a stronger than he : Jesus has carried the fortress of the heart by storm, and driven out the foe. Satan is not inside our heart now ; he entered into Judas, but he cannot enter into us ; for our soul is filled by another who is well able to hold His own. The wicked one has been expelled by the Holy One, who now lives and reigns within our nature as Lord of all.

Moreover, these young men have overcome the wicked one, not only in breaking away from his power and in driving him entirely out of possession so that he is no longer master, but they have overcome him in the very fact of their opposition to him. When a man resists Satan, he is victorious over Satan in that very resistance. Satan's empire consists in the yielding of our will to his will; but when our will revolts against him, then already we have in measure overcome him. Albeit that sometimes we are much better at willing than we are at doing, as the Apostle Paul was; for he said, "To will is present with me; but how to perform that which is good I find not"; yet, still, the hearty will to be clean from sin is a victory over sin; and as that will grows stronger and more determined to resist the temptations of the evil-one, in that degree we have overcome sin and Satan. What a blessed thing this is! for fail not to remember that Satan has no weapons of defence, and so, when we resist him, he must flee. A Christian man has both defensive and offensive weapons, he has a shield as well as a sword: but Satan has fiery darts, and nothing else. I never read of his having any shield whatever; so that when we resist him he is bound to run away. He has no defence for himself, and the fact of our resistance is in itself a victory.

But, oh, brothers and sisters, besides that, some of us who are young men in Christ have won many a victory over Satan. Have we not been tempted, fearfully tempted? But the mighty grace of God has come to the rescue, and we have not yielded. Cannot you look back, not with Pharisaic boasting, but with gracious exultation, over many an evil habit which once had the mastery over you, but which is master of you no longer? It was a hard conflict. How you bit your lip sometimes, and feared that you must yield! In certain moments your steps had

almost gone, your feet had well-nigh slipped; but
here you are, conqueror yet! Thanks be to God who
giveth us the victory through our Lord Jesus Christ.
Hear what the Spirit saith to you when John writes
to you; because you have overcome the wicked one,
he says, " Love not the world, neither the things that
are in the world."

In Christ Jesus we have entirely overcome the
wicked one already; for the enemy we have to contend with is a vanquished foe—our Lord and Master
met him and destroyed him. He is now destitute of
his boasted battle-axe, that terrible weapon which has
made the bravest men to quail when they have seen
it in his hand. " What weapon is that? " say you.
That weapon is death. Our Lord overthrew him
that had the power of death, that is, the devil, and
therefore Satan has not the power of death any
longer. The keys of death and of hell are at the
girdle of Christ. Ah, fiend, we who believe in Jesus
shall defeat thee, for our Lord defeated thee! That
bruise upon thy head cannot be hidden! Thy crown
is dashed in pieces! The Lord has sore wounded
thee, O dragon, and never can thy deadly wound be
healed! We have at thee with dauntless courage;
for we believe the promise of our Lord, that He will
bruise Satan under our feet shortly. As certainly as
thou wast bruised under the feet of our crucified
Lord, so shalt thou be bruised under the feet of all
His seed, to thine utter overthrow and contempt. Let
us take courage and abide steadfast in the faith; for
we have in our Lord Jesus overcome the wicked one.
We are more than conquerors through Him who hath
loved us.

SARAH, A WOMAN OF FAITH.

SARAH was calm and quiet, and was not put in fear by any terror. There were several occasions on which she might have been much disquieted and put about. The first was in the breaking-up of her house life. You see her husband, Abraham, gets a call to go from Ur of the Chaldees. Well, it is a considerable journey, and they move to Haran. There are some women—unbelieving women—who would not have understood that. "Why does he want to go away from the land in which he lives, and from all our kindred, away to Haran?" That would have been her question had she not been a partaker in her husband's faith. An unbelieving woman would have said, "A call from God? Nonsense! Fanaticism! I do not believe it," and when she saw that her husband would go she would have been afraid with great amazement. When Abraham went to Haran with his father Terah, and Terah died in Haran, and then God called him to go further, they had to cross the Euphrates and get right away into a land which he knew nothing of, and this must have been a sterner trial still. When they packed up their goods on the camels and on the asses, and started with their train of servants and sheep and cattle, she might very naturally have said, if she had been an unbelieving woman, "Where are you going?" "I do not know," says Abraham. "What are you going for? What

are you going to get?" "I do not know," says
Abraham; "God has bidden me go, but where I am
going to, I do not know; and what I am going for I
cannot exactly say, save that God has said, ' Get thee
out from thy country and thy kindred, and I will bless
thee and multiply thee, and give thee a land wherein
thou shalt dwell.' " We do not read that Sarah ever
asked these questions, or was ever troubled at all
about them. The things were put on the camels'
backs, and away she journeyed, for God had called
her husband to go, and she resolved to go with
him. Through floods or flames, it mattered not
to her, she felt safe with her husband's God, and
calmly journeyed on. She was not afraid with any
amazement.

Then, though we do not hear much about her, we
know that all those years she had to live in a tent.
You know the man is out abroad attending to his
business, and he does not know much about the
discomforts of home, not even in such homes as ours.
But if you were called to give up your houses and go
and live in tents—well, the master might not mind it,
but the mistress would. It is a very trying life for a
housewife. Sarah travelled from day to day, and what
with the constant moving of the tent, as the cattle
had to be taken to fresh pastures, it must have been a
life of terrible discomfort; yet Sarah never said a
word about it. Up to-morrow morning; every tent-
pin up; and all the canvas rolled away, for you must
move to another station. The sun scorches like an
oven, but you must ride across the plain; or if the
night is cold with frost and heavy dews, still canvas
is your only wall and roof. Remember, they were

dwelling in tents as pilgrims and strangers, not for one day, or two, nor for a few days in a year, but for scores of years at a stretch. It was bravely done by this good woman that she was not afraid with any amazement.

And then there was a special time when Abraham put on his harness and went to war. He hears that Chederlaomer has come down with tributary kings and swept away the cities of the plain, and taken captive his nephew, Lot. Abraham says, " I will go and deliver him ; " and she might have said, " My husband, you are an old man. Those grey locks should not be touched with the stains of warfare." She said nothing of the sort, but doubtless cheered him on and smiled as he invited some of his neighbours that dwelt near to go with him. She is under no distress that her husband is gone, and all the herdsmen and servants round about the tents all gone, so that she is left alone with her women servants. No ; she sits at home as a queen, and fears no robbers, calmly confident in her God. Abraham has gone to battle, and she fears not for him, and she needs not, for he smites the kings, and they are given like driven stubble to his bow, and he comes back laden with spoil. God was pleased with Sarah's quiet faith, because in troublous times she was not afraid with any amazement.

Then there came, a little while after, that great trial of faith which must have touched Sarah, though its full force fell on her husband. She observed the sudden disappearance of her husband and his servant. " Where is your master ? He does not come into breakfast." The servants say, " He was up a great while before day, and he has gone with the servant, and with the ass, and with Isaac." He has not told her ; for Abraham had struggled enough with himself to take Isaac away to the mountain and offer him, and he could not bear to repeat the struggle in Sarah. He was gone without telling Sarah of his movements. This was a new state of things for her. He did not return all day. "Where has your master gone ? I never knew him to go away before without informing me. And where is Isaac ? " Oh, that Isaac ! How she feared for her jewel, her delight, the child of promise, the wonder of her old age. He did not come home that night, nor Abraham either ; nor the next day, nor the next. Three days passed, and I can hardly picture the anxiety that would have fallen upon you if you had been Sarah, unless you had enjoyed Sarah's faith, for by faith in this trying case she was not afraid with any amazement. I dare-say it took three days for Abraham to come back again, so that it was a week nearly, and no Abraham and no Isaac. One would have thought she would have wandered about, crying, "Where is my husband, and where is my son ? " But not so. She calmly waited, and said within herself, " If he has gone, he has gone upon some necessary errand, and he will be under God's protection ; and God, who promised to bless him and to bless his seed, will not suffer any evil to harm him." So she rested quietly, when others would have been in dire dismay. She was not afraid with any amazement. We hear so little said about Sarah, that I am obliged thus to picture what I feel she must have been, because human nature is so like itself, and the effect of events upon us is very like the effect which would have been produced upon the mind of Sarah.

Now, this is a point in which Christian women should seek to imitate Sarah : we should not let our hearts be troubled, but rest in the Lord, and wait patiently for Him.

What is this virtue? It is a calm, quiet trusting in God. It is freedom from fear, such as is described in another place in these words : " He shall not be afraid of evil tidings : his heart is fixed, trusting in the Lord." Or, as we read in David's words, " Yea, though I walk through the valley of the shadow of death, I will fear no evil : for Thou art with me ; Thy rod and Thy staff they comfort me." It is composure of mind, freedom from anxiety, the absence of fretfulness, and clean deliverance from alarm ; so that, whatever happens, trepidation does not seize upon the spirit, but the heart keeps on at its own quiet pace, delighting itself in a faithful God. This is the virtue which is worth a king's ransom, and Sarah had it. " Whose daughters ye are, if ye are not afraid with any amazement."

When is this virtue to be exercised by us? Well, it should be exercised at all times. If we are not self-composed when we are happy we are not likely to be calm when we are sad. I notice that if I am at all pleased with the praise of a friend, I become in that degree open to be grieved by the censure of a foe. By so much as you are elated by prosperity, by so much are you likely to be depressed when adversity comes ; but if you are calm, quiet, happy—no more than that—when everything goes well, then you will be calm, quiet, happy—not less than that—when everything goes ill. To keep up an equable frame of mind is a thing to aim at, even as the gardener desires an even temperature for his choice flowers. You enquire, "Who are to exercise this virtue?" We are all to do so; but the text is specially directed to the sisterhood. I suppose women are exhorted to it, because some of them are rather excitable, a little hysterical, and apt to be fearfully depressed and utterly carried away. I am not saying that this fault is general or common among women, neither am I blaming them, but only stating the fact that some are thus afflicted, and it is a happy, happy thing if they can master it, so that they are not afraid with any amazement.

But this virtue especially serves in *time of trouble*, when a very serious trial threatens us. Then the Christian is not to say, "What shall I do now? I shall never endure it. I cannot live through it. Surely God has forgotten me. This trouble will crush me. I shall die of a broken heart." No. Do not talk so. If you are God's child do not even think so. Try in patience to lift up your head, and remember Sarah, "whose daughters ye are, if ye are not afraid with any amazement."

And so must it be in times of personal sickness. How many are the pains and sufferings that fall to the lot of the sisterhood! But if you have faith, you will not be afraid with any amazement. I saw one who was about to suffer from the surgeon's knife. It was a serious operation, about which all stood in doubt; but I was happy to see her as composed in the prospect of it as though it had been a pleasure rather than a pain. Thus calmly resigned should a

Christian be. I went to see an aged sister close upon fourscore years of age, dying with dropsy, and, being unable to lie down in bed, was obliged to sit up always—a posture which allows little or no rest. When I entered her room she welcomed me most heartily, which, perhaps was not wonderful, for she was greatly attached to her minister ; the wonder lay in the fact that she expressed herself as being full of happiness, full of delight, full of expectancy of being with Christ. I went to comfort her ; but she comforted me. What could I say ? She talked of the goodness of God with an eye as full of pleasure as if she had been a maiden speaking to her young companion of her marriage day. I was charmed to see one with such evident marks of long-continued pain upon her face, but with such sweet serenity there too—yea, with more than serenity—with unspeakable joy in the Lord, such as I fear some in health and strength have not yet learned. A Christian woman should not be afraid with any amazement either in adversity or in sickness, but her holy patience should prove her to be a true daughter of Sarah and Abraham.

Christian women in Peter's day were subject to persecution as much as their husbands. They were shut up in prison, scourged, tortured, burned, or slain with the sword. One holy woman in the early days of the Church was tossed upon the horns of bulls ; another was made to sit in a red-hot iron chair : thus were they tortured, not accepting deliverance. In the early days of martyrdom the women played the man as well as the men. They defied the tyrant to do his worst upon their mortal bodies, for their conquering spirits laughed at every torment. If persecuting times should come again, or if they are here already in some measure, O daughters of Sarah, do well, and be not afraid with any amazement.

And so if you should be called to some stern duty, if you should be bound to do what you feel you cannot do, recollect that anybody can do what he can do. It is the believing man who does what he cannot do. We achieve impossibilities by the power of the Almighty God. Be not afraid, then, of any duty, but believe that you will be able to do it, for grace will be sufficient for you.

At last, in the prospect of death, may you not be afraid with any amazement! Oftentimes a death-bed is vantage-ground for a Christian. Where others show their fear, and sometimes their terror, there should the believer show his peacefulness and his happy expectancy, not afraid with any amazement, whatever the form of death may be.

What is the excellence of this virtue? I shall answer that question by saying it is due to God that we should not be afraid with any amazement. Such a God as we have ought to be trusted. Under the shadow of such a wing fear becomes a sin. If God were other than He is we might be afraid; but while He is such a God it is due to Him that fear be banished. Peacefulness is true worship. Quiet under alarming conditions is devotion. He worships best who is most calm in evil times.

Moreover, the excellence of this virtue is that it is *most impressive to men.* I do not think anything is more likely to impress the ungodly than the quiet peace of mind of a Christian in danger or near to death. If we can be happy then, our friends will ask,

"What makes them so calm?" Nor is the usefulness confined to others. It is most useful to ourselves; for he who can be calm in time of trouble will be most likely to make his way through it. When you once become afraid you cannot judge wisely as to your best course. You generally do wrong when you are frightened out of your confidence in God. When the heart begins palpitating, then the whole system is out of order for the battle of life. Be calm, and watch your opportunity. Napoleon's victories were to a large extent due to the serenity of that masterly warrior; and, depend upon it, it is so with you Christian people: you will win if you can wait. Do not be in a hurry. Consider what you should do. Do not be so alarmed as to make haste. Be patient; be quiet; wait God's time, and so wait your own time. Wait upon God to open your mouth. Ask Him to guide your hand, and to do everything for you. Calmness of mind is the mother of prudence and discretion; it gives the firm foothold which is needful for the warrior when he is about to deal a victorious blow. Those who cannot be amazed by fear shall live to be amazed with mercy.

How can we obtain it? That is the question. Recollect, it is an outgrowth of faith, and you will have it in proportion as you have faith. Have faith in God, and you will not be afraid with any amazement. Very early in my preaching days I had faith in God in times of thunderstorm. When I have walked out to preach, it has happened that I have been wet through with the storm, and yet I have felt no annoyance from the thunder and lightning. On one occasion I turned in by reason of the extreme severity of the rain to a little lone cottage, and I found a woman there with a child who seemed somewhat relieved when she had admitted me, but previously she had been crying bitterly with sheer alarm and terror. " Why," she said, "this is a little round lodge-house, and the lightning comes in at every window. There is no place into which I can get to hide it from my eyes." I explained to her that I liked to see the lightning, for it showed me that an explosion was all over, and since I had lived to see the flash it was clear it could now do me no harm. I told her that to hear the thunder was a splendid thing, it was only God saying, " It is all over." If you live to see the lightning flash there is nothing to be afraid of; you would have been dead, and never have seen it, if it had been sent to kill you. I tried to console her on religious grounds, and I remember well praying with her and making her as happy as a bird. It was my being so calm and quiet and praying with her that cheered her up; and when I went on my way I left her in peace. You may depend upon it that unless our own souls have peace we cannot communicate it to others. In this way we must believe in God about everything. It so happened that about that matter— the thunder and lightning—I did believe in God up to the very last degree, and therefore I could not be alarmed on that score ; so if you believe in God upon any other subject, whatever it is, you will have perfect peace with God about it. If you can believe God when you are in a storm at sea, that He holds the water in the hollow of His hand, you will be at peace about the tempest. It is the thing that troubles you that you must believe about ; and when faith makes an application of her hand to the particular trial, then will peace of mind come to you.

This holy calm comes, also, *from walking with God.* No spot is so serene as the secret place of the tabernacles of the Most High. Commune with God, and you will forget fear. Keep up daily fellowship with Christ in prayer, in praise, in service, in searching the Word, in submitting your heart to the work of the eternal Spirit : and as you walk with God, you will find yourself calm. You know how our poet puts it :—

> " Oh, for a closer walk with God,
> A calm and heavenly frame."

These go together.

If you would feed upon certain truths which will produce this calm of mind, recollect, first, that God is full of love, and therefore nothing that God sends can harm His child. Take everything from the Lord as a love-token, even though it be a stroke of His rod, or a cut of His knife. Everything from that dear hand must mean love, for He has said, " I have graven thee upon the palms of My hands " When you accept every affliction as a love-token, then will your fear be ended.

SARAH, A WOMAN WHO DID WELL.

"Look unto Abraham your father, and unto Sarah that bare you."—Isaiah li. 2.

"Even as Sara obeyed Abraham, calling him lord: whose daughters ye are, as long as ye do well, and are not afraid with any amazement."—1 Peter iii. 6.

WHAT a happy circumstance it is when a godly, gracious man has an equally godly and gracious wife! It is ill when there is a difference, a radical difference, between husband and wife,—when one fears God, and the other has no regard to Him. What a pain it is to a Christian woman to be yoked with an unbelieving husband! In a case which I remember, the husband lived all his life indifferent to Divine things, while the wife was an earnest Christian woman, and saw all her children grow up in the ways of the Lord. The father lived unregenerate, and died without giving any testimony of a change of heart. When our sister speaks of him, it is with fearful anguish; she does not know what to say, but leaves the matter in the hands of God, often sighing, "O that, by a word or a look, I could have been enabled to indulge a hope that my poor husband looked to Jesus at the last." The same must be the case of a husband who has an ungodly wife. However much God may bless him in all other respects, there seems to be a great miss there, as if a part of the sun were eclipsed,—a part of that life which should be all light left in thick darkness. Oh, let those of us who have the happiness of being joined together in the Lord, thank and bless God every time we remember each other. Let us pray God that, having such a privilege, so that our prayers are not hindered by irreligious partners, we may never hinder our prayers ourselves. God grant that we may give unto His name great glory because of His choice favour to us in this respect! Abraham had cause to praise God for Sarah, and Sarah was grateful for Abraham. I have not the slightest doubt that Sarah's character owed its excellence very much to Abraham; I should not wonder, however, if we discover when all things are revealed that Abraham owed as much to Sarah. They probably learned from each other; sometimes the weaker comforted the stronger, and often the stronger sustained the weaker. I should not wonder if a mutual interchange of their several graces tended to make them both rich in the things of God. Mayhap Abraham had not been all that Abraham was if Sarah had not been all that Sarah was. We thank God if we, like Abraham, are favoured with holy consorts, whose amiable tempers and loving characters tend to make us better servants of God.

God does not forget the lesser lights. Abraham shines like a star of the first magnitude, and we do not at first sight observe that other star, with light so bright and pure, shining with milder radiance but with kindred lustre, close at his side. The light of Mamre, which is known under the name of Abraham, resolves itself into a double star when we apply the telescope of reflection and observation. To the common eye Abraham is the sole character, and ordinary people

overlook his faithful spouse, but God does not overlook. Our God never omits the good who are
obscure. You may depend upon it that there is no
such difference in the love of God towards different
persons as should make Him fix His eye only
upon those that are strong, and omit those who are
weak. Our eyes spy out the great things, but God's
eye is such that nothing is great with Him, and
nothing is little. He is infinite, and therefore nothing
bears any comparison to Him. You remember how
it is written that He who telleth the stars, and calleth
them by name, also bindeth up the broken in heart,
and healeth all their wounds. He who treasures the
names of His apostles, notes also the women
that followed in His train. He who marks the
brave confessors and the bold preachers of the
gospel, also remembers those helpers who labour
quietly in the gospel in places of retirement into
which the hawk's eye of history seldom pries. God
forgets not the less in His care for the greater.
Sarah was in life covered with the shield of the
Almighty as well as Abraham, her husband ; in
death she rested in the same tomb ; in Heaven she
has the same joy ; in the Book of the Lord she has
the same record.

It would be well for us to imitate God in this : in
not forgetting the lesser lights. I do not know that
great men are often good examples. I am sorry
when, because men have been clever and successful,
they are held up to imitation, though their motives
and morals have been questionable. I would sooner
men were stupid and honest than clever and tricky ;
it is better to act rightly and fail altogether than

succeed by falsehood and cunning. I would sooner bid my son imitate an honest man who has no talent, and whose life is unsuccessful, than point him to the cleverest and greatest that ever lived, whose life has become a brilliant success, but whose principles are condemnable. Learn not from the great but from the good; be not dazzled by success, but follow the safer light of truth and right. But so it is that men mainly observe that only which is written in big letters; but you know the choicest parts of God's Book are printed in small characters. They who would only know the rudiments may spell out the words in large type which are for babes; but those who want to be fully instructed must sit down and read the small print of God, given us in lives of saints whom most men neglect. Some of the choicest virtues are not so much seen in the great as in the quiet, obscure life. Many a Christian woman manifests a glory of character that is to be found in no public man. I am sure that many a flower that is "born to blush unseen," and, as we think, to "waste its fragrance on the desert air," is fairer than the beauties which reign in the conservatory, and are the admiration of all. God has ways of producing very choice things on a small scale. As rare pearls and precious stones are never great masses of rock, but always lie within a narrow compass, so full often the fairest and richest virtues are to be found in the humblest individuals. A man may be too great to be good, but he cannot be too little to be gracious. Do not, therefore, always be studying Abraham, the greater character. Does not the text say, " Look unto Abraham, your father, and

unto Sarah that bare you "? You have not learned
the full lesson of patriarchal life until you have been
in the tent with Sarah as well as among the flocks
with her husband.

God does not by His grace lift us out of our place.
A man is made gentle, but he is not made a fool. A
woman is made brave, but grace never made her
masterful and domineering. Grace does not make the
child so self-willed that he disobeys his father ;—it is
something else that does that. Grace does not take
away from the father his authority to command the
child. It leaves us where we were, in a certain sense,
as to our position, and the fruit it bears is congruous
to that position. Thus Sarah is beautified with the
virtues that adorn a woman, while Abraham is
adorned with all the excellences which are becoming
in a godly man. According as the virtue is required,
so is it produced. If the circumstances require
courage, God makes His servant heroic ; if the circumstances require great modesty and prudence,
modesty and prudence are given. Faith is a wonderful magician's wand ; it works marvels, it achieves
impossibilities, it grasps the incomprehensible. Faith
can be used anywhere—in the highest Heaven touch-
ing the ear of God, and winning our desire of Him,
and in the lowest places of the earth amongst the
poor and fallen, cheering and upraising them. Faith
will quench the violence of fire, turn the edge of the
sword, snatch the prey from the enemy, and turn the
alien to flight. There is nothing which it cannot do.
It is a principle available for all times, to be used on
all occasions, suitable to be used by all men for
all holy ends. Those who have been taught the

sacred art of believing God are the truly learned : no
degree of the foremost university can equal in value
that which comes with much boldness in the faith. If
Abraham walks before God and is perfect—if he
smites the kings who have carried Lot captive, if he
does such deeds of prowess as become a man—the
self-same faith makes Sarah walk before God in her
perfectness, and she performs the actions which
become her womanhood, and she, too, is written
among the worthies of faith who magnified the
Lord.

There were two fruits of faith in Sarah,—she did
well, and she was not afraid with any amazement.

She did well as *a wife*. She was all her husband
could desire, and when, at the age of one hundred and
twenty-seven years, she at last fell on sleep, it is said
that Abraham not only mourned for her, but the old
man wept for her most true and genuine tears of
sorrow. He wept for the loss of one who had been
the life of his house. As a wife she did well. All
the duties that were incumbent upon her as the
queen of that travelling company were performed
admirably, and we find no fault mentioned concerning
her in that respect.

She did well as *a hostess*. It was her duty, as her
husband was given to hospitality, to be willing to
entertain his guests ; and the one instance recorded
is, no doubt, the representation of her common
mode of procedure. Though she was truly a
princess, yet she kneaded the dough and prepared
the bread for her husband's guests. They came
suddenly, but she had no complaint to make. She
was, indeed, always ready to lay herself out to

perform that which was one of the highest duties of a God-fearing household in those primitive times.

She did well also as *a mother.* We are sure she did, because we find that her son Isaac was so excellent a man ; and you may say what you will, but in the hand of God the mother forms the boy's character. Perhaps the father unconsciously influences the girls, but the mother has evidently most influence over the sons. Any of us can bear witness that is so in our own case. There are exceptions, of course ; but, for the most part, the mother is the queen of the son, and he looks up to her with infinite respect if she be at all such as can be respected. Sarah by faith did her work with Isaac well, for from the very first, in his yielding to his father when he was to be offered up as a sacrifice, we see in him evidence of a holy obedience and faith in God which were seldom equalled, and were never surpassed.

Besides that, it is written that God said of Abraham, " I know Abraham, that he will command his children and his household after him." There is one trait in Abraham's character that, wherever he went, he set up an altar unto the Lord. His rule was, a tent and an altar. Do you always make these two things go together—a tent and an altar ? Where you dwell is there sure to be family worship there ? I am afraid that many families neglect it, and often it is so because husband and wife are not agreed about it, and I feel sure that there would not have been that invariable setting up of the worship of God by Abraham in his tent unless Sarah had been as godly as himself.

She did well, also, as *a believer*, and that is no mean point.   As a believer, when Abraham was called to separate himself from his kindred, Sarah went with him.   She would adopt the separated life, too, and the same caravan which travelled across the desert with Abraham for its master, had Sarah for its mistress. She continued with him, believing in God with perseverance.   Though they had no city to dwell in, she continued the roaming life with her husband, looking for "a city which hath foundations, whose Builder and Maker is God."   She believed God's promise with all her heart, for though she laughed once, because when the promise neared its realization it overwhelmed her, it was but a slip for the moment, for it is written by the apostle in the eleventh of Hebrews, "Through faith also Sarah herself received strength to conceive seed, and was delivered of a child when she was past age, because she judged Him faithful who had promised."

She did well to her parents, well to her husband, well to her household, well to her guests, well before her God.   Oh, that all professing Christian people had a faith that showed itself in doing well!

But never let it be forgotten that, though we preach faith as the great means of salvation, yet we never say that you are saved unless there is a change wrought in you, and good works are produced in you; for "faith without works is dead, being alone."   Faith saves, but it is the faith which causes men to do well; and if there be a faith (and there is such a faith) which leaves a man just what he was, and permits him to indulge in sin, it is the faith of devils; perhaps not so good as that, for "the devils believe and tremble," whereas these hypocrites profess to believe, and yet dare to defy God, and seem to have no fear of Him whatsoever. Sarah had this testimony from the Lord, that she did well ; and her daughters ye are, all of you who believe, if ye do well. Be no discredit to your queenly mother. Take care that you honour your spiritual parentage, and maintain the high prestige of the elect family.

AFTER TWENTY-FIVE:

For Young Men and Women.*

N O parable teaches all sides of truth. It is wrong to attempt to make a parable run on all-fours ; it is intended to convey some one lesson, and if it teaches that, we must not attempt to draw everything else out of it. This parable sets forth the great God as a householder going forth to find men to work for Him ; but let no man imagine that God needs any of us. He was perfect—perfectly happy and perfectly glorious,—long before wing of angel moved in space, or time even existed. God ever was and still is self-contained and all-sufficient ; and if He chooses to make any creatures, or to preserve or use any of the creatures He has formed, that is not because He needs them, or is in the least degree dependent upon them. If God comes forth, in wondrous grace, to call any of us to work in His vineyard, it is not because He needs us, but because we need Him ; He does not set us to work because He needs workers, but because we need work. He calls us, not because He requires us, but because we require to be called.

Out of the various men who are mentioned, no one went to the vineyard, either early in the morning or later in the day, and requested to be employed. The householder came out into the market-place, and engaged his men. At the third hour, the sixth hour, and the ninth hour, not one had come of his

* Matt. xx. 3, 4.

own free will ; but in every case the first overture
was from the householder : "He went out to hire
labourers into his vineyard." And at the eleventh
hour, though the day was waning to a close, and the
sun was almost down, yet even then men were not
wise enough to wish to conclude the day in the right
service ; but they still remained, as they had been all
day, idling in the market-place until the generous employer came out, and expostulated with them, and
induced them to enter the vineyard. No man ever
comes to God till God first comes to him, so it is my
earnest desire that the impulses of Divine grace may
be even now felt in many hearts. God the Holy
Ghost is able to work upon the judgment, the understanding, the affections, the fears, the hopes, the will
of men ; and as He works upon them, He makes
men willing in the day of God's power, so that they
turn to Him, and enter into His service. That is, I
think, the first meaning of God's going out.

Personally, to most there is a time of God's going
forth, when they are specially moved to holy things.
It happens to some in childhood ; while they are yet
young, God speaks with them as He did with Samuel.
Perhaps, even on their little bed at night He appears
to them, and says, " Samuel, Samuel," and then helps
them to answer, " Here am I, for Thou didst call
me." To others, God comes a little farther on, when
it is the second hour of the day, while yet they are in
the heyday of their youth. It was the great privilege
of some of us for the Lord to call us while we were
yet young men ; and it is a great blessing when God
comes to us at that important period of our history.
To others, He appears when they are advanced in

life ; and, blessed be God, He comes also to some when the day is well-nigh closed, when the furrows of care are on their brows, and the snows of age are on their heads. He comes with power, by the effectual calling of the Holy Ghost, and He speaks to them, and they yield to His speaking, and give themselves up to be His servants for the rest of life.

I have heard or read a good many sermons to the young, or I have heard of them, sermons to those who are called by God early in the morning ; and I know there have been a great many sermons to those who have reached the eleventh hour ; so I thought that I would specially address those who have come to the third hour. What kind of people are those who are at the third hour ? What is the third hour ? Let us calculate a little. To the Jews, there were always twelve hours in the day, whether it was summertime or winter, so that the hour altered every day,—a very difficult way of computing time, for, as the day lengthened or shortened, they still divided the daylight into twelve hours. Well, think of human life as a period of twelve hours, and then form a calculation of what each hour must be. Take the whole of life roughly at 70, 72, 73, 74, or 75, as you like. Then you have to leave out the very earliest hours, —that period of life in which God does not call children to intelligent faith because they have not yet understanding enough to be capable of intelligent faith. Strike off a little for that ; and I should give the first three hours of life to be over at about 20, 21, 22, 23, or 24, if you please ; and I should say that the third hour of life would range from twenty-five to thirty-five. That is the period in which the man has come to perfection, and in which the woman has reached the fulness of her strength. There will be little growing after this; if not the zenith of life, yet certainly a considerably-developed period of life has now been reached. Very earnestly do I pray the Master to come out to you who have come to the third hour of your day, and to say to you, "Go ye also into the vineyard, and whatsoever is right I will give you."

Now, my friend—between twenty and forty years of age—I want *you* to become the servant of my Lord and Master; first, because already you have wasted some of the best hours of the day. There are no hours of the day like the early morning, when the dew is upon everything, and the smoke of care and trouble has not yet dimmed the landscape. Give me for enjoyment the earliest hours of a summer morning, when the birds are singing at their sweetest, and all Nature seems to be begemmed with her wedding jewels, her most delightful ornaments. There is no time for work like the first hours of the day; and there is no time for serving the Lord like the very earliest days of youth. I recollect the joy I had in the little service I was able to render to God when first I knew Him. I was engaged in a school all the week; but there was Saturday afternoon, and that Saturday afternoon, though I might rightly have used it for rest, and though I was but a boy myself, was given to a tract-district, and to visiting the very poor within my reach, and the Sabbath-day was devoted to teaching a class, and later on, addressing the Sunday-school. Oh, but how earnestly I did it all! I often think that I spoke better then than I did in later years, for I spoke so tremblingly, but my heart went with it all. And when I began to talk a little in the villages on the Sunday, and afterwards every night in the week, I know that I used to speak then what came fresh from my heart. There was little time for gathering much from books ; my chief library was the Word of God and my own experience, but I spoke out from my very soul,—no doubt with much blundering and much weakness, and much youthful folly, but oh, with such an intense desire to bring men to Christ ! I remember how I felt that I could cheerfully lay down my life if I might but save a poor old man, or bring a boy of my own age to the Saviour's feet. There is nothing in after life quite like those early morning works. Yet, my friend, you have let that period pass away ; you are five-and-twenty, you are thirty, are you even five-and-thirty, and still unsaved ! Then, do not waste any more precious time ; go at once to the Crucified, my adorable Lord and Master. There He stands, with a thorn-crown about His brow. Give Him, at least, the rest of your days ; and beg Him to pardon you for having lived so long without loving and serving Him.

Besides, I must plead with you at this age that you come to Christ, because already habits of idleness are forming upon you. "Nay," you say, "it is not so." I mean, spiritual idleness. You have not done anything yet for Christ, you have not even looked to see what you could do, you have not meditated upon what place in the vineyard you could occupy,— whether you could trim the vines, or water them, or gather the grapes, or tread the winefat. No, you have done nothing as yet ; and what I am afraid of

10

is that soon you will get settled down into this do-
nothing style, and you will go back to the dust from
whence you sprang, having achieved nothing for Him
who gave Himself that He might save us from our
sins.   Do not stay in that condition a moment
longer.   The wax is not very soft now, it is beginning to harden ; ere yet it is quite set, let the stamp
of sovereign grace be pressed upon it that your life
may yet bear the impress of Christ.

Moreover, Satan is very ready with his temptations ; and, you know, he always—

> " Finds some mischief still,
> For idle hands to do."

You have not gone into any gross open sin, I hope.
Peradventure, you have been kept, like the young
man in the narrative we read, quite pure and clean
outwardly.   Well, but, do you not see that—so good
a fellow as you are in your own estimation,—you are
extremely likely to be assailed by Satan ; and if he
can get you to indulge the lusts of the flesh, or some
other vain and sinful pleasure, he will take great
delight in ruining you?   Oh, how I wish that I could
get you enlisted into my Lord's army !   Here, take
the shilling.   I mean, believe on the Lord Jesus
Christ, and accept Him as your Saviour, and become
His faithful servant.   I wish I could put a hoe into
your hands, or a pruning-knife, or something with
which you should be induced to go into the vineyard
of my Master, to serve Him.   You who have reached
five-and-twenty, or thirty, or five-and-thirty, I want
you to come to Christ, because your sun may go down
at noon.   Such things do happen.

It seems to me that if God will spare you, there is

a fair opportunity of work yet before you. As I look at men and women in the prime of life, and know that many of them are not yet converted to God, I feel that Satan must not have you, and the world must not have you, and sin must not have you, but Christ *must* have you. He is such a glorious Saviour and Lord that I would fain have all the world at His feet. He deserves so much that, if all kings fell down before Him, and all princes called Him blessed, He deserves it well ; and, if you will do so, it shall be but right. What a life you may yet lead ! What usefulness, what happiness, what blessedness, may yet be your portion ! If you could look through a telescope that could reveal what you might be if your heart were consecrated to God, what a heaven below and what a heaven above awaits you, I feel sure that you would now yield to the calling of the Great Householder, and enter His vineyard.

In a literal sense, many are altogether idling. There are, still, many who ought to be Christians, who are really idle. Sometimes, when I have been by the seaside, I have seen a great many well-to-do folk who had nothing the matter with them, they were perfectly well, yet they were idling their time away day after day ; and I have almost thought, " If they were thrown into the Mediterranean, who would lose anything by them ? " Are there not plenty of people just like that even among those who come to our places of worship ? They consume so much bread and meat, and if they do not mind they will get consumed one of these days, for they do no good to anybody. What a pity it is that a man who stands nearly six feet in his shoes should be doing nothing, and that a woman who is made for love and kindness should not be scattering that love and kindness on all sides, and serving the Lord! To those of you who are of the ages from thirty to forty, who yet are idle, I do wish to say, with all earnestness, in the name of the Lord Jesus Christ, come to Him by faith, confess your idleness and all your other sins, seek His grace and mercy, and then enter His vineyard, and serve Him while you may.

There are also others who are laboriously idle, wearied with toils which accomplish nothing of real worth. The man who is spending all his life in his business, living simply to get money, has but trifling aims, for temporary objects engross him. He who lives for God, for Christ, for the good of men, lives for an object worthy of an immortal being ; but he who lives only for his own aggrandisement, lives for such a temporary and trifling object that he may be said to be idle though he wears himself to death with his labour. Oh, if this be all you do, the Master thinks you idle! You are doing nothing for Him, nothing worth the doing, nothing that can be written in the roll and record of history as a great feat done by a soul redeemed with the blood of Christ. O ye laborious idlers, I pray that you may be made to go and work in the Master's vineyard.

There are some who are idling because of their constant indecision. They are not altogether bad, but they are not good. They do not serve the devil except it be by neglecting to serve God. Though they are idle, they are full of good intentions ; but so they have long been. If they were now what they resolved to be ten years ago, there would be a great change in them. But no ; and, apparently, in ten years' time they will be as they are now ; that is to say, if God spares them. They will go no farther, for they are of the sort that resolve, and resolve, and yet remain the same. I almost wish that they would say that they would be lost, sooner than say that they will be saved, and yet not mean it ; for, if they said that they would be lost, they would recoil from it with horror after having said it. But now they play with God, and with eternity, and Heaven, and hell, and say, " I will, I will, I will ; " and always it is, " I will," yet they never will to make " I will " a thing of the present moment. If a house were on fire, and you were in the upper story, it would be a pity to say, " I will escape by-and-by when the flames have reached another story ; but I must wait a little while." No ; you would be eager to escape at once, I am sure that you would ; and wisdom dictates that a man should not always parley, and say, " I will," and yet never come up to the mark. Wisdom dictates that, by the grace of God, he should say, " I have reached the end of my indecision ; I will begin to live for God, if He will give me spiritual life. I will cast off the works of darkness if God will give me spiritual light. I will lay myself at Jesu's feet, and cry, ' Save me, O Lord, for I long to escape from my sin, and to be an idler no longer.' "

One would think, from what you hear from some men, that the service of God was a very difficult, dreary, dismal, hard, toilsome business ; but it is not so. The work which the Lord would have us do is very proper and fit for us. He would have us recognize that we are sinners, and He therefore would

have us come and be washed ; and when we are
washed, He would have us realize that it is our joy,
our duty, our privilege, our delight, to show forth the
praises of Him who has thus saved us. The service
of God is the most fit employment for a man to be
engaged in ; it never degrades him, it never wearies
him, for in the service of God we gain fresh strength ;
and the more we serve Him, the more we can serve
Him.

The Lord invites you to a service in which He will
give you all the tools and all the strength you need.
When He sends you to His vineyard, He does not
expect you to go home and fetch a basket of tools.
God does not expect sinners to bring their own
Saviour, and He never sends His soldiers on a warfare at their own charges. He who yields himself up
to be a servant of God shall find himself singularly
prepared and specially helped to do all that God asks
him to do.

More than that, if you will come into God's vineyard,
you shall work with God, and so be ennobled. That
seems to me the most wonderful thing about our service, that we are " workers together with God." To
bend the tendril of that vine, and find a hand almighty softly working with our own ;—to take the
sharp pruning-knife, and cut off the too-luxuriant
bough, and feel that there is a knife sharper than ours
cutting as we cut ;—to take a spade, and dig about
the vine, and all the while to feel and know that there
is a secret Worker digging deeper than we are digging, and so making what we do effectual. If you
are building for God, and you lift the trowel, or the
hammer, and feel that there is another hand lifting

another trowel, and another hammer, building with you and building by you, you are divinely honoured. You are of the nobility of Heaven if God works with you ; and it is to that position He invites you when He says, " Go ye also into the vineyard."

Let me tell you that, if you engage in this work, it shall be growingly pleasant to you. The little difficulties at the commencement shall soon be gone. The service of God may seem, at first, like swimming against the stream ; but afterwards you shall discover that there is a pleasure even in the opposing element, for the live fish always prefers to swim up the stream. You shall find a delight in your difficulties, a sacred joy in that which seems at first so arduous ; and as you live and labour for your Lord, it shall become joy upon joy to serve Him and glorify His holy name.

We must remember that the householder went out again at the sixth hour ; say, thirty-five to forty-five. He called those whom he found then, and when he called them, they went into the vineyard. You who are between thirty-five and fifty, in the very strength of your days, Christ will not refuse to employ you if you will come at His call.

Then the householder went out again at the ninth hour ; say, fifty, fifty-five, sixty,—or, farther on, sixty-five. It was getting late, but still they could do a good stroke of work if they threw all their energies into it. No man need despair of doing a life-work even now ; if you cannot do long work, you can do strong work. There are some who begin work very late, but they go at it with such vigour and earnestness that they get through a good deal. I do not see

why you should not ; at any rate, come in now. Old
men have done great things in the past ; if they have
not the vivacity of youth, they have more wisdom ;
if they have not all the strength, they have more
prudence. There is a place for you to fill, though so
many years have flown over your head. If you come
to Christ even now, He will use you in His vineyard.

Ah ! but, best of all, the householder went out
even at the eleventh hour. He might have said, " It
is of no use to go out now, for if I bring them in,
there is only one hour left for them to work in."
Still, as I have told you, it was not because he
needed men, but because they needed the money, that
he employed them. So, to show that, as he did
not need them at the first hour, and did not need
them at the third, or the sixth, or the ninth hour,
much less could he need them at the eleventh hour,
yet he would still go out. There they are ! I see
them ; they are a pack of old men and old women.
You would not engage them, I am sure ; you would
say, " They will take half their time for talking, and
the other half for wiping the sweat from their brows,
and doing nothing. There is not any strength left in
the poor old souls, they had better have an alms-
house, and a basin of gruel, and sit by the fireside."
But this good householder's engagement of the men
was not for his own sake, but for their sakes ; he
felt that he might as well engage these as he had
done the rest ; so he said to them, " Here, it is the
eleventh hour, but go and work in my vineyard, and
whatsoever is right I will give you." I feel it a great
joy to have been called to work for my Lord in the
early hours of life's day ; and I hope by-and-by to

be able to say, " O God, Thou hast taught me from my youth : and hitherto have I declared Thy wondrous works. Now also when I am old and greyheaded, O God, forsake me not ; until I have shewed Thy strength unto this generation, and Thy power to every one that is to come."

It is the best and the happiest thing of all, if we have served our Lord from our youth ; but if you have missed that privilege, to your own grief and sorrow, if you are old, yet even now the Lord invites you ; He calls you, He bids you come and welcome, and if you do but come to Him, He will give you your penny, too, even as He gives it to those who have begun their working day so early.

If I remember, there was a man who was converted at the age of 103. He was sitting under a hedge, I think in Virginia, and he remembered a sermon that he had heard Mr. Flavel preach at Plymouth ; and recalling a striking part of it, he turned to God, and found peace and pardon. He was spared to live three years more, and when he died, this inscription was put over his grave, " Here lies a babe in grace, aged three years, who died, according to nature, aged 106."

JOASH AND HIS FRIEND JEHOIADA.*

THERE is a book called *The Museum of Natural History*, and the most singular animal in that museum is man. It would be far more easy to understand any other creature than to understand a human being. He is worthy of great study; and the more he is studied, the more will he surprise you. There are certain characters that are great curiosities. Alas, there are also other characters that are great monstrosities! You can never tell, from what a man is, what he will be. The case before us is a very extraordinary one, because here is a man with every possible advantage, who through a number of years exhibited the brightest form of character; and yet in the end he was not thought worthy to be laid in the sepulchres of his fathers with others of the kings of Judah; neither was he worthy of any royal interment, for the latter part of his life blackened and defiled the whole of his career, and he who began his reign like the dawning of the day ended it like the middle of the night.

I wonder whether any we know will turn out to be very sinful and wicked before life is over; I mean, those who have begun well, who are now the hope and joy of those who know them, but who will end badly, in dishonour to themselves, and grief to their households? Probably you can find them out by this one test. Those who say, "It is impossible that it should

---

2 Chronicles xxiv.

be so with us," are probably the persons ; while those who are afraid lest it should be so, and ask for grace that it may not be so, are probably those who will be preserved, and whose path will shine brighter and brighter unto the perfect day.

What need there is to go below the surface in the examination of moral and spiritual character! In appearance Joash was all that we could wish ; yet, had he really been what he seemed to be, he would have continued so. If there had been that work of grace within his soul which there appeared to be in his life, he would not have turned aside as he did ; for where a work of grace is real and true, it is known by its abiding influence throughout the whole of life. Where godly principles have been imparted, and a Divine life has been infused, these things are not taken from a man. "They went out from us, but they were not of us ; " said the apostle John, "for if they had been of us, they would no doubt have continued with us : but they went out, that they might be made manifest that they were not all of us." So was it with Joash. He turned aside from God because he had never truly known the Lord at all, and his last end was worse than the first because his beginning was really not such as it had seemed to be.

Although Joash came of a bad family, yet he had a good aunt, who was married to the high priest, and the aunt and the uncle took care of young Joash. When he was but an infant, they stole him away, so that Athaliah might not kill him with the rest of the seed royal ; and thus Joash had this remarkable privilege that : " He was with them hid in the house of God six years." That is a splendid beginning for any life, to be hid in the house of God six years. I do not think we ever value enough those first six years of a child's life; impressions then made have a remarkable influence over the rest of life. Joash was where God's praise was sung from day to day, and where holy prayer was perpetually offered. He was seldom beyond the fragrance of the perfumed incense, or away from the sight of the white-robed priests. He heard nothing that could defile him, but everything that could instruct and purify him. He was hidden in the house of the Lord so as not even to go out of it, concealed with godly people for the first six years of his life.

The first thing that you can remember is your mother taking you to a place of worship; you can never forget the time when father also led you there, and did not seem to be happy unless his boy was trotting by his side when he went to hear the gospel. Amongst our earliest recollections are the memories of holy hymns, and the sayings of gracious people, in whom, as children, we took an interest when they came to our father's house. It is a grand thing that the first days of one's life should bear the impress of the Divine finger. It is well when the vessel begins to revolve upon the wheel, and the clay is soft and plastic, that the first fingers that should touch and shape it should be the fingers of God's servants. God grant that they may be as the very finger of God upon our souls! Thus Joash began his career by being hid in the house of the Lord six years.

After he was seven years of age, he was started on his life's business in a very admirable way. He was to be the king, but there had to be great care taken to sweep away the usurper from the throne, and to put the little king upon it, and Jehoiada managed the whole affair with great skill. He also drew up a covenant for the king to sign, a covenant with God that he would be obedient to Jehovah as the supreme King, and a covenant with the people that he would rule according to equity and right, and not tyrannize over them. It was all done so well that no objection was ever taken to it ; and Joash reigned with great prosperity and happiness over a people who were blessed by his rule, Jehoiada all the while being his faithful prime minister and guide. It is a grand thing to be started in life aright ; it is half the battle, you know, to begin well. Some young men, and some young women, too, are launched in life wrongly ; it seems almost a matter of course that they should be too strongly tempted, and in all probability yield to the temptation. But many of you were not started so ; you began with a father's blessing, and with a mother's prayers. You recollect your first going out into life ; some of us remember the ride on the coach when, early in the morning, we had to leave our father's house for the first time. Perhaps it was a cold and bitter frosty morning when we started in those old days to go across the country ; we recollect it well, and how God cared for us, and blessed us ; and we desire to praise Him that He has preserved us even unto this day.

I am showing you the bright side of Joash's career first. After the six years in the house of God, he had a grand start in life with everything to his advantage. Alas, alas, alas, that, with such a bright beginning, he should come to such a sad end !

Notice also that, being thus well started, " Joash
did that which was right in the sight of the Lord all
the days of Jehoiada the priest." While that good
man lived, the king was under his influence ; he con-
sulted him in every matter of importance, he seems
even to have been guided by him to some extent in
the matter of his marriage. He was plastic under
his uncle's hand, and he did that which was right in
the sight of the Lord, not only that which was right
in the sight of good people. His life seems to have
been at least outwardly obedient to the law of
Jehovah, and he yielded himself up, apparently, at
any rate, to be a loyal servant of the great King ;
and that he did, not for a short time only, but all the
days in which Jehoiada lived. Well, now, have we
not known men and women, whose lives have been
under the benign influence of some kind elderly
person, uncle or aunt, father or mother, and they
have done what was right year after year, as long as
their godly relatives lived ? They have been diligent
in going up to God's house, apparently devout in
Bible-reading and prayer, willing to assist in holy
work in the school and all sorts of service for the
Lord, and leading outwardly most useful, admirable
lives all the time that these higher influences were
over them.

More than this, he was zealous for the externals
of religion : " It came to pass after this, that Joash
was minded to repair the house of the Lord." He
actually chided Jehoiada, his uncle, because of the
slowness of the Levites : " The king called for
Jehoiada the chief, and said unto him, Why hast
thou not required of the Levites to bring in out of

Judah and out of Jerusalem the collection?" Yes,
and there are some whose hearts are not right
towards God, who nevertheless are very zealous
about the externals of divine worship. It is a much
easier thing to build a temple for God than it is be a
temple for God; and it is a much more common
thing for persons to show zeal in repairing temples
than in reforming their own manners. So this young
man, you see, went even beyond his uncle in intense
zeal for the cause of God, just as there are many
who, trained up in the ways of the Lord, are inde-
fatigable in rendering some external service to the
cause of the Lord Jesus Christ. They would give to
the building of a church; they would work hard to
promote the paying for it, and so forth; but, alas,
you may give, and you may work, and you may
attend to all the externals of religion, and yet have
no part nor lot in the matter! Bunyan says that,
when he was an ungodly man, he yet had such a
reverence for the outwards of religion that he would
fain have kissed the ground that the clergyman
walked upon, and every nail in the door of the church
seemed holy to him. That is all very fine; but
unless there is a great deal more than that in us, we
shall fall far short of the requirements of God.

All this while, Joash influenced other people for
good. As king, he kept back the nation from the
worship of idols; as king, he threw the cloak of his
patronage over those who worshipped Jehovah; and
things seemed to go well for years, "all the days of
Jehoiada the priest." As long as Jehoiada lived,
Joash seemed to be all that he should be.

THE LAST DAYS OF JOASH.

EARLY PROMISE NOT REALIZED.

ALL that Joash had done was to give his heart to Jehoiada, not to Jehovah. It is very easy to be outwardly religious by giving your heart to your mother, or your father, or your aunt, or your uncle, or some good person who helps you to do what is right. You are doing all this out of love to them, which is at best but a very secondary motive. God says, "My son, give *Me* thine heart." If your religion is taken up to please any creature, it is not the religion which pleases the Creator. Your homage is due, not to any-one here below, but to Him who sitteth in the heavens, whose kingdom ruleth over all.

This yielding to godly influences may exist without any personal, vital godliness whatever. You may meet with God's people, and yet not be one of God's people. You may give attention to God's servant, and yet not be yourself God's servant. A young man may yield to his mother's advice, and yet never be really repentant on account of sin. He may listen to his father's word, and pay respect to the externals of his father's religion, but yet never have believed in the Lord Jesus Christ. You must your-selves repent, and yourselves believe in Christ, or else all the rest will aggravate your sin by increasing your responsibility, but it will not go even a hair's breadth towards your salvation. I would have every person

11

examine himself to see whether his religion is vital to his own soul. Have you been born again ? I enquire not now about your mother, or father, or friends. Have *you* been born again ? Are you now condemned under sin, or are you justified by faith in Jesus Christ ? There can be no proxies, and no sponsors here ; every man must give account for himself to God ; and each man, each woman, must come to the Saviour personally, and accept Him, and be saved by Him, or else eternal ruin is certain.

I do believe also that a character like that of Joash, a yielding character, an externally pious character, may even prevent men from being saved at all. I mean, you may take it for granted that you are saved ; but you must not take anything for granted between God and your soul. I charge you to make sure work here ; take your wealth for granted if you like ; take the title-deeds of your estate for granted if you please ; but between God and your soul let everything be settled, and straight, and clear, and sure, and have no mistakes about this matter. It is so easy to have been under religious influence from our youth up, and then to go on, year after year, never having raised the question whether we are Christians or not, saying to ourselves, " Of course it is all right." You will be much nearer the truth if you say, " Of course it is all wrong." You will be much more likely to come to an honest conclusion if you rather suspect yourself too much than believe in yourself too much ; I am sure that, in speaking thus, I am giving you sound teaching.

After all, to be under godly influences year after year, without any great trial or temptation, may leave the personal character altogether undeveloped. Some put children under restraint continually, never suffering them to have any sort of temptation. It is so with children sometimes in large institutions ; they have not any money, and they cannot steal any, because there is nobody else who has any ; they are kept out of the world altogether, they live only amongst their own company, and there is very much of prayer and everything that is good ; and often, when they go out into the world, those who have trained them are altogether disappointed with them ; yet they need not very much wonder. If a person on dry land thinks he can swim, it is not certain that he will swim when he gets into the sea. We must have some kind of test, or else we cannot be sure of the character ; we cannot know whether a child is honest or not if it never has any chance to take that which is not its own. You cannot be sure about principle being in any young man if he has been kept under a glass case, and if his principles have never been tried. That was the condition of Joash ; the real character of the man had never come out at all, because Jehoiada, as it were, covered him. He was guided and influenced by the high priest ; but his own disposition only wanted an opportunity of developing itself.

I have heard of an officer in India, who had brought up a young leopard. It was completely tamed, apparently it was as tame as a cat, and the officer had no fear of his leopard. It went up and down the stairs, and entered into every room of his house ; he never suspected for a single moment that it would be guilty of blood-shedding ; but, while he was asleep, one afternoon, in his chair, the leopard licked his hand in all tenderness as a cat might have done ; but after licking for a while, it licked too hard, and a little blood began to flow. It no sooner tasted blood than the old leopard spirit was up, and his master was his master no more. So does it happen to many that, by being shut in, and tamed, as it were, but not changed, subdued but not renewed, kept in check but not converted, there has come a time afterwards when the taste of blood has called out the old nature, and away the man has gone. You would never have thought that he could act as he did ; but he did so because he had not a new nature.   It was human nature held in check for a while, not the Spirit of God creating a new life, and infusing a new character into the soul.

Do you see where I am coming to ?   I am speaking to those who have not passed from death unto life, to you who have never been renewed in the spirit of your mind.   I do pray you not to imagine that natural religion is spiritual religion. Do not mistake the lessons learnt at your mother's knee for the teachings of the Holy Ghost, do not confuse *a* change with *the* change ; and do not think that anything that can come to you by your first birth can serve your turn without a second birth.   "Ye must be born again," or else, though you spent the first six years of your life in the house of God, and though you were started under the most hallowed influences, you only want an opportunity, a temptation, a peculiar stress laid upon you, and you will go off whither the old nature carries you, and you will find out for yourself, and to the horror of others, that all your early training had effected nothing, because it stopped short of the kingdom of God and His righteousness.

We like young people to be obedient, we are very glad to have to do with those plastic characters that are readily shaped ; but, at the same time, we ought never to be too sure about them. A person with grit in his character, if really affected by the grace of God, may turn out a far better man than your too plastic, pliable character. How many we know who are very good, but there is nothing in them at all! We have known some others who were dreadfully hard to manage, and to get at ; but when at last a change has been wrought by Divine grace, that very obstinacy and wilfulness of theirs, when sanctified, has given a strength to their character, and instead of being a drawback, it has been a help.

This young Joash was exceedingly supple in the hand of Jehoiada, but alas ! Jehoiada was dead. Other counsellors came and flattered him : " Now after the death of Jehoiada came the princes of Judah, and made obeisance to the king." Do you not see those gentlemen coming, bowing and scraping a hundred times before they get up to him ? They " made obeisance to the king." Jehoiada had not often made much obeisance to him ; he had treated him with due respect as his king, but he had also spoken to him honestly and faithfully. Joash had somebody to look up to while Jehoiada lived, and now he found himself a great man with everybody looking up to him ; and the princes of Judah, the fashionable part of the realm, the respectable people who never had been worshippers of Jehovah, but who had always preferred the more recondite, ritualistic, and sensuous service of Baal, the philosophical god, came, and bowed, and made obeisance to the king.

I think I can hear what they said : "Royal sir, we congratulate you upon being released from leading-strings. Now you can think for yourself. It is a fine thing for a young man to be delivered from the power of his old uncle; he was no doubt a very excellent person, we were present at his funeral, and we paid him all due respect ; still, he was a regular old fossil, one who never had made any progress at all. He clung to the worship of Jehovah, and served the God of his fathers. Royal sir, we congratulate you upon the liberty to which you have attained. Besides that, we fear that you have been considerably priest-ridden. This Jehoiada was a priest, and of course you respected and venerated his character ; but you could not indulge yourself as long as he lived. We have always had high thoughts of you, royal sir, we always believed that you would break out one of these days ; and now that the good man is laid asleep, we are sure that you will not let his dead hand rest upon you, but you will wake up, and be abreast of the age, and keep up with the spirit of the times."

You know how they do it ; it is always being done, this pouring of drops of poison into the ear, these soft, subtle flatteries. Even when a man has reached Joash's age, he is not beyond the power of flattery ; I wonder how old a man would be when he would be too old to love flattery. Of course, he always likes to be told, " Ah, dear sir, I know that you could not bear flattery," being at that moment more highly flattered than at any other time in his life. So these princes of Judah did ; and poor Joash, good Joash, Joash who repaired the temple, Joash who was even more intensely earnest than Jehoiada himself, was led astray by the soft words of the deceivers, and we find him burying his religion with his uncle. In Jehoiada's grave he buried all his piety. Some whom I have known, and over whom I have wept, have acted in the same way.

After that, he went off to sin. The images which he had broken down were set up again ; the groves which he had cut down were planted again ; and he who seemed so zealous a servant of Jehovah had now become a worshipper of the foul Ashtaroth, and bowed before the accursed Baalim. Oh, sad, sad, sad mischief this ! There was a want of principle in Joash, and it is of that I want to warn all. Do not be satisfied with the practice without the principles of piety. It is not enough to have a correct creed ; you must have a renewed heart. It is not sufficient to have an ornate ritual ; you must have a holy life, and to be holy you must be renewed by the Holy Spirit. If this change is not wrought in you by the Holy Ghost, you who yield so readily to good will yield just as quickly to evil.

What happened next? Joash refused reproof. God sent prophets to the people, and they came, and warned them, testifying against the idolaters : " But they would not give ear." This Joash, who had spent his first six years in the temple, now would not give ear to the Lord's prophets. He was always ready to listen to Jehoiada, but now he would not give ear. He was a tremendous zealot for repairing the temple, with most costly architecture, and gold

and silver without limit; but now he will not give
heed to God's servants at all.   They may speak with
all their heart and soul; but he is as the deaf adder
that will not hear the voice of the charmer, charm he
never so wisely.

Yet he was once your good young man, your pious
young man!   Oh, what a sifter London has been to
many like Joash!   Many do I remember whose story
was like this.   They had been to the house of God
always; they were brought up where there was a
family altar in the house; everybody reckoned them
to be Christians; and they came to London.   At
first, they went where their father exhorted them to
go, to some humble place where the gospel was
preached; but after a time they thought it was not
wrong to go on the Sunday to see one of the more
showy religious places.   That done, they went to
some showy place that was not religious.   They
worked so hard all the week that they must go out a
little into the fresh air on the Sunday; and by
degrees they found companions who led them, little
by little, from the path of integrity and chastity,
till "the good young man" was as vile as any on
the streets of London, and he who seemed to be
a saint became not only a sinner, but the maker of
sinners.

What did Joash do next?   He slew his friend's
son.   Old Jehoiada's son, Zechariah, one of those
who had helped to put the crown upon young Joash's
head, was at last moved to come out, and speak in
the midst of the temple service to the people, as he
had a right to do; and he began to upbraid them for
turning aside from Jehovah to the worship of the foul

idol gods. Now, see, the tiger's blood is up! Joash bids them kill him. How dare he testify against his king? True, he is the son of his best friend, he is his own cousin, he is one who helped him to ascend the throne ; but what matters all that to this once good young man ? The milk of human kindness is soured now. The oil that was so soft burns fiercely when it once takes fire. " Let Zechariah die. Kill him in the temple. Bespatter the sacred altar with his blood. Stone him. He has dared to speak against me." See your soft clay, how hard and coarse, and rough it has become! I have seen this change come over men. I believe that the worst persecutors in the world are generally made of those who once were tender and soft-hearted. Nero would at first scarcely sign the death-warrant of a criminal; and yet he lived to delight in wholesale murder. When the son of perdition was wanted to betray his Lord, the raw material of the traitor was found in an apostle. You cannot make an out-and-out bad man except from one who seems to be good. You must take the man who has been six years in the temple, the man who has done that which is right in the sight of the Lord all the days of Jehoiada, to make such a devil as Joash turned out to be when he killed the son of his benefactor in the court of the house of the Lord. Oh, I could look steadily in the face of some, and in the spirit of prophecy I could burst out into tears to think of what they will yet be, what they will yet do, and what they will yet say! Perhaps you ask, " Is thy servant a dog that he should do this thing ? " Oh, sir, you are worse than a dog ; there lurks within you a heart "deceitful above all things, and desperately wicked, who can know it?" Oh, that you did know it, and would turn to God, and say, "O Lord, renew me! Lord, make a new creature of me! Lord, save me, that I never may do such things as now, to-day, I think it impossible that I should ever do!"

This Joash, perishing, miserable, having no faith in God, robbed the temple, and gave all the gold and treasures unto Hazael the Syrian. Personally, he was full of disease, and by-and-by his own servants, disgusted with him for his conduct towards Jehoiada's son, slew him on his bed. What a death for the young man who was six years hidden away in the house of the Lord!

Oh, if I could tell some of you what will become of you, you would be so angry with me! If I could prophesy to some good young fellow—I mean, outwardly good as Joash was at first, but without a new heart, without the grace of God in his soul,—if I could prophesy to him what he will be, he would spit in my face in indignation that I should dare to foretell such a thing. There is not a man or woman who is safe from the most abominable sin until they yield themselves to Christ. There is not one who is sure that the deepest damnation of hell will not be your portion unless you come and commit your soul into the hands of Jesus, who is a faithful Keeper of them that put their trust in Him. Can there be a Character Insurance Society? There can be no such society formed by men that can insure our character; yet God has formed one. "The righteous also shall hold on his way; and he that hath clean hands shall be stronger and stronger." The Lord will keep him, and preserve him from evil, for "the path of the just is as the shining light, that shineth more and more unto the perfect day." I do adjure you, by the living God, my hopeful young friend, yield yourself to Jesus Christ, and seek His guardian care, lest the fair blossom of to-day should never bring forth fruit, but end in disappointment!

A BOLD AND EARNEST PROFESSION.

DAVID said, "O Lord, *truly* I am Thy servant." "Truly." The word of caution is, If you become the servant of God, become the servant of God *truly*. God is not mocked. It is the curse of our churches that we have so many merely nominal Christians in them. It is the plague of this age that so many put on Christ's livery, and yet never do Him a hand's turn. Oh, if you serve God, mean it! If a man serves the devil, let him serve the devil; but if he serves God, let him serve God. Some people serve their business very actively, but not their God. There was, years ago, a brother who used to pray at the prayer-meeting occasionally in a low tone, as if he had no lungs left. Seldom could you hear what he said, and if you listened and strained your ear there was still nothing to hear. I thought that the brother had a bad voice, and so I never called on him to pray any more. But, stepping one day into his shop, I heard him say in a commanding voice, "John, fetch that half-hundred!" "Oh, dear!" I thought, "that is the kind of voice he has in his business, but when he comes into the service of God, that little squeak is all he can give." Is there not much of this hypocrisy abroad? God is to have the cheese-parings of a man's life, and he flings these down as if they were all that God was worth. But as for the world, that is to have the vigour of his life and the cream of his being. God does not want nominal

servànts. " O Lord, truly I am Thy servant," said
David ; and he that does not mean to be *truly* God's
servant, let him not pretend to be one at all.

Now, I want every young man who is a Christian
to make it known by an open avowal of his disciple-
ship. I mean that there should not be one who
follows the Lord Jesus Christ in a mean, sneaking,
indistinct, questionable way. It has become the
custom of many to try to be Christians and never
say anything about it. This is beneath contempt.
But I urge you true servants of Christ to " out with
it," and never to be ashamed, because if ever a bold
profession was required it is required now. You may
not be burned at the stake for saying that you are a
Christian, but I believe that the old enmity to Christ
is not removed, and a true believer will still be called
upon to take up the cross. In many a house in
London a young man will have to run the gauntlet
if he is known to be a Christian. Run the gauntlet,
then ! You have an honourable opportunity. It is
a grand thing to be permitted to endure reproach for
Christ's sake ; and you should look at it as a choice
privilege that you are counted worthy not only to
believe in the Lord Jesus Christ, but also to suffer for
His sake. Nowadays the world wants decided men.
Everywhere it seems to be imagined that you may
believe what you like, or believe nothing ; and do as
you like, or do nothing, and the result will be all the
same both to the unbeliever and the man of faith.
But it is not so. It is time for the out-and-out
servant of the Lord to put down his foot and say,
" I have believed ; therefore have I spoken. I am a
Christian, and while I leave you to your individual

liberty I mean to have mine, and I mean to exercise that liberty by being openly and unquestionably on the side of Christ, and on the side of that which is pure, and sober, and right, and true, and good."

Is not this well deserved by Christ? Oh, if He never was ashamed of us we never ought to be ashamed of Him! If the Lord of life and glory stooped to die for us, could we ever stoop at all even if we rolled into the mire or dropped into the grave for Him? Surely, our blessed Lord deserves to be followed by heroes. Every man in the presence of the cross-bearing Jesus should feel that to take up his cross and follow Christ is the simplest and most natural thing that can be; and he should resolve in God's strength that he will do it, and continue to obey the Lord, though all the world should ridicule. Let me tell you that it is the easiest thing to do, after all: as compared with compromise it is simplicity itself. I have known many young Christians who have come up to London, and they have determined that they would serve God if they could, but that they would keep it very quiet, and so they have attempted to be Christians on the sly; but they have failed. If you are a genuine Christian it will be found out as surely as you are a living man. If you go down to Mitcham when the lavender is ripe, you may shut all your windows, but you will find that the perfume of the lavender will get into your house somehow. Christianity has a perfume about it which will spread abroad, so that all in the house enquire, "What is all this?" The wicked wags will whisper that you are "a Christian young man"; and if you have not come out at first it will be very hard for you afterwards. Begin as you mean to go on, young man. Do not hide your flag and try to sail under false colours, for both good and bad will be against you in that case. You will be hunted from place to place if the dogs find that you will run : you will make rare sport for the hunters if you take to your heels. Come straight out and let them do their best or their worst. Live a most consistent life, and the other young fellows will know whereabouts you are. They will soon reckon you up, and if you are sincere, before long they will let you alone ; and if they do not, forbearance is still yours. If they continue to persecute you, so much the worse *for them ;* for you, by your quiet, holy life, will make them feel that it is hard for them to kick against the pricks. But, any-how, do come out bravely. Some young fellows are like rats behind the wainscot—you do not mind coming out of a night to eat the crumbs on the floor but there you are, back again directly : I mean that you will join in religious exercises if it is not known to the shop, but you would not for the world become suspected of real religion. Is that how true Christians should act? No ; put on your livery. "But I do not care about joining a church," says one. Very likely ; but do you not know that it is found to be a convenient and proper thing in warfare that a soldier should wear regimentals? At first Oliver Cromwell's Ironsides were dressed anyhow and everyhow ; but in the *mêlée* with the Cavaliers it sometimes happened that an Ironside was struck down by mistake by the sword of one of his own brethren, and so the general said, "You wear red coats, all of you. We must know our own men from the enemy." What

Cromwell said he meant, and they had to come in their red coats, for it is found essential in warfare that men should be known by some kind of regimental. Now, you that are Christ's, do not go about as if you were ashamed of His Majesty's service. Put on your red coats : I mean, come out as acknowledged Christians. Unite with a body of Christian people, and be distinctly known to be Christ's. How are the ordinances of the Lord's house to be sustained if every man is to go to Heaven alone by the back way? Come out boldly. If any man wants to laugh at a Christian, step out, and say, " Laugh at me. If anybody wants to abuse a fellow, and call him a hypocrite, a Presbyterian, a Methodist, come on ! I am ready for you." If you have once done that, and come right out on the straight, you shall find it the easiest thing in life to bear the reproach of Christ.

Young men, if you should meet with any reproach for Christ, a reward awaits you. Shall I tell you a parable? There was once a king's son who went upon a journey incognito, and he journeyed into a far country ; but there he was ill-treated, and because of his language and his appearance the people of the land set him in the pillory, which was of old the place of scorn. They set him there, and the mob gathered round him, and threw all kinds of filth and ordure upon him. This prince unknown must needs be pelted thus, and made as the offscouring of all things. But there was among them one man who loved the prince, and who recognized him, and determined to bear him company. He mounted the pillory and stood by his side, and wiped his face with his handkerchief, and whenever he could he put himself in the

12

way of the mire and dirt that he might catch it and screen the prince from it. Years went on, and it came to pass that the prince was back in his kingdom in all his glory, and the courtiers were standing round about the throne. This man who had been a poor man in his own country was summoned to the court, and when he arrived at the palace, the prince saw him, and said to the peers of the realm, "Stand aside and make way for this man. He was with me when I was ill-treated and scorned, and now he shall be with me in my glory, chief among you here." Do you not know the story of how our Lord Jesus came down to earth and suffered many things, and how He was despised and rejected of men? Young man, are you the man who would wipe His blessed face and share His shame, and take half turns with the man of Nazareth in all the obloquy and scorn? Are you that man? Then there shall come a day when the great Father on His throne shall spy you out and say, "Make a lane, ye angels! Stand back, seraphim and cherubim! Make way for this man. He was with My Son in His humiliation, and now he shall be with Him in His glory." Will you receive that mark of honour? Not unless you are prepared to put on the badge of Christ, and say, "I am His servant and His follower from this day to life's end." God help you to do it! O Holy Spirit, lead scores of young men to shoulder the cross!

Were you ever in bonds? Did you ever feel *the bonds of guilt?* Are you believing in Christ? Then those bonds are loosed, for your sin is forgiven you for Christ's sake, and you are delivered from all condemnation. Now, you are clean delivered from

the bonds of guilt and despair, you are also saved
from *the power of sin*. The habits that were your
masters are now destroyed. The lusts that lorded it
over you are now slain ; and you are free. Will you
not wish to be bound to Christ henceforth because
He has loosed your bonds? I know some men in
this world who talk a great deal about being free, but
they are always in chains. There is a man I know
for whom the devil makes a nauseous mixture—at
least, to me it is very nauseous ; and he says, " Drink
a quart of it ; " and he drinks. " Drink another,"
says the devil; and he does so. " Drink another,"
says the devil ; and his brain begins to reel, and
he is all on fire. " Drink it," says the devil ; and
he lets it run down his throat, for he is in chains.
I know another who, against his better self, will go
into sin, which he knows to be sin, and knows to
be injurious to him. Yet he goes in a silly manner
and harms himself more and more. He is led by
the nose by the devil, and he says that he cannot
resist. He is a slave in the worst sense. Oh,
blessed is the man who can say, " Thou hast loosed
my bonds ; no evil habit enslaves me now, no passion
controls me, no lust enchains me " ! Young friend, if
you can stand up and say, " I am free from myself ; I
am no longer the slave of sin ! "—you are a blessed
man, and you may well be God's servant for ever !

What a mercy it is to be delivered from the bonds
of the fear of man ! Some young men dare not call
their souls their own for fear of their employers. A
great many more are dreadfully in fear of the young
man who sleeps in the next bed. Oh, dear, they
dare not do what is right ! Poor babies that they

are, they must ask permission to keep a conscience!
When they are about to do anything they are always
saying, "What will So-and-so think of it?" Does it
matter to any true man what all the world thinks
about him? Has he not risen out of that? Is he
still a serf? "Go," says the brave man; "think what
you will, and say what you will. If I serve God, I
am no servant of yours; by your censures I shall not
fall, as by your praises I shall not rise." Be afraid of
such a thing as I myself, and ask the leave of another
man what I shall think, what I shall believe, what I
shall do! I will die first! When God brings a man
to know himself, and to be His servant, He sets him
free from this cowardly crime of being afraid of a
man that shall die.

So, too, He sets him free from all the maxims and
customs of the world. Young man, when you go
into business, they will tell you that you must do
so-and-so, because it is "the custom of the trade."
"Why," say you, "it is lying!" You will be told
that it is not exactly lying, because your customer is
used to your tricks, and quite understands that a
hundred means eighty, and the best quality means a
second-class article. I am told that half the business
in London is robbery in some form or another if the
customs of the trade are not understood. If it be so
that it is all understood, it might just as well be done
honestly for the matter of that, and it would pay as
well. Yet, somehow, men feel as if they must do
what others have done, or else they will be out of the
race. Slaves! Serfs! Be honest! He is not free
that dares not be honest. Shall I not speak my
mind? Shall I not act out my integrity? If I

cannot, then I cannot say with David, " Thou hast loosed my bonds."

What a blessing it is when God frees us from the fear of death ! " Thou hast loosed my bonds." What will it matter to you, young man, if you become the servant of God by faith in Jesus Christ, whether you live or die ? If you die early, so much the sooner in Heaven. If you live long, so much the longer in which to serve your God on earth. Give your heart to Christ; trust your salvation in those dear hands that were pierced for sinners ; thus become the servant of God, and you shall be provided for, for His children shall not lack. You shall be led, guided, taught, educated, prepared for Heaven ; and one of these bright days a convoy of celestial spirits shall think it an honour to be permitted to bear your joyful spirit up to the throne of God.

Who will be the servant of the Most High, then ? I always wish when I have done with sermons that I could preach them over again, because I have not done well enough ; but all I care to preach for is that I may touch your hearts. I would not care a snap of the fingers to be an orator, or to put sentences prettily. I want to put the truth so that some young man will say, " I will serve God." I remember young men who began life when I began, who are now—I will not say what. Ah ! I remember hearing their names mentioned as models, they were such fine young men, and had just gone up to London. Yes, and they are to-night, if not in jail, in the workhouse. It all came about in this way : the young man sent word home to his mother what the text was on the Sunday, yet he had not been to hear a sermon at all.

He had been to some amusement, to spend a happy day : wherever he went he had neglected the house of God ; and by-and-by there was a little wrong in his small accounts—just a little matter ; but that man could not pick himself up again, once having lost his character. There was another. There was nothing wrong in his accounts, but his habits were loose. By-and-by he was ill. Who could wonder ? When a man plays with edged tools he is very likely to cut himself. It was not long before he was so sickly that he could not attend to business, and ere long he died ; and they said—I fear it was true— that he killed himself by vice. And that is how thousands do in London. Oh, if you become the servant of God this will not happen to you ! You may not be rich ; you may not be famous ; you may not be great : you need not want these things. They are gilded vanities full often. But to be a man—to the fulness of your manhood ; to be free and dare to look every other man in the world in the face, and speak the truth, and do the right ; to be a man who can look God in the face because Christ has covered him with His glorious righteousness—this is the ambition with which I would fire the spirit of every young man ; and I pray God that the flame may burn in his life by the power of the Divine Spirit. Come then, bow your heads and say, "We will be servants of the living God henceforth and forever."

LYDIA, OF THYATIRA.

IN Lydia's conversion there are many points of interest. Observe that it was brought about by providential circumstances. She was a seller of purple, of Thyatira. That city was famous for its dyeing trade, which had flourished there ever since the days of Homer. The mode of producing a peculiarly delicate and valuable purple seems to have been known to the women of Thyatira. It may be that Lydia had come to Philippi upon a journey, or that while her manufactures were carried on at Thyatira, she resided during a part of the year at Philippi, to dispose of her goods. The communication between the two places was very easy, and she may have frequently made the journey; at any rate, Providence brings her there when the hour of her conversion is come. You will remember that Thyatira was situated in that part of the country into which Paul was forbidden by the Spirit to go and preach; therefore, had Lydia been at home, she could not have heard the truth; and as " Faith cometh by hearing, and hearing by the Word of God," she must have remained unconverted. But Providence brings her to Philippi at the right time. Here is the first link of the chain.

But how is Paul to be brought there? He must, first of all, be shut out of Bithynia; and he must be silenced in his journey through Mysia; he must be brought to Troas, close by the margin of the sea ; he must look across the blue sea, and muse upon Europe's needs ; he must fall asleep, and in the visions of the night, he must be prompted to cross to Macedonia ; he shall ask for a ship—that ship shall be bound for Samothracia, and for no other place ; he must land at Neapolis, and by the same instinct, he must make his way to Philippi ; he cannot go in any other direction ; he must be brought there at the very time when Lydia is present ; he must find out the little oratory by the river's brink, for God ordains that Lydia shall be saved.   Now, how many different threads were all interwoven here, to make up the fabric of her providential conversion !   In this case, God rules and overrules all things to bring that woman and that apostle to the same spot ; and every-thing in God's providence is working together for the salvation of the elect.

In Lydia's case there was not only preventing providence, but there was also grace in a certain manner preparing the soul.   The woman did not know the Saviour ; she did not understand the things which made for her peace, yet she knew many truths which were excellent stepping-stones to a knowledge of Jesus.   If not a Jewess by birth, she was a proselyte of the gate, and therefore well acquainted with the oracles of God ; she was one who worshipped God ; nay, she was one of the most devout of God's worshippers among the Jews.   Though she was far away from the synagogue—some forget the Sabbath when they travel in foreign lands—yet when the day came round, she was found with that little handful at the river-side oratory.   I doubt not that she had read

Esaias the prophet, that she could carry in her heart and remember such words as these, " He is despised and rejected of men ; a man of sorrows, and acquainted with grief. . . . He is brought as a lamb to the slaughter, and as a sheep before her shearers is dumb, so He openeth not His mouth." As in the case of the Ethiopian eunuch, the Scriptures she had read, though they were not understood for want of some man to guide her, had prepared her mind : the ground had been ploughed ready for the good seed ; it was not a hard rock, as in the gaoler's case. She worshipped God ; worshipped Him in sincerity ; worshipped Him looking for the coming of the Messiah, Israel's consolation ; and so her mind was prepared for the reception of the gospel. Doubtless, in many of us there was a preparation for Christ before Christ came to us in quickening grace. I know that in some of our cases the pious example of a godly father, and the loving instruction of a tender mother, had softened us somewhat, so that though still we were unsaved and still out of Christ, yet we were like the man who laid at the pool of Bethesda, we were close by the edge of the healing stream, and there was not in our case that sudden, that astounding change which we have seen in others. Still, we ought to ascribe all this preparatory work to sovereign grace, for grace— free favour—does much in which no grace of effectual salvation is perceptible. I mean that before grace renews the heart there is grace preparing us for grace ; grace may be setting the mind in activity, clearing us from prejudice, ridding us of a thousand infidel and sceptical thoughts, and so raising a platform from which Divine grace conducts us into the region of the new life. Such was the case of Lydia, such is the case of many ; Providence and grace co-work before the effectual time is come.

Her conversion took place in the use of the means. On the Sabbath she went to the gathering of her people. Although God works great wonders and calls men when they are not hearing the Word, yet usually we must expect that, being in the way, God will meet with them. It is somewhat extra-ordinary that the first convert in Europe was converted at a very small prayer-meeting. There were only a few women there ; we have no reason to think that there were any more males than just Paul and his friend Luke ; and these, you see, had called in, as we say, accidentally, and had been moved to give an address at the prayer-meeting, and that address it was which was the means in God's hand of opening her heart. Let us never neglect the means of grace ; wherever we are, let us not forget the assembling of ourselves together, as the manner of some is. May you ever have, even if as yet you are unconverted, a love for the courts of the Lord's house, and for the place where His people meet together. Love the prayer-meeting ; do not say of it, " Only a prayer-meeting ! " God loves to put honour upon prayer, upon the assembly of His people directly for His worship ; and you may hope, that even if the sermon shall not have been useful, and if the common Sab-bath-day service may not have been blessed, yet perhaps, on the Monday evening—perhaps, too, in that little cottage, when there are only a few women present—you may meet with God, who did not appear to you in the greater assembly. Be diligent in the use of the means ; be constantly in God's house, as often as the doors are open and your engagements will permit, for Lydia's conversion takes place in the use of the means.

It was assuredly a work of grace, for we are expressly told, " whose heart the Lord opened." She did not open her own heart. Her prayers did not do it ; Paul did not do it ; the Lord Himself must open the heart, to receive the things which make for our peace. To operate savingly upon human hearts belongs to God alone. We can get at human brains, but God alone can arouse human affections. We may reach them, we grant you, in the natural and common way, but so to reach them, as that the enemy of God shall become His friend, and that the stony heart shall be turned into flesh, is the work of grace, and nothing short of Divine power can accomplish it. Lydia was baptized, but her good works did not end at the water ; she then would have the apostles come to her house. She will bear the shame of being thought to be a follower of the crucified Jew, a friend of the despised Jewish apostle, the renegade, the turncoat— she will have him in her house ; and though he saith Nay, out of his bashfulness to receive aught, yet she constrains him, for love is in her heart, and she has a generous spirit ; and while she hath a crust it shall be broken with the man who brought her to Christ ; she will give not only the cup of cold water in the prophet's name, but her house shall shelter him. I do not think much of a conversion where it does not touch a man's substance ; and those people who pretend to be Christ's people, and yet live only for themselves, and do nothing for Him or for His Church, give but sorry evidence of having been born again. A love to the people of God has ever been a distinguishing mark of the true convert. Look, then, at Lydia, and remembering that she is but a specimen of many, let her case rest before you, and let the prayer go up, " Lord, bring in Lydias, according to Thy mighty grace."

" The Lord opened Lydia's heart, to attend to the things that were spoken." No doubt the Lord removed prejudice. This prejudice is an evil which we have to fight against in very many. In Lydia's case it would be Jewish prejudice ; perhaps the report had reached her, as it had most of the Jews, concerning Jesus of Nazareth ; she knew that her race had hounded Him to the death, that her nation had even said, " His blood' be on us, and on our children." Paul, the apostle, was the subject of much of this prejudice among the Jews, insomuch that when writing his Epistle to the Hebrews, you will have observed that he does not begin with his name, as he does in all the other Epistles, because he felt that the very name Paul, from the fact of his having been an eminent Pharisee, and having become a Christian, was distasteful to the Hebrew people. But God removed all this prejudice from Lydia's mind ; she sat down to listen to Paul with a determination to give him a fair hearing, and to weigh the matter and see whether these things were so or not—somewhat like the Bereans of old, who also had their hearts in a measure opened, for they searched the Scriptures to see whether things were so. The devil often covers men from head to foot in a coat of mail, so that when they come where the arrows of God are flying, there is very little hope of their being wounded, because there is scarce a joint of the harness which the devil has not protected by an iron rivet of prejudice.

When her heart was opened her desires were awakened. She felt now a wish to understand this matter, and if there was anything in what the apostle was saying about eternal salvation—about complete pardon by the blood of Him who was the " Lamb slain from before the foundation of the world," she said to herself, " I should like to know about it ; I hope it may be true ; I wish I may get an interest in these things." So she listens, anxiously desiring to be impressed by the Word. She has a hunger and a thirst ; and those people have this blessing—"They shall be filled." When we get people, by God's grace, as far as hungering and thirsting, then we are very thankful to say, this is the opening of the heart. As the oyster, when the tide comes up, openeth its shell, so when the tide of grace is coming, God often makes men open their hearts, so that now they may get the spiritual supply.

Well, there was a desire awakened, but this was not all ; there came another kind of opening, her understanding was now enlightened. So her understanding was opened ; she had a clear view of the gospel ; she could see in its height, and depth, and length, just that which her soul wanted.

Then came something else ; now her affections were excited, she felt growing within her a love to Him who, though He was equal with God, yet took upon Himself the form of a servant. As she heard

Paul describe His sufferings, as she pictured to herself
the scene around the cross, she thought she could
hear the death-shriek and mark the flowing blood,
and she seemed to think, " Yes, I love that Man : I
love that God ; my heart goeth after Him ; O that He
were mine ! Yes," said she, " I love that preaching ;
sweet to my ears are those doctrines of mercy." She
began already to rejoice, and " Blessed are the people
that know the joyful sound," for if they do not yet
walk in the light of God's countenance, yet they shall,
for so the promise runs. All this, I think, is included
in the term, " Her heart was opened." Her affections
were now kindling towards Divine things. And then
came faith ; she believed the whole of the record.
She took it to be absolutely true, as Paul had stated,
that there had been a Messiah ; that He, according to
Scripture, was the Son of God, and was also the Son
of man ; that He had suffered, the just for the unjust,
and that she, believing in Him, had her sins forgiven.
Faith came now through hearing. She took God at
His word ; she simply and humbly put her soul at the
feet of that cross where the blood was dropping,
believing that, as it fell from Heaven, it pleaded for
her, and as it dropped on her it gave her peace with
God through Jesus Christ.

Faith being given, all the graces followed. Now
she hated her sins, she repented. Now she loved
righteousness, she sought after holiness. Now she
had a bright hope of the many mansions in the
Father's house. Now she began to run with holy
and happy feeling in the ways of obedience
to Christ's commands, and she became, not merely
a believer in the elements of Christianity, but she

went on towards perfection, adding to her faith
courage, and to her courage experience, and to
experience brotherly kindness, and to brotherly
kindness love. Onward she went in the way of
her God. All this the Master did by opening her
heart to attend to the things that were spoken of
by Paul.

THE QUEEN OF SHEBA, SOLOMON'S PUPIL.

QUEENS have many cares, multitudes of occupations and engagements, but the Queen of Sheba neither considered it beneath her dignity to search into the wisdom of Solomon, nor a waste of valuable time to journey to his dominions. How many offer the vain excuse that they cannot give due attention to the religion of Jesus Christ for want of time ; they have a large family, or a very difficult business to manage. This woman rebukes such, for she left her kingdom, and threw off the cares of state to take a long journey, that she might listen to the royal sage.

Her royal court was, doubtless, already stored with wisdom. The princes of the Eastern realms were always careful to gather to themselves a band of wise men, who found in their patronage both subsistence and honour. In the court of so great a lover of learning as was the Queen of Sheba, there would certainly be a little congress of magi and wise men ; but yet she was not content with what she knew already, she was determined to search after this Divine wisdom, of which she had heard the fame. In this she rebukes those of you who think you know enough ; who suppose that your own home-spun intelligence will suffice, without sitting at the feet of Jesus. If you dream that human wisdom can be a sufficient light without receiving the brighter beams of revelation ; if you say, " These things are for the unintelligent and for the poor, we will not listen to them," this queen, whose court was full of wisdom, and yet who leaves it all to find the wisdom which God had given to Solomon, rebukes you. The wisdom of Jesus Christ as much surpasses all human knowledge as the sun outshines a candle. Comparison there can be none, contrast there is much. He who will not come to the fountain which brims with wisdom, but trusts to his own leaking cisterns, shall wake up too late to find himself a fool.

Consider, too, that the queen came from a very great distance to hear the wisdom of Solomon. The journey from Arabia Felix, or from Abyssinia, which-ever the country may have been, was a long and dangerous one—a much more serious matter than it would be in these times ; and performed by the slow process of the camel-back, the journey must have occupied a very long season. Coming, as Matthew says, " from the uttermost parts of the earth," there were doubtless mountains to be climbed, if not seas to be navigated, and deserts to be crossed ; but none of these difficulties could keep her back. She hears of wisdom, and wisdom she will have. So she boldly ventures upon the journey with her numerous train, no matter how far she may have to travel. Very many have the gospel brought to their doors, and yet will not leave their chimney-corners to listen to it. The Queen of Sheba, toiling across the desert, of the weaker sex though she was, shall rise up in judgment against those who neglect the great salvation, and treat the Saviour as though it were nothing to them that Jesus should die.

Do not forget, too, that this woman was a foreigner to Solomon, and that she had a religion already—

probably one of the older forms of idolatry, perhaps the Sabean worship of the sun. Now, many persons argue in these times, "Would you have me change my religion?" Yes, that I would, if your religion is false. If your religion has not changed you, I would that you would change your religion, for a religion which does not renew a man's character and make him holy—which does not change his confidence, and make him rest upon Christ—a religion which does not make altogether a new man of him, from top to bottom, is a religion of no value, and the sooner he gives it up the better. Because my mother or my grandmother happened to be blind, why am I to be blind too, if there is sight to be had? Remember, to your own Master you stand or fall on your own account. Each soul enters through the gate of life alone; and through the iron gate of death it departs alone. Every man should search in solitary earnestness, apart from all the rest of the world, to know what the truth is, and knowing it, it is his to come out alone on the Lord's side. Yes, we would have you give attention to the things of God, even though you should have been brought up in other customs, and should have honestly espoused another form of religion. Prove the spirits whether they be of God. If your soul has been deceived, there is yet time to be set right. God help you, that you may find out the truth!

It is worthy of observation that this woman, coming from afar, made a journey which cost her very much expense. She came with a great train, with camels bearing spices and very much gold and precious stones. She looked upon the treasures of her kingdom as only valuable, because they would admit her into the presence of the keeper of the storehouse of wisdom. Now, our Lord Jesus Christ asks nothing of men except their hearts. He doth not sell the truth to any of them, but gives it freely without money and without price. And what if men will not have it, if they refuse to lend their ears, and to give their thoughts to Divine things, shall they not be utterly inexcusable when this heathen queen shall rise up and shall declare that she gave her rubies and her pearls, her spices and her camels, to King Solomon, that she might learn his human wisdom? The gospel presents freely to every needy soul just that which he requires. It cries, " He that hath no money, let him come, buy wine and milk without money and without price." If you have refused the invitation of Christ's gospel, well may you tremble at the thought that the Queen of Sheba shall rise up in judgment against you.

Note that this queen had received no invitation; King Solomon never bade her come; she came unsought for, unexpected. You have been bidden to come—" The Spirit and the Bride say, Come." The Bible is God's written invitation, and ye may search it if you will. Therefore, if you, followed with invitations, and urged with line upon line and precept upon precept, will not come when God's providence brings the gospel to your very gates, if you will not seek King Jesus, then shall ye be condemned indeed by this Queen of Sheba. The object which she journeyed after was vastly inferior to that which is proposed to our enquiry. We bid the careless soul bethink himself of the Son of God; she went that distance to see a son of man. She journeyed all that way to see one who was wise himself, but who had power to impart but a very small portion of his wisdom ; whereas we invite the sinner to come to One who is made of God unto us wisdom, righteousness, sanctification, and redemption ; we tell him that all Christ hath He is ready to bestow, that His abundance is only an abundance for others, and His fulness is that out of which all of us have received. She went to hear a man who had wisdom ; we bid you come to One who *is* wisdom—wisdom itself consolidated. Talk ye of the royalty of Solomon ?—we invite you to a greater King than he, who is Lord of Heaven, and earth, and hell. Speak ye of his riches ?—we tell you of One who hath unspeakable riches of grace and glory. True, she *might* gain by the journey, it was but a probability, but whosoever cometh to Christ, becomes rich to all the intents of bliss. No soul ever trafficked with our Solomon without being at once enriched ; if he came empty-handed, poor, feeble, naked, and sinful, to accept from our Jesus His great salvation, he was never sent away empty. Let us observe, to this queen's worthy commendation, how she conducted the enquiry.

Observe that she did it in person. She did not depute an ambassador to go and search into the matter, but personally, and on her own account, she set out to see Solomon himself. Was it not the Duke of Wellington who, on one occasion, rebuked one of his officers for railing against the Bible, by asking him if he had ever read it, and when the other frankly confessed he had not, showed him how base it was to find fault with that which he did not understand ? Most persons who object to the religion of Christ have never investigated it. This I am sure of, no man has ever had an intelligent idea of the person of the Saviour, of the graciousness of His work, who ever could think or speak against Him afterwards. Watts is correct when he says :—

> " His worth, if all the nations knew,
> Sure the whole world would love Him too."

The queen went first of all to Solomon. *She* went, and she went *to Solomon.* The way to learn the faith of our Lord Jesus Christ, is to go to *Him.* "*She told him all that was in her heart.*" This is the way to know the Lord ; tell Him all that is in your heart— your doubts, your fears, your hardness of heart and impenitence ; confess the whole. That man is near to knowing Christ who begins to know himself; and he who will tell out as much as he knoweth of his own corruption and depravity, and sinfulness and necessities, and inabilities, shall soon have a gracious answer of peace. Tarry not because thy heart is vile—it is viler than thou thinkest it is—but go with it just as it is, and tell Jesus all. Art thou like the woman with the issue of blood ? I pray thee tell Him all the truth, and He will say, " Thy faith hath made thee whole." Why dost thou try to hide anything from Omniscience ? He knows the corners of thy heart, the deep places and the dark places thereof are in His hands. If thou shouldest tell Him He will know no more, wherefore then dost thou hesitate ? Tear off the veil from thy heart, and then thou shalt find mercy.

Moreover, she proposed to Solomon her hard questions. I do not know what they were, and I do not particularly care. The Jewish rabbis have invented a few very stupid ones, which they say were her hard questions. But I know if you come to our Solomon, to Christ, these will be your hard questions, "My Lord, how can mercy and justice kiss each other? How can God forgive sin and yet punish it?" Jesus will point you to His wounded hands and feet, He will tell you of His great atonement, how by a substitution God is dreadful in His justice and boundless in His love. Then you will put to Him the question, "How can a sinful creature be accepted in the sight of a holy God?" He will tell you of His righteousness, and you will see how, covered with the imputed righteousness of the Redeemer, a sinful soul is as acceptable before the Lord as though it had never offended. You will say to Him, "Canst thou tell me, Jesus, how it is that a weak soul with no power, shall yet be able to fight with the devil and overcome the world, the flesh and the devil?" And Jesus will answer, "My grace is sufficient for thee; My strength shall be perfect in thy weakness;" and so, all the knotty questions will be answered.

This good woman, in pursuing her enquiry, listened carefully to what Solomon told her. It is said, he told her all her questions. Oh! there is a blessed communion between Christ and a trembling soul. If you will tell Him all your failings, He will tell you all His merit; if you will tell Him your weakness, He will tell you all His strength ; if you will tell Him your distance from God, He will tell you His nearness to God ; if you will show Him how hard your heart is, He will tell you how His heart was broken that you might live. Be not afraid, only make a clear revelation to Him and trust in Him, and He will make a sweet revelation to you.

She then did what was the best proof of her truthfulness, she gave to Solomon of her treasures—" She gave the king a hundred and twenty talents of gold, and of spices very great store, and precious stones : there came no more such abundance of spices as these which the Queen of Sheba gave to King Solomon." And so souls that know the beauty of Christ give Him all they have. There are no such spices as those which come from newly-converted souls. Nothing gives Christ greater delight than the love of His people. We think our love to be a very poor and common thing, but He does not think so—He has set such a store by us that He gave His heart's blood to redeem us, and now He looks upon us as being worth the price He paid. He never will think that He had a bad bargain of it, and so He looks upon every grain ot our love as being even choicer spices than archangels before the throne can render to Him in their songs. What are we doing for Christ ? Are we bringing Him our talents of gold ? Perhaps you have not one hundred and twenty, but if you have one bring that ; you have not very many spices, but bring what you have—your silent, earnest prayers, your holy, consistent life, the words you sometimes speak for Christ, the training up of your children, the feeding of His poor, the clothing of the naked, the visitation of the sick, the comforting of His mourners, the winning of His wanderers, the restoring of His backsliders, the saving of His blood-bought souls—all these shall be like camels laden with spices, an acceptable gift to the Most High.

When she had done this, Solomon made her a present of his royal bounty. She lost nothing ; she gave all she had, and then Solomon gave her quite as much again, for I will be bound to say King Solomon would not be outdone in generosity, such a noble-hearted prince as he, and so rich. I tell you Jesus Christ will never be in your debt. Oh, it is a great gain to give to Christ ; we give Him pence and He gives us pounds; we give Him years of labour and He gives us an eternity of rest ; we give Him days of patient endurance and He gives us ages of joyous honour; we give Him a little suffering and He gives us great rewards. "I reckon that the sufferings of this present life are not worthy to be compared with the glory which shall be revealed in us." Besides what He gives us in the covenant of grace, you note He does for us what Solomon did for her—He gives us all that is in our heart, all that we can desire. What a King is our Saviour, who will not let His people have one ungratified wish, if that wish is a good one ! Knock and the gate shall open. "Open thy mouth wide, and I will fill it," saith the Lord. "According to your faith so be it done unto you." "Whatsoever ye ask in prayer believe that ye have it, and ye shall have it." What precious promises, and all these are given to those who come with a humble enquiry, willing to get Christ first and then to get the rest afterwards.

"HE PROPHESIETH OF THE TIMES THAT ARE FAR OFF."*

ONE would have thought that if the glorious Lord condescended to send His servants to speak to men of the way of salvation, all mankind would delight to hear the message. We should naturally conclude that the people would immediately run together in eager crowds to catch every word, and would be obedient at once to the heavenly command. But, alas! it has not been so. Man's opposition to God is too deep, too stubborn for that. The prophets of old were compelled to cry, "Who hath believed our report?" and the servants of God in later times found themselves face to face with a stiff-necked generation, who resisted the Holy Ghost as did their fathers. Men display great ingenuity in making excuses for rejecting the message of God's love. They display marvellous skill, not in seeking salvation, but in fashioning reasons for refusing it; they are dexterous in avoiding grace, and in securing their own ruin. They hold up first this shield and then the other, to ward off the gracious arrows of the gospel of Jesus Christ, which are only meant to slay the deadly sins which lurk in their bosoms. The evil argument which is mentioned in the text has been used from Ezekiel's day right down to the present moment, and it has served Satan's turn in ten thousand cases. By

---

* Ezek. xii. 27.

its means men have delayed themselves into hell. The sons of men, when they hear of the great atonement made upon the cross by the Lord Jesus, and are bidden to lay hold upon eternal life. in Him, still say concerning the gospel, " The vision that he seeth is for many days to come, and he prophesieth of times that are far off." That is to say, they pretend that the matters whereof we speak are not of immediate importance, and may safely be postponed. They imagine that religion is for the weakness of the dying and the infirmity of the aged, but not for healthy men and women. They meet our pressing invitation, " All things are now ready, come ye to the supper," with the reply, " Religion is meant to prepare us for eternity, but we are far off from it as yet, and are still in the heyday of our being ; there is plenty of time for those dreary preparations for death. Your religion smells of the vault and the worm. Let us be merry while we may. There will be room for more serious considerations when we have enjoyed life a little, or have become established in business, or can retire to live upon our savings. Religion is for the sere and yellow leaf of the year's fall, when life is fading, but not for the opening hours of spring, when the birds are pairing and the primroses smiling upon the returning sun. You prophesy of things that are for many days to come, and of times that are far off." Very few young people may have *said* as much as this, but that is the secret thought of many ; and with this they resist the admonition of the Holy Ghost, who saith, " To-day, if ye will hear His voice, harden not your hearts." They put off the day of conversion, as if it were a day of tempest and terror, and not, as it really is, a day most calm, most bright, the bridal of the soul with Heaven.

Let every unconverted person recollect that God knows what his excuse is for turning a deaf ear to the voice of a dying Saviour's love. You may not have spoken it to yourself so as to put it into words; you might not even dare to do so, lest your conscience should be too much startled; but God knows it all. He sees the hollowness, the folly, and the wickedness of your excuses. He is not deceived by your vain words, but makes short work with your apologies for delay. Remember the parables of our Lord, and note that when the man of one talent professed to think his master a hard man, he took him at his word, and out of his own mouth condemned him; and in the case of the invited guests who pleaded their farms and their merchandise as excuses, no weight was attached to what they said, but the sentence went forth, " None of these men that are bidden shall taste of my supper." God knows the frivolity of your plea for delay, He knows that you yourself are doubtful about it, and dare not stand to it so as to give it anything like a solemn consideration. Very hard do you try to deceive yourself into an easy state of conscience concerning it, but in your inmost soul you are ashamed of your own falsehoods.

Suppose that you are spared for threescore years and ten. Young man, suppose that God spares you in your sins till the snows of many winters shall whiten your head; young woman, suppose that your now youthful countenance shall still escape the grave until wrinkles are upon your brow; yet, still, how short will your life be! You, perhaps, think seventy years a

long period, but those who are seventy, in looking
back, will tell you that their age is a hand-breadth.
I feel that every year flies more swiftly than the last ;
and months and weeks are contracted into twinklings
of the eye. The older one grows, the shorter one's
life appears. I do not wonder that Jacob said, " Few
and evil have the days of the years of my life been,"
for he spake as an extremely old man. Man is short-
lived compared with his surroundings, he comes into
the world and goes out of it, as a meteor flashes
through yonder skies which have remained the same
for ages. Listen to the brook which murmurs as
it flows, and the meditative ear will hear it warble,—

> " Men may come and men may go,
> But I go on for ever."

Look at yonder venerable oak, which has for five
hundred years battled with the winds, and what
an infant one seems when reclining beneath its shade!
Stand by some giant rock, which has confronted the
tempests of the ages, and you feel like the insect of an
hour. There are persons of seventy years of age who
look back to the days of their boyhood as if they were
but yesterday. Ask them, and they will tell you that
their life seems to have been little more than a wink
of the eye ; it has gone like a dream, or a lightning's
flash,—

> " What is life ? 'Tis but a vapour,
> ·Soon it vanishes away."

Therefore do not say, " These things are for a far-off
time ;" for even if we could guarantee to you the
whole length of human existence, it is but a span.

But there comes upon the heels of this a reflection

never to be forgotten—that not one among us can promise, with anything like certainty, that he shall ever see threescore years and ten. We may survive, and by reason of strength we may creep up to fourscore years ; yet not one of us can be sure that he shall do so ; the most of us will assuredly be gone long before that age. Nay, more, we cannot promise that we shall see half that length of time. Young men and women cannot be certain they shall reach middle life. You cannot be certain that you will see this year out, and hear the bells ring in a new year. Yea, close upon you as to-morrow is, boast not yourselves of it, for it may never come ; or, should it come, you know not what it may bring forth to you, perhaps a coffin or a shroud. Ay, and this very night, when you close your eyes and rest your head upon your pillow, reckon not too surely that you shall ever again look on that familiar chamber, or go forth from it to the pursuits of life. It is clear, then, that the things which make for your peace are not matters for a far-off time, the frailty of life makes them necessities of this very hour. You are not far from your grave, you are nearer to it than when this discourse began ; some of you are far nearer than you think.

To some this reflection comes with remarkable emphasis, for your occupation has enough of danger about it every day to furnish death with a hundred roads to convey you to his prison-house in the sepulchre. Can you look through a newspaper without meeting with the words " fatal accident," or " sudden death " ? Travelling has many dangers, and even to cross the street is perilous. Men die at home, and when engaged about their lawful callings

many are met by death.   How true is this of those
who go down to the sea in ships, or descend into the
earth in mines!   But, indeed, no occupations are
secure from death ; a needle can kill as well as a
sword ; a scald, a burn, a fall, may end our lives,
quite as readily as a pestilence or a battle.   Does
your business lead you to climb a ladder ; it is no very
perilous matter, but have you never heard of one who
missed his footing and fell, never to rise again ?   You
work amidst the materials of a rising building ; have
you never heard of stones that have fallen and have
crushed the workers ?

> " Dangers stand thick through all the ground
>   To push us to the tomb,
> And fierce diseases wait around
>   To hurry mortals home."

Notwithstanding all that can be done by sanitary
laws, fevers are not unknown, and deadly strokes
which fell men to the ground in an instant, as a
butcher slays an ox, are not uncommon.   Death has
already removed many of your former companions.
You have ridden into the battle of life, like the
soldiers in the charge at Balaklava ; and, young as
you are in this warfare, you have seen saddles emptied
right and left around you ; you survive, but death has
grazed you.   The arrow of destruction has gone
whizzing by your ear to find another mark ; have you
never wondered that it spared you?   There are
persons of delicate constitution.   It grieves me to see
so many fair daughters of our land with the mark of
consumption upon their cheeks.   Full well I know
that lurid flame upon the countenance, and that
strange lustre of the eye—signs of exhausting fires

feeding upon life and consuming it too soon. Young men and women, many of you, from the condition of your bodily frames, can only struggle on till middle life, and scarcely that ; for beyond thirty or forty you cannot survive. I fear that some of you have, even in walking, sometimes felt a suspicious weariness, which augurs exhaustion and decline. How can *you* say, when we talk to *you* about preparing to die, that we are talking about things that are far off? Do not be so foolish. I implore you let these warnings lead you to decision. Far be it from me to cause you needless alarm, but is it needless? I am sure I love you too well to distress you without cause, but is there not cause enough? Come now, I press you most affectionately, answer me and say, does not your own reason tell you that anxiety for you is not misplaced? Ought you not at once to lay to heart your Redeemer's call, and obey your Saviour's appeal? The time is short, catch the moments as they fly and hasten to be blest.

Remember, also, that even if you knew that you should escape from accident and fever and sudden death, yet there is one grand event that we too often forget, which may put an end to your day of mercy on a sudden. Have you never heard that Jesus Christ of Nazareth, who was crucified on Calvary, died on the cross, and was laid in the tomb? Do you not know that He rose again on the third day, and that after He had spent a little while with His disciples, He took them to the top of the Mount of Olives, and there before their eyes ascended into Heaven, a cloud hiding Him from their view? Have you forgotten the words of the angels, who said, "This same Jesus who is taken up from

14

you into Heaven shall so come in like manner as ye have seen Him go into Heaven"? Jesus will certainly come a second time to judge the world. Of that day and of that hour knoweth no man—no, not the angels of God. He will come as a thief in the night to an ungodly world; they shall be eating and drinking, and marrying and giving in marriage, just as they were when Noah entered into the ark, and they knew not until the flood came and swept them all away. In a moment—we cannot tell when, perhaps it may be ere next the words escape my lips—a sound far louder than any mortal voice will be heard above the clamours of worldly traffic, ay, and above the roaring of the sea. That sound as of a trumpet will proclaim the day of the Son of man. "Behold, the Bridegroom cometh : go ye out to meet Him," will sound throughout the Church ; and to the world there will ring out this clarion note, "Behold, He cometh with clouds, and every eye shall see Him, and they also which crucified Him." Jesus may come to-night. If He were to do so, would you then tell me that I am talking of far-off things? Did not Jesus say, "Behold, I come quickly"? His tarrying may be long to us, but to God it will be brief. We are to stand hourly watching and daily waiting for the coming of the Lord from Heaven. Oh, I pray you do not say that the Lord delayeth His coming, for that was the language of the wicked servant who was cut in pieces, and it is the mark of the mockers of the last days, that they say, "Where is the promise of His coming?" Be ye not mockers, lest your bands be made strong ; but listen to the undoubted voice of prophecy and of the Word of God, "Behold, I come quickly." "Be ye also ready, for in such an hour as ye think not the Son of man cometh."

Now, then, it is clear enough that even if the gospel message did concern only our life in another world, yet still it is unwise for men to say, " The vision is for many days to come, and he prophesieth of the times that are far off."

SOMETHING TO DO WITH THE FUTURE.

THE gospel of Jesus Christ has to do with the whole of life. If you receive Jesus Christ you will have that faith which will operate upon your whole existence throughout time and eternity. If you are saved while yet you are young you will find religion to be a great preventive of sin. What a blessing it is not to have been daubed with the slime of Sodom, never to have had our bones broken by actual vice. Many who have been saved from a life of crime will nevertheless be spiritual cripples for life! To be snatched out of the vortex of vice is cause for great gratitude, but to have been kept out of it is better. It is doubly well, if the grace of God comes upon us while still we are untainted by the pollution of the world, and have not gone into excess of riot. Before dissolute habits have undermined the constitution, and self-indulgence has degraded the mind, it is above all things well to have the heart renewed. Prevention is better than cure, and grace gives both. Thank God that you are still young, and pray earnestly that you may now receive grace to cleanse your way by taking heed thereto, according to His Word.

Grace will also act as a preservative as well as a preventive. The good thing which God will put in you will keep you. I bless God I have not to preach a temporary salvation. That which charmed me about the gospel when I was a lad was its power to preserve from sinning. I saw some of my school companions who had been highly commended for their character, and were a little older than myself, become sad offenders when they left home. I used to hear sad stories of their evil actions when they had gone to London to be apprenticed, or to take positions in large establishments, and I reasoned thus with myself: " When I leave my father's house I shall be tempted, too, and I have the same heart that they have—indeed, I have not been even as good as they have been ; the probabilities are, therefore, that I shall plunge into sin as they have done." I felt horrified with that. I could not bear that I should cause my mother to shed tears over a dissolute son, or break my father's heart with debauchery. The thought could not be endured, and when I heard that whosoever believed in the Lord Jesus Christ should be saved, I understood that he would be saved from sinning, and I laid hold upon Jesus to preserve me from sin, and He has done it. I committed my character to Christ, and He has preserved me to this day, and I believe He will not let me go. I recommend to you, young men, a character-insurance, in the form of believing in Jesus Christ Dear young woman, may that modest cheek of yours never need to blush for deed of shame ; may your delicate purity of feeling never be lost through gross defiling sin ; but remember, it may be so unless the Lord keeps you. I commend to you the blessed preserving power of faith in Jesus Christ, which will secure for you the Holy Spirit to dwell in you and abide in you, and sanctify you all your days. I know I speak to some who shudder at the thought of vice. Trained as you

have been by Christian parents, and under the holiest
influences, you would rather die than act as some who
disgrace their father's name; I know you would.
But you must not trust your own hearts; you may
yet become as bad as others, or worse than they,
unless your natures are renewed, and only Jesus
Christ can do that by the power of the Holy Spirit.
Whosoever believeth in Him has passed from death
unto life; he shall not live in sin, but he shall be preserved in holiness even to the end.

You have not fully entered into the battle of life
yet. You have your way to make, your professions
and trades to choose. You, young women, are still
under the parental wing; you have domestic relationships yet to form. Now, consider how well prepared
you will be for life's work and service if you give
your hearts to Jesus. Young man, you will be the
right man to enter a large establishment : with the
grace of God in your heart you will be a blessing
there. Though surrounded by her snares in this
wicked city, the strange woman will in vain hunt for
your precious life ; and other vices will be unable to
pollute you. Young woman, you will have wisdom
to choose for your life's companion no mere fop and
fool, but one who loves the Lord as you will do, with
whom you may hope to spend happy and holy days.
You will have placed within yourself resources of joy
and pleasure which will never fail; there will be a well
of living water within you which will supply you with
joy and comfort and consolation, even amid trial and
distress. You will be prepared for whatever is to
come. A young Christian is fit to be made an emperor or a servant, if God shall call him to either

post.   If you want the best material for a model
prince, or a model peasant, you shall find it in the
child of God ; only, mark you, the man who is a
child of God is less likely to sink into utter destitution,
because he will be saved from the vices of extrava-
gance and idleness, which are the frequent causes of
poverty ; and, probably, on the other hand, he is less
likely to become a prince, for seldom has God lifted
His own children to places so perilous.   You will be
ready, young man, for any future, if your heart be
right with God.   And do you know when I think of
you, and of what the Lord may make of you, I feel
an intense respect, as well as love, for you.   I hope
none of us will be lacking in respect to old age, it is
honourable, and it is to be esteemed and reverenced ;
but I feel frequently inclined to do homage to your
youth.   When a celebrated tutor entered his school-
room, he always took off his hat to his boys, because,
as he said, he did not know which of them might yet
turn out to be a poet, a bishop, a lord chancellor, or a
prime minister.   When I look at young men and
women, I feel much the same, for I do not know what
they are to be.   I may be addressing a Livingstone,
or a Moffat.   I may be speaking to a John Howard,
or a Wilberforce.   I may be addressing a Mrs. Judson,
or an Elizabeth Fry.   I may be speaking to some
whom God will kindle into great lights to bless the
sons of men for many a day, and afterwards to shine
as the stars for ever and ever.   But you cannot shine
if you are not lighted.   You cannot bless God and
bless the sons of men unless God first blesses you.
Unregenerate, you are useless.   Born again, you will
be born for usefulness, but while you are unconverted

your usefulness is being lost. I will not insinuate that I expect everyone to become famous. It is not even desirable ; but I do know this, that everyone whose heart shall be given to Jesus, will be so useful and so necessary to the Church and to the world, that this world without them would lack a benefactor, and Heaven's company would be incomplete unless they joined its ranks.

Thus far concerning this life ; but now let me remind you, dear young friends, that if your hearts be given to Christ you need not tremble about the end of life. You may look forward to it with hope. It will come. Thank God, it will come ! Have you never wished that you could ride to Heaven in a chariot of fire, like Elijah ? I did once, till I reflected that if a chariot of fire should come for me I should be more afraid to get into it than to lie down and die upon my bed ; and of the two one might prefer to die, for to die in the Lord is to be made like to our glorious Head. I see no joy in the hope of escaping death. Jesus died, and so let me die. On His dear face the seal of death was set, so let it be on mine, that I may talk of resurrection as they cannot who shall be changed at His coming. You need not be afraid to depart and be with Christ, which is far better. Young people, whether you die in youth or old age, if you are resting in Jesus you shall sit upon the banks of Jordan singing,—

" Never mind the river."

The parting song will be sweet, but oh, the glory ! Oh, the glory ! I will not try to paint it. Who can ? The judgment will come, but you will not

tremble at it. On the right hand shall you stand, for
who can condemn those for whom Christ has died ?
The conflagration of the globe will come, the elements shall melt with fervent heat ; but you will not
tremble, for you shall be caught up together with the
Lord, and so shall you be for ever with the Lord.
Hell shall swallow up the unjust, they shall go down
alive into the pit ; but you shall not tremble for that,
for you are redeemed by the precious blood. The
millennial glory, whatever that may be ; and the reign
with Christ, and the triumph over death and hell ;
and the giving up of the kingdom to God, even the
Father, when God shall be all in all ; and eternity
with all its infinite glory ; these shall be all yours.
If you had to go through hell to reach this glory, it
would be worth the cost ! But you have not to do
any such thing ; you have only to believe in Jesus,
and even faith is the Lord's own gracious gift.
" Look unto Me and be ye saved, all ye ends of the
earth." This is the gospel.

A MESSAGE FOR THE PRESENT TIME.

W E plead with you, young men and women, and
tenderly remind you that you are at this
hour acting unjustly and unkindly towards your
God. He made you, and you do not serve Him ; He
has kept you alive, and you are not obedient to Him.
He has sent the word of His gospel to you, and you
have not received it ; He has sent His only begotten
Son, and you have despised Him. This injustice is a
thing of the present ; and the appeal we make to you
about it is, that in all reason such conduct should
come to an end. Oh, may God's Holy Spirit help
you to end it ! If I feel that I have done any man
an injustice, I am eager to set it right ; I would not
wait till to-morrow, I wish to make him amends at
once. Yes, and even when I have forgotten to render
assistance to some needy widow, I chide myself, and
feel uneasy till I have attended to the matter. Do
you not feel the same ? Would you wilfully wrong
or neglect another ? I feel sure you would not.
How is it, then, that you can be content to be unjust
to God, cruel to the dear Lover of the souls of men,
and antagonistic to the loving pleadings of the Holy
Spirit ? That first chapter of Isaiah—how striking it
is ! Why, if men had hearts that were at all tender
it would break them. " Hear, O heavens, and give
ear, O earth. I have nourished and brought up
children, and they have rebelled against Me. The ox
knoweth his owner, and the ass his master's crib : but

Israel doth not know ; My people doth not consider."
It is the wail of God Himself over man's unkindness
to his Maker! Young man of honour, young man of
integrity, does nothing speak to your conscience in
this ? " Will a man rob God ? " You would not rob
your employer. You would not like to be thought
unfaithful or dishonest towards man ; and yet your
God, your God, your God—is He to be treated so
basely, notwithstanding all His goodness ? As Jesus
said, " For which of these works do you stone Me ? "
so does Jehovah say, " I have made you ; I have kept
the breath in your nostrils ; I have fed you all your
life long; and for which of all these good things do
you live without Me, and neglect Me, and perhaps
curse My name, and sin with a high hand against My
sacred law ? " Now, can you think it right to remain
in so wantonly unjust a course of life as this ? Can
it be right to continue to wrong your God and grieve
His matchless love? Provoke Him no more, I pray
you. Let conscience lead you to feel that you have
dealt ill with the Lord, and come ye to Him for
forgiveness and change of heart. O Spirit of God,
make this appeal to be felt by all our beloved youths
and maidens !

Again, our message has to do with the present, for
we would affectionately remind you that you are now
at enmity with your best Friend—the Friend to whose
love you owe everything. You have grieved Him, and
are, without cause, His enemy ; can you bear this
thought ? I know a little child who had done something wrong, and her kind father talked to her, and
at last, as a punishment, he said to her in a very sad
voice, " I cannot kiss you to-night, for you have

grieved me very much." That broke her little heart. Though not a stroke had been laid upon her, she saw sorrow in her dear father's face, and she could not endure it. She pleaded and wept, and pleaded again to be forgiven. It was thought wise to withhold the kiss, and she was sent to bed, for she had done very wrong ; but there was no sleep for those weeping eyes, and when the mother went up to that little one's chamber she heard frequent sobs and sighs, and a sorrowful little voice said, " I was very, very naughty, but pray forgive me, and ask dear father to give me a kiss." She loved her father, and she could not bear that he should be grieved. Child of mercy, erring child of the great Father of spirits, canst thou bear to live for ever at enmity with the loving Father? " Would He forgive me ? " say you. What makes you ask the question? Is it that you do not know how good He is ? Has He not pourtrayed Himself as meeting His prodigal son and falling upon his neck and kissing him ? Before the child had reached the father, the father had reached the child. The father was eager to forgive, and therefore, when the son was yet a great way off his father saw him, and ran, and had compassion. Say no longer that we are talking of things of a far-off time. It is not so. I am speaking of that which I pray may be true of you now, that you may not remain enemies to God even another hour, but now may become His dear repenting children, and fly into your tender Father's arms.

I have to remind you, however, of much more than this—namely, that you are in danger. On account of your treatment of God, and your remaining an enemy

to Him, He will surely visit you in justice and punish
you for your transgressions. He is a just God, and
every sin committed is noted in His book ; and there
it stands recorded against His judgment day. The
danger you are in is that you may this moment go
down into the pit ; you may bow your head in death
and appear before your Maker in an instant, to
receive the just reward of your sins.

We tell you that there is immediate pardon for
all the sins of those who will believe in the Lord
Jesus Christ, and that if you will believe in Jesus,
your sins, which are many, are all forgiven you.
Know ye not the story (ye have heard it many
a time) that the Lord Jesus took upon Himself
the sins of all who trust Him, and suffered, in
their room and stead, the penalty due to their sins ?
He was our substitute, and as such He died, the just
for the unjust, to bring us to God. He laid down His
life for us, that " whosoever believeth in Him should
not perish, but have everlasting life." Will you refuse
the salvation so dearly purchased but so freely pre-
sented ? Will you not accept it here, and now? Can
you bear the burden of your sins? Are you content
to abide for a single hour in peril of eternal punishment? Can you bear to be slipping down into the
open jaws of hell as you now are ? Remember God's
patience will not last for ever ; long enough have you
provoked Him. All things are weary of you. The
very earth on which you stand groans beneath the
indignity of bearing a sinner upon its surface. So
long as you are an enemy to God, the stones of the
field are against you, and all creation threatens you.
It is a wonder that you do not sink at once to

destruction. For this cause we would have you pardoned *now* and made free from Divine wrath *now*. The peril is immediate, the Lord grant that so the rescue may be! Do I hear you say, "But may pardon be had at once? Is Jesus Christ a present Saviour? We thought that we might perhaps find Him when we came to die, or might obtain a hope of mercy after living a long life of seeking." It is not so. Free grace proclaims immediate salvation from sin and misery. Whosoever looks to Jesus at this very moment shall have his sins forgiven. At the instant he believes in the Lord Jesus, the sinner shall cease to be in danger of the fires of hell. The moment a man turns his eye of faith to Jesus Christ he is saved from the wrath to come. It is present salvation that we preach to you, and the present comfort of that present salvation, too.

Many other reasons tend to make this weighty matter exceedingly pressing; and among them is this, that there is a disease in your heart, the disease of sin, and it needs immediate cure. I do not hear persons say, if they discover an incipient disease in their systems, that they will wait a while till the evil is more fully developed, and will then resort to a physician. The most of us have sense enough to try to check disease at once. Young man, thou hast a leprosy upon thee. Young woman, thou hast a dreadful malady within thy heart. Dost thou not desire to be healed now? Jesus can give thee immediate healing if thou believest in Him. Wilt thou hesitate to be made whole? Dost thou love thy mortal malady? Is hideous sin so dear to thee? O that thou wouldst cry to be saved immediately, then

will Jesus hear thee. His Spirit will descend upon
thee, and cleanse thee, give thee a new heart, and a
right spirit—yea, and make thee whole from this time
henceforth and for ever ; canst thou wish to have so
great a blessing postponed ? Surely a sick man can
never be cured too soon ?

The gospel will also bring you present blessings.
In addition to present pardon and present justification,
it will give you present regeneration, present adoption,
present sanctification, present access to God, present
peace through believing, and present help in time of
trouble, and it will make you even for this life doubly
happy. It will be wisdom for your way, strength for
your conflict, and comfort for your sorrow. If I had
to die like a dog I would still wish to be a Christian.
If there were no hereafter—though the supposition is
not to be tolerated—yet still let me live for and with
Jesus, my beloved Lord. Balaam chose the righteous
man's death, I choose it too ; but quite as much do I
choose his life, for to have the love of God in the
heart, to have peace with God, to be able to look up
to Heaven with confidence, and talk to my Heavenly
Father in childlike trustfulness, is a present joy and
comfort worth more than worlds. Young men and
women, in preaching to you the gospel, we are preaching that which is good for this life as well as for the
life to come. If you believe in Jesus you will be
saved now, this moment, and you will now enjoy the
unchanging favour of God, so that you will go your
way henceforth not to live as others do, but as the
chosen of God, beloved with special love, enriched
with special blessings, to rejoice every day till you
are taken up to dwell where Jesus is. Present salva-

tion is the burden of the Lord's message to you, and therefore it is not true, but infamously false, that the vision is for many days to come, and the prophecy for times that are far off. Is there not reason in my pleadings? If so, yield to them. Can you answer these arguments? If not, I pray you cease delaying. Again would I implore the Holy Spirit to lead you to immediate decision!

A STORY OF AN ECCENTRIC WOMAN.*

THE Evangelists are, of course, the historians of
the time of Christ ; but what strange historians
they are! They leave out just that which worldly
ones would write, and they record just that which the
worldly would have passed over. What historian
would have thought of recording the story of the
widow and her two mites? Would a Hume or a
Smollett have spared half a page for such an incident?
Or think you that even a Macaulay could have found
it in his pen to write down a story of an eccentric
woman, who broke an alabaster box of precious
ointment upon the head of Jesus? But so is it.
Jesus values things, not by their glare and glitter, but
by their intrinsic value. Christ was sitting, or reclining, at the table of Simon the leper. A sudden
thought strikes this woman. She goes to her home ;
she gets her money, and expends it in an alabaster
box of ointment, or perhaps she had it in store, all
ready laid up. She brings it ; she hastens into the
house. Without asking anyone's leave, or com-
municating her intention, she breaks the alabaster
vase, which was itself of great value, and forth flows a
stream of the most precious ointment, with a very
refreshing fragrance. This she poured on His head.
So plenteous was the effusion that it streamed right
down to His feet, and the whole house was filled with

* Matt. xxvi. 13.

the odour of the ointment. The disciples murmured, but the Saviour commended. Now, what was there in the action of this woman worthy of commendation, and of such high commendation, too, that her memory must be preserved and transmitted with the gospel itself throughout all ages ?

I think, in the first place, this act was done from the impulse of a loving heart, and this it was that made it so remarkable. The heart is better than the head, after all, and the renewed heart is infinitely superior to the head ; for, somehow or other, though doubtless grace will renew the understanding, yet it takes longer to sanctify the understanding than it doth the affections ; or, at least, the heart is the first affected, it is that which is first touched, and being swifter in its goings forth than the head, it is generally more uncontaminated by the atmosphere around, and more clearly perceives that which is right. We in our day fall into the habit of calculating whether a thing is our duty or not ; but have we never an impulse of the heart more impressive, and more expressive, than the mere arithmetic of moral obligations ?   Our heart says to us, " Arise, go and visit such and such an one who is sick." We stop and say, " Is it my duty ?   If I do not go, will not somebody else go ?   Is the service absolutely requisite ? "   Or thy heart has said, perhaps, once upon a time, " Devote of thy substance largely to the cause of Christ." If we obeyed the heart we should do it at once ; but, instead of that, we stop and shake the head, and we begin to calculate the question whether it is precisely our duty. *This woman* did no such thing. It was not her duty—I speak broadly—it was not her positive duty to take the alabaster box and break it on the head of Christ. She did not do it from a sense of obedience ; she did it from a loftier motive. There was an impulse in her heart, which gushed forth like a pure stream overflowing every quibble and questioning,—" Duty or no duty, go and do it : "—and she takes the most precious things she can find, and out of simple love, guided by her renewed heart, she goes at once and breaks the alabaster box, and pours the ointment on His head. If she had stayed a minute to consider, she would not have done it at all ; if she had pondered, and reckoned, and reasoned, she never would have accomplished it ; but this was the heart acting, the invincible heart, the force of a spontaneous impulse, if not of a very inspiration, while the head with its various organs hath not been allowed time to hold a council. It was the heart's dictate fully and entirely carried out. Now, in these times, we lace ourselves so tight that we do not give our hearts room to act ; we just calculate whether we *should* do it—whether it is precisely our duty. Oh, would to God our hearts could grow bigger ! Let our heads be as they are, or let them be improved ; but let the heart have full play, and how much more would be done for Christ than ever has been done as yet ! But I would have you remark that this woman, acting from her heart, did not act as a matter of form.

Will you give to Christ no more than His due, as you give to Cæsar, when you pay your tax ? What ! if the *custom* be but a shekel, is the shekel all He is to have ? Is such a Master as this to be served by calculations ? Is He to have His every-day penny, just as the common labourer ? God forbid we should indulge such a spirit! Alas! for the mass of Christians, they do not even rise so high as that ; and if they once get there they fold their arms, and they are quite content. " I do as much as anybody else ; in fact, a little more ; I am sure I do my duty ; nobody can find any fault ; if people were to expect me to do more, they would be really unreasonable." Ah! then, you have not yet learned this woman's love, in all its heights and depths. You know not how to do an unreasonable thing—a thing that is not expected of you—out of the Divine impulse of a heart fully consecrated to Jesus. The first era of the Christian Church was an era of wonders, because, then, Christian men obeyed the prompting of their hearts. What wonders they used to do! A voice within the heart said to an apostle, " Go to a heathen country and preach." He never counted the cost—whether his life would be safe, or whether he would be suc- cessful ; he went and did whatever his heart told him. To another it spake, "Go thou, and distribute all that thou hast ; " and the Christian went and did it, and cast his all into the common store. He never asked whether it was his duty ; his heart bid him do it, and he obeyed at once. Now, we have become stereotyped ; we run in the ancient cart-rut ; we all do what other people do ; we are just content with performing the routine, and accomplishing the for- malism of religious duties. How unlike this woman, who went out of all order, because her heart told her to do so, and she obeyed from her heart. This, I think, is the first part of the woman's act that won a deserved commendation.

The second commendation is—what this woman

did was done purely to Christ, and for Christ. Why did she not take this spikenard, and sell it, and give the money to the poor? "No," she might have thought, "I love the poor, I would relieve them at any time; to the utmost of my ability would I clothe the naked, and feed the hungry; but I want to do something for *Him*." Well, why did she not get up, and take the place that Martha did, and begin to wait at the table? "Ah!" she thought, "Martha is at the table, dividing her services; Simon the leper, and Lazarus, and all the rest of the guests, have a share in her attention. I want to do something directly *for Him*, something that He will have all to Himself, something that He cannot give away, but which He must have and which must belong to Him." Now, I do not think that any other disciple, in all Christ's experience, ever had that thought. I do not find, in all the Evangelists, another instance like this. He had disciples, whom He sent out by two and two to preach, and right valiantly did they do it, for they desired to benefit their fellow-men in the service of their Lord. He had disciples, too, I doubt not, who were very, very happy when they distributed the bread and the fishes to the hungry multitudes, because they felt they were doing an act of humanity in supplying the needs of the hungry; but I do not think He had one disciple who thought about doing something exactly and directly for *Him*—something of which no one else could partake, something that should be Christ's, and Christ's alone.

The very beauty of this woman's act lay in this, that she did it all for the Lord Jesus Christ. She felt she owed Him all; it was He who had forgiven her sins;

it was He who had opened her eyes, and given her to see the light of heavenly day ; it was He who was her hope, her joy, her all ; her love went out in its common actings to her fellow-men—it went out towards the poor, the sick, and the needy ; but, oh ! it went in all its vehemence to Him.   That Man, that blessed Man, the God-Man, she *must* give something to *Him*. She could not be content to put it in that bag there ; she must go and put it right on His head. She could not be content that Peter, or James, or John, should have a part of it ; the whole pound must go on His head : and though others might say it was waste, yet she felt it was not, but that whatever she could give unto Him was well bestowed, because it went to Him to whom she owed her all.   The scene is a very simple one, but it is extremely captivating. You will do your acts in religion far better, if you can cultivate always the desire to do them all for Christ.

This woman did an extraordinary thing for Christ. Not content with doing what other people had done, nor wishful to find a precedent, she ventured to expose her ardent attachment though she might have known that some would call her mad, and all would think her foolish and wasteful, yet she did it—an extraordinary thing—for the love she bore her Lord. It seems to me that Jesus praised this woman, and handed down this memorial, because her act was so beautifully expressive.   There was more virtue in it than you could see.   The manner, as well as the matter, of her votive sacrifice, might well excite the rebuke of men, whose practical religion is mercenary and economical.   It is not enough that she pours out

the ointment with such reckless profusion, but she is
so rash and extravagant she must needs break the
box. Marvel not, but admire the rapt enthusiasm of
her godly soul. Why! love is a passion. If ye did
but know and feel its vehemence, ye would never
marvel at an act so expressive. Her love could no
more tarry to conform to the rubrics of service, than it
could count the cost of her offering. A mighty impulse of devotion carried her soul far above all ordinary
routine. Her conduct did but symbol the inspiration of
a grateful homage. A sanctified heart, more beautiful
than the transparent vase of alabaster, was that hour
broken. Only from a broken heart can the sweet
spices of grace give forth their rich perfume. " Love
and grief, our heart dividing," we sometimes sing—
but, oh! let me say it—love, grief and gratitude, the
spikenard, myrrh and frankincense of the gospel blend
together here ; the heart must expand and break, or
the odours would never fill the house. Every muscle
of her face, every involuntary motion of her frame,
frenzied as it might appear to the unsympathizing
looker-on, was in harmony with her heart's emotion.
Her every feature gives evidence of her sincerity.
What they could coldly criticise, Jesus delivers to
them for a study. Here is one on whom a Saviour's
love has produced its appropriate effects. Here is a
heart that has brought forth the most precious fruits.
Not only admiration for her, but kindness to us, moved
our Lord, when He resolved henceforth to illustrate
the gospel, wherever it is published, with this portrait
of saintly love, in one instant breaking the delicate
vase, and bursting the tender heart. Why, that woman
meant to say to Christ, " Dear Lord, I give myself

away." She went home ; she brought out the most precious thing she had ; if she had had anything worth ten thousand times as much, she would have brought that ; in fact, she did really bring Him all.

"She hath wrought a good work upon Me." Note these two last words, " *Upon Me !* " " Why," say they, " it is not a good work to go and spill all that ointment, and perpetrate so much waste." " No," says Jesus, " it is not a good work in relation to you, but it is a good work upon Me." And, after all, that is the best sort of good work—a good work that is wrought upon Christ—an act of homage such as faith in His name, and love to His person, would dictate. A good work upon the poor is commendable ; a good work upon the Church is excellent ; but a good work upon Christ, surely this is one of the very highest and noblest kinds of good works. But I will be bound to say that neither Judas nor the disciples could comprehend this ; and there is a mystic virtue in the acts of some Christian men that common Christians do not and cannot comprehend. That mystic virtue consists in this, that they do it " as unto the Lord, and not unto men," and in their service they serve the Lord Jesus Christ.

Moreover, our Lord protects the woman with another apology. " Do not trouble her ; do not reflect upon what might have been done for the poor, ' for ye have the poor always with you, but Me ye have not always.' Ye can always do good to them, whenever you please." Why, He seems here to retort upon her accusers. " If there are any poor about, give to them yourselves ; empty that bag of Mine out, Judas ; don't be hiding that away in your girdle. ' Whensoever *ye* will, ye may do them good.' Don't begin talking about the poor, and about what might have been done ; go you, and do what might have been done yourselves ; this poor woman hath done a good thing for Me ; I shall not be here long ; don't trouble her." And so, if you murmur at men because they do not go in your ordinary ways, because they venture a little out of the regular line, there is plenty for you to do ; your errand, perhaps, is not there exactly, but there is plenty for you to do ; go and do it, and do not blame those who do extraordinary things. There are multitudes of ordinary people to attend to ordinary things. If you want subscribers to the guinea list, you can have them ; it is those who give all they have, that are the varieties. Do not trouble those men. There are not many of them. They will not trouble you. You will have to travel from here to John o' Groat's house before you knock against many dozen. They are rare creatures not often discovered. Do not trouble them ; they may be fanatical, they may be excessive ; but if you should build an asylum to put them all in, it would require but a very small sort of a house. Let them alone ; there are not many who do much for their Master—not many who are irrational enough to think that there is nothing worth living for but to glorify Christ and magnify His holy name.

This woman thought she was just anointing Christ. "Nay," says Christ, "she is anointing Me for my burial." There was more in her act than she knew of. And there is more in the spiritual promptings of our heart than we shall ever discover to the day of judgment. When first of all the Lord said to Whitefield, "Go and preach out on Kennington Common," did Whitefield know what was to be the result? No ; he thought, doubtless, that he should just stand for once on the top of a table, and address some five thousand people. But there was a greater intent in the womb of Providence. The Lord meant that to set the whole country in a blaze, and to bring forth a glorious renewal of Pentecostal times, the like of which had not been seen before. Only seek to have your heart filled with love, and then obey its first spiritual dictate. Stop not. However extraordinary may be the mandate, go and do it. Have your wings outstretched like the angels before the throne, and the very moment that the echo vibrates in your heart, fly, fly, and you shall be flying you know not whither—you shall be upon an errand higher and nobler than your imagination has ever dreamed.

GRACE A MATTER OF GROWTH.

IN the Christian Church there is an order of Christians who have grown so much that they can no
longer be called *babes in grace*, but yet they are not so
far matured that they can be exactly called *fathers*.
These, who form the middle-class of the spiritual-
minded, are styled *young men*. Age, according to
the flesh, often differs much from the condition of the
spirit : many old men are still no more than "babes";
some children in years are even now " young men "
in grace, while not a few young men are " fathers " in
the Church while young in years. God has endowed
certain of His servants with great grace, and made
them mature in their youth : such were Joseph,
Samuel, David, Josiah, and Timothy. It is not age
according to the family register that we speak about,
but age according to the Lamb's Book of Life.

Grace is a matter of growth, and hence we have
among us babes, young men, and fathers, whose
position is not reckoned according to this fleeting,
dying life, but according to that eternal life which
has been wrought in them of the Spirit of God. It is
a great mercy when young men in the natural sense
are also young men in the spiritual sense. The fathers
need not be ashamed of their spiritual seed. In
speaking to young men in Christ, I am speaking to a
numerous body of Christians who make up a very
efficient part of the army of Christ. I would ask
them not to be either so modest or so proud as to

decline to be thus classed. You are no longer
weaklings ; do not, therefore, count yourselves mere
babes, lest you plead exemption from hard service.
You are hardly yet mature enough to rank with the
fathers ; do not forget the duties of your real place
under cover of aspiring to another. It is honour
enough to be in Christ, and certainly it is no small
thing to be in spiritual things a man in the prime
of life.

These young men are not babes. They have been
in Christ too long for that : they are no longer
novices, to whom the Lord's house is strange. They
have been born unto God probably now for years :
the things which they hoped for at first they have to
a large extent realized ; they know now what once
they could not understand. They are not now
confined to milk diet ; they can eat meat and digest
it well. They have discernment, having had their
senses exercised by reason of use, so that they are
not so liable to be misled as they were in their
infancy. And while they have been longer in the
way, so also have they now grown stronger in the
way. It is not a weak and timorous faith which they
now possess ; they believe firmly and stoutly, and are
able to do battle for the "faith once delivered to the
saints," for they are strong in the Lord and in the
power of His might. They are wiser now than they
used to be. When they were children they knew
enough to save them, for they knew the Father, and
that was a blessed knowledge ; but now they know
far more of the Word of God which abideth in them
through their earnest, prayerful, believing reception
of it. Now they have a clearer idea of the breadth

and length, and depth and height of the work of redemption, for they have been taught of God. They even venture to enjoy the deep things of God ; and the covenant is by no means an unknown thing among them. They have been under the blessed teaching of the Spirit of God, and from Him they have received an unction, so that they know all things. In knowledge they are no more children, but men in Christ Jesus. Thus they are distinguished from the first class, which comprehends the babes in Christ.

They are not yet fathers because they are not yet so established, confirmed, and settled as the fathers are, who know what they believe, and know it with a certainty of full assurance which nothing can shake. They have not yet had the experience of fathers, and consequently have not all their prudence and foresight : they are richer in zeal than in judgment. They have not yet acquired the nursing faculty so precious in the church as the product of growth, experience, maturity, and affection ; they are going on to that, and in a short time they will have reached it, but as yet they have other work to do more suitable to their vigour. Do not suppose that when we say they are not to be called "fathers," that they are not, therefore, very valuable to the community ; for in some senses they are quite equal to the fathers, and in one or two respects they may even be superior to them. The fathers are for contemplation, they study deep and see far, and so they "have known Him that is from the beginning"; but a measure of their energy for action may have gone through stress of years. These young men are born to fight ; they are the militia of the Church, they have to contend for her faith, and to extend the Redeemer's kingdom. They should do so, for they are strong. This is their lot, and the Lord help them to fulfil their calling. These must for years to come be our active spirits : they are our strength and our hope. The fathers must soon go off the stage : their maturity in grace shows that they are ready for glory, and it is not God's way to keep His shocks of corn in the field when once they are fully ripe for the garner—perfect men shall be gathered up with the perfect, and shall enter into their proper sphere. The fathers, therefore, must soon be gone ; and when they are gone, to whom are we to look for a succession but to these young men ? We hope to have them for many years with us, valiant for the truth, steadfast in the faith, ripening in spirit, and growingly made meet to take their seats among the glorified saints above. Judge ye whether ye are fairly to be ranked among the young men. Have no regard to the matter of sex, for there is neither male nor female in Christ Jesus Judge whether ye be fit to be ranked among those whose full-grown and vigorous life entitles them to stand among the effectives of the Church, the vigorous manhood of the seed of Israel.

These Christians of the middle class are emphatically strong. This does not imply that any measure of spiritual strength was in them by nature ; for the Apostle Paul clearly puts it otherwise concerning our natural state, saying, "When we were yet without strength, Christ died for the ungodly"; so that by nature we are without strength to do anything that is good and right. We are strong as a wild bull, to dash headlong into everything that is evil : strong as a lion to fight against all that is good and Godlike ; but for all spiritual things and holy things we are utterly infirm and incapable ; yea, we are as dead men until God the Holy Spirit deals with us.

Neither does the apostle here at all allude to the strength of the body in young men, for in a spiritual sense this is rather their weakness than their strength. The man who is strong in the flesh is too often for that very reason strongly tempted to sins of the flesh ; and hence the apostle bids his young friend " flee youthful lusts." Whenever you read the life of Samson you may thank God you had not Samson's thews and sinews ; or else it is more than probable that you would have had Samson's passions, and they might have mastered you as they mastered him. The time of life in which a young man is found is full of perils ; and so is the spiritual condition of which it is the type. The young man might almost wish that it were with him as with the older man in whom the forces of the flesh have declined, for though age brings with it many infirmities it also has its gain in the abatement of the passions. So you see the young man cannot reckon upon vigour of the flesh as contributing towards real " strength ; " he has rather to ask for more strength from on high lest the animal vigour that is within him should drag down his spirit. He is glad to be in robust health that he may bear much toil in the Lord's cause ; but he is not proud of it, for he remembers that the Lord delighteth not in the strength of the horse, and taketh not pleasure in the legs of a man.

These young men in grace are strong, first of all,

16

in faith, according to that exhortation, " Be strong !
fear not ! "   They have known the Lord now for some
time, and they have enjoyed that perfect peace which
comes of forgiven sin : they have marked the work of
the Spirit within themselves, and they know that is
no delusion, but a Divine change ; and now they not
only believe in Christ, but they know that they believe in Him.   They know whom they have believed,
and they are persuaded that He is able to keep that
which they have committed to Him.   That faith
which was once a healing touch has now become a
satisfying embrace ; that enjoyment which was once a
sip has now become a draught, quenching all thirst ;
ay, and that which was once a draught has become an
immersion into the river of God, which is full of
water : they have plunged into the river of life and
find waters to swim in.   Oh, what a mercy it is to be
strong in this fashion ! Let him that is strong take
heed that he glory only in the Lord, who is his
righteousness and strength ; but in Him and His
strength he may indeed make his boast and defy the
armies of the aliens.   What saith Paul—" I can do
all things through Christ that strengtheneth me."
Take good heed that ye never lose this strength.
Pray God that you may never sin so as to lose
it ; may never backslide so as to lose it ; may
never grieve the Spirit so as to lose it ; for I reckon
that to be endowed with power from on High, and to
be strong in faith, giving glory to God, is the truest
glory and majesty of our manhood, and it were sad
to lose it, or even to deface it.   Oh, that all Christians
were so much advanced as to enter the enlisted
battalion of the Lord's young men !

This strength makes a man strong to endure. He is a sufferer, but mark how patient he is! He is a loser in business, and he has a hard task to earn his daily bread, but he never complains, he has learned in every state to be content. He is persecuted, but he is not distressed thereby; men revile him, but he is not moved from the even tenor of his way. He grows careless alike of flattery and calumny; so long as he can please God he cares not to displease men. He dwells on high, and lives above the smoke of human opinion. He bears and forbears. He bows his neck to the yoke and his shoulders to the burden, and has fellowship with Christ in His sufferings. Blessed is that man who is so strong that he never complains of his trials, never whimpers and frets because he is made to share in the humiliations and griefs of His covenant head. He expected to bear the cross when he became a follower of the Crucified, and he is not now made weary and faint when it presses upon him. It is a fair sight to see young Isaac bearing the wood for the sacrifice; young Joseph bearing the fetters in prison with holy joy; young Samson carrying away the gates of Gaza, bars and all; and young David praising God with his harp though Saul is feeling for his javelin. Such are the exploits of the young men who count it all joy when they fall into manifold trials for Christ's sake. O young man, be strong; strong as an iron column which bears the full stress of the building and is not moved.

This strength shows itself, next, in labouring for Christ. The young man in Christ is a great worker. He has so much strength that he cannot sit still; he

would be ashamed to leave the burden and heat of
the day to be borne by others. He is up and at it
according to his calling and ability. He has asked
his Lord as a favour to give him something to do.
His prayer has been, " Show me what Thou wouldst
have me to do," and having received an answer he is
found in the vineyard trenching the soil, removing
the weeds, pruning the vines, and attending to such
labours as the seasons demand. His Master has said
to him, " Feed My sheep," and "Feed My lambs ;" and,
therefore, you shall see him through the livelong day
and far into the night watching over the flock which is
committed to him. In all this toil he greatly rejoices,
for he is strong. He can run and not be weary ; he
can walk and not faint. " By my God have I leaped
over a wall," saith he. Nothing is hard to him ; or, if
it be, he remembers that the diamond cuts the diamond, and so he sets a harder thing against a hard
thing, and by a firm and stern resolution he overcomes. That which ought to be done he declares
shall be done in the power of God, and lo, it is accomplished ! Blessed is the church that hath her
quiver full of these ; she shall speak with her adversaries in the gate. These are the men that work our
reformations ; these are the men who conduct our
missions ; these are the men who launch out into the
deep for Christ. They make the vanguard of the
host of God, and largely compose the main body of
her forces.

So, also, are these young men strong to resist
attack. They are assaulted, but they carry with them
the shield of faith wherewith they quench the fiery
darts of the enemy. Wherever they go, if they meet

with other tempted ones, they spring to the front to espouse their cause. They are ready in the day of battle to meet attacks upon the faith with the sword of the Spirit : they will yield no point of faith, but defend the truth at all hazards. Clad in the panoply of truth, they meet no deadly wound ; for by grace they are so preserved that the wicked one toucheth them not. They resist temptation, and are unharmed in the midst of peril. Do you want a specimen? Look at Joseph! Where ten thousand would have fallen he stands in snow-white purity. Joseph as contrasted with David is an instance of how a young man may bring greater glory to God than an older man when assailed by a kindred temptation. Joseph is but young, and the temptation forces itself upon him while he is in the path of duty. He is alone with his temptress, and no one need know of the sin if it be committed ; on the other hand, if he refuses, shame, and possibly death, may await him through the calumny of his offended mistress ; yet he bravely resists the assault, and overcomes the wicked one. He is a bright contrast to the older man, a father in Israel, who went out of his way to compass an evil deed, and committed crime in order to fulfil his foul desire. From this case we learn that neither years, nor knowledge, nor experience can preserve any one of us from sin ; but old and young must be kept by the power of God, or they will be overthrown by the tempter.

Furthermore, these young men are not only strong for resistance, but they are strong for attack. They carry the war into the enemy's territory. If there is anything to be done, they are like Jonathan and his armour-bearer, eager for the fray : these are very zealous for the Lord of hosts, and are prompt to undertake toil and travail for Jesus' sake. These smite down error, and set up truth ; these believe great things, attempt great things, and expect great things, and the Lord is with them. The archers have sorely grieved them, and shot at them, and hated them ; but their bows abide in strength, for the arms of their hands are made strong by the mighty God of Jacob. One of them shall chase a thousand, and two put ten thousand to flight.

OPEN THE YOUNG MAN'S EYES.*

FOR certain of our friends we pray that their eyes may be opened to see the enemy of their souls under the many disguises which he assumes. We fear that many are ignorant of his devices. Young men, especially, are too apt to mistake the great enemy for a friend. They believe his false and flattering words, and are seduced to ruin. He holds forth to them the sparkling cup; but in its beaded bubbles death is lurking. He talks of "pleasure"; but in the lusts of the flesh the pleasure is a shadow, and misery is the substance. He wears the mask of prudence, and admonishes young men to "mind the main chance", and leave religion till they have made their fortunes; but that gain which comes of thrusting God aside will prove to be an everlasting loss. The devil as a serpent does more mischief than as a roaring lion. If we had to meet the devil, and knew him to be what he is, we might far more easily conquer him; but we have to deal with him disguised as an angel of light, and here is the need of a hundred eyes, each one of them opened by God, that we may see. Even worse than this is the fact that, at times, he does not meet us at all, but he undermines our path; he digs pits for our feet; he shoots his arrows from afar, or sends forth a pestilence which walks in darkness. Then have we need of a better sight than

---

* 2 Kings vi. 17.

nature gives. I would pray for the young man who
is just leaving home to go into the world, " O Lord,
open the eyes of the young man, that he may see ! "
May he be able to detect the falsehood which may
hide itself beneath the truth, the meanness which may
wrap itself about with pride, the folly which may robe
itself in learning, the sin which may dress itself in the
raiment of pleasure! I would not have you taken,
like birds, in a snare. I would not have the youth
led, like a bullock to the shambles, by the hand of
temptation. Let us breathe such a prayer as that of
Elisha for each person who is beginning life. God
grant that his eyes may be opened to see sin as sin,
and to see that evil never can be good, and a lie never
can be true, and rebellion against our God can never
be the way to happiness !

We want men's eyes to be opened to see God as
everwhere, observing all things. What an opening
of the eyes this would be to many! It is a sad but
true saying, that God may be seen everywhere, but
that the most of men see Him nowhere. He is blind
indeed who cannot see HIM to whom the sun owes
its light. Until our eyes are opened, we rise in the
morning, and we fall asleep at night, and we have not
seen God all day, although He has been every moment
around us and within us. We live from the first day
of January to the last day of December, and while the
Lord never ceases to see us, we do not even begin to
see Him till, by a miracle of grace, He opens our
eyes. We dwell in a wonderful world which the
great Creator has made, and filled with His own
handiwork, and cheered with His own presence, and
yet we do not see Him : indeed, there are some so

blind as to assert that there is no Creator, and that they cannot perceive any evidence that a supremely wise and mighty Creator exists. Oh, that the Lord Jesus would open the eyes of the wilfully blind! Oh, that you, also, who are blinded by forgetfulness rather than by error, may be made to cry with Hagar, "Thou God seest me"; and with Job, "Now mine eye seeth Thee"! If God will graciously convince men of His own Divine presence, what a benediction it will be to them, especially to the young in commencing life! A clear perception that the Lord observes all that we do will be a very useful protection in the hour of temptation. When we remember the Divine eye, we shall cry, like Joseph, "How can I do this great wickedness, and sin against God?" To see yourself is well; but to see God is better. Let us pray, "O Lord, open the young man's eyes, that he may see THEE!"

When a man begins to see his great enemy, and his best Friend, we may next pray, "Lord, open his eyes to see the way of salvation through the appointed Saviour". There is no seeing the Lord Jesus but by His own light. We look *to* Him with a look which comes *from* Him. I have tried to explain salvation to people many a time, in simple words and figures; but there is a great deal more wanted than an explanation. It is right to be very plain; but more is needed than a clear statement. No matter how bright the candle, a blind man sees none the better. I continually pray, "Lord, open my mouth!" but I perceive that I must also pray, "Lord, open men's eyes!" Until God opens a man's eyes, he will not see what faith means, nor what atonement means, nor

what regeneration means.   That which is plain as a
pikestaff to a seeing man is invisible to the blind.
" Believe, and live " ; what can be plainer?   Yet no
man understands it till God gives grace to perceive
His meaning.   It is our duty, as preachers, to put the
gospel as plainly as possible ; but we cannot give a
man spiritual understanding.   We declare, in baldest
and boldest terms, " Believe on the Lord Jesus Christ,
and thou shalt be saved " ; but men ask, like simple-
tons, " What do you mean ? "   We cry, " Look unto
Jesus, and live "; but when our explainings are over,
we learn that they have mistaken our meaning, and
are still looking to themselves, and turning their backs
on the Lord Jesus.   To believe, or trust, is no mystery,
but the simplest of all simplicities ; and for that very
reason men cannot be persuaded to think that we
mean what we say, or that God means what He says.
We need to pray—" Lord, open their eyes, that they
may see ; for seeing, they do not see ; and hearing,
they do not perceive ! "

Blessed be the Lord, how sweetly they do see it the
moment their eyes are opened by His own omnipotent
touch !   Then they wonder that they did not see it
before, and call themselves ten thousand fools for not
perceiving what is so plain.   Faith in the Lord Jesus
is the veriest A B C of Divine revelation :· it belongs
to the rudiments and elements of heavenly knowledge,
and we are dolts indeed not to take it as we find it in
the Word, and leave off mystifying ourselves over so
plain a matter.   Once let the miracle-working power
of God open our eyes, and we see well enough ; but
till then we grope in the noon-day for that which is
right before us.   Sin cannot so darken the mind but

that God can pour light into it. If we cannot make men see, we can at least lead them to the Master Oculist, who can rectify their sight.

We should pray that our friends may have their eyes opened to see all manner of spiritual truth. These optics of ours can only see natural objects: that is all they are intended for. We should be very grateful that our eyes can see as much as they do see; but spiritual objects are not discernible by the eyes of the body, which are for material objects only. The things which pertain to the spiritual kingdom must be perceived by eyes of a spiritual sort, eyes opened by the Lord. God must give to us spiritual senses before we can discern spiritual things: let this never be forgotten. The flesh cannot grasp, perceive, or discern the things of the Spirit. We must become spiritual, and receive spiritual faculties, before we can perceive spiritual things; in a word, we must be "born again." "The natural man receiveth not the things of the Spirit of God: for they are foolishness unto him: neither can he know them, because they are spiritually discerned." Hence the need of the prayer, ' Lord, open thou the eyes of the young man, that he may see!''

Already the horses and chariots of fire were round about Elisha; but his servant could not see one of them, because they were spiritual chariots and spiritual horses — angelic beings belonging to the purely spiritual domain; and as yet the youth had not entered the spiritual region, and had no eyes with which to see into it. When God had given him spiritual eyes, then there began to break upon his vision that strange sight — ethereal, aerial, nay, spiritual, but yet most real; that sight which revived his soul with the conviction that the prophet was safe, since the ministers of God, as flames of fire, flashed to and fro; and like an army, with horses and chariots, showed themselves strong for the defence of the servant of Jehovah. How surprised he was! How great his amazement! How content his mind! He and his master were mysteriously defended, beyond all fear of danger. Strangers to the things of God, if the Lord would open your eyes at once, you would be astonished indeed; for as yet you have no idea, you cannot have any idea, what the spiritual life is, nor what spiritual realities must be; neither can you have any true idea of them till you are quickened of the Lord. You may talk about spiritual subjects, and discuss them, and think yourselves theologians; but you resemble deaf persons criticising music, and blind men describing pictures. You are not qualified even to express an opinion upon the matter till you are created anew in Christ Jesus, and brought within range of the spiritual and the heavenly. "Except a man be born again, he cannot see the kingdom of God." Let the prayer go up, then, from all enlightened hearts, for those who are not as yet walking in the light : "Lord, open the eyes of the young men, that they may see!"

Elisha's prayer for this young man was not, and our prayer for others is not, that they may do something which they can do, that they may use some faculty which they already possess; but that a new sight may be granted to them, and that a new nature may be created within them, by a power altogether above and beyond themselves. We call in the hand of God. We ask the Lord to work a marvel. We would have you receive what no education can ever give you, what no graduation at any university can ever bestow upon you ; we want you to obtain what no years of experience or of study can achieve ; we want you to possess what no imitation of other people will gain for you ; we want you to experience a change which only the Lord Himself can work in you. We would have you pass from nature's darkness into God's marvellous light, from an awful blindness into a clear vision of things otherwise invisible.

PRAYER FOR YOUNG MEN—THE REASONS FOR IT.*

THE first reason for our prayer is, because we ourselves have been made to see. Had this miracle of grace not taken place within us, we should have had no thought of prayer for you ; but now our whole heart goes with the plea. Once we were as you are. Our eyes were blinded so that we saw neither our foes in all their terror, nor the glory of the Lord round about us. Like blind Samsons, we went through the weary drudgery of earth surrounded by our foes. At length a glimmering of the light fell upon us, like a lightning flash, showing us our sin ; and after we were thus illuminated we endured a great fight of afflictions. Without were fightings, within were fears. Our enemies were round about us, and we knew not what to do. But some man of God prayed for us, and one day our eyes were turned toward the hills from whence cometh all aid to terror-stricken men. The Lord was there, though we knew Him not ; but yet we looked to Him and were enlightened, and our faces were not ashamed ; for round about Him the mountain was full of chariots and horses of fire. " For God, who commanded the light to shine out of darkness, hath shined in our hearts, to give the light of the knowledge of the glory of God in the face of Jesus Christ."

We call upon the Lord for this second reason,

---

* 2 Kings. vi. 17.

because only by His power can men be made to see. This we found in our own experience. In vain we struggled to behold the salvation of God; in vain we sought the help of godly people; no sight came to our souls, nor were the eyes of our understanding enlightened, until the Lord Himself laved our eyes in the waters that go softly. Then we came seeing. And this we also discover when we try to lead others to the light. We speak to them of the glories we ourselves behold, and set before them the truth of God; but we cannot make them see. To bestow spiritual vision is as great a wonder as to make a world, and requires the same fiat of omnipotence. Only He who created the eye can give this second sight. "Since the world began was it not heard that any man opened the eyes of one that was born blind." What folly, then, to attempt the greater task of bestowing the sight of the heart! How vain the boast of those who attempt to invade God's prerogative, and imagine that human ordinances or observances can open blind eyes! Let us, after we have done our best to make the people see the glory of the gospel, ever fall back on the God of the gospel, and entreat Him to do His own blessed work. Do not try to hold up your tallow candles to reveal the chariots of fire, nor parade your vain philosophy, as if that could clear away the darkness of the soul. Leave room for God to work; and, in a moment, at the touch of His finger, in response to the prayers of His people, the wondrous work shall be accomplished.

Most importunately do we pray when we see the people enquiring. The cry, "What shall we do?"

sends us to our knees ; for we know that what is necessary is, not something to be done, but something to be seen. And we feel persuaded that the Lord who awoke the desire in the hearts of the seekers, will surely, also, open their eyes to behold His glory. The very fact that we feel drawn to pray for them, is already a token to us that, ere long, the scales shall fall from their eyes; and through their vision of the splendour and sufficiency of the provision that God hath made for those who trust in Him, the name of the Lord will be greatly glorified. Therefore, with much expectancy, we again utter our prayer, " Lord, open their eyes, that they may see ! "

Another reason for this prayer is—you are not aware of your own blindness. You are trusting in yourselves that you can see well enough all you need to see. That young man, of whom I am thinking now, has no idea whatever that his eyes are stone blind to eternal things. He thinks himself a sharp and clever fellow ; and I do not deny that he is so, in his own line of things. I am glad that he has such quick faculties for this life. God bless him ; and may he prosper in his business, and in the enterprise upon which he is just entering ! May the good Lord be with him concerning the matter on which his heart is set ! But still I am rather afraid of your cleverness ; I am somewhat frightened at that keenness of yours, because I have seen sharp men cut themselves, and I have seen the self-reliant make miserable failures. Something is to be said for confidence in its proper place ; but self-congratulation is a proof of inward weakness, and forebodes a breakdown. If you are

17

depending on an arm of flesh, at the very best you are resting on a broken reed ; you require a strength beyond your own to fight the moral and spiritual battle of life. Your self-reliance, in this case, is a piece of groundless self-conceit. Do you not remember one, of whom we read, that, when he was forewarned of what he would yet do, he exclaimed, in astonishment, " Is thy servant a dog, that he should do this great thing ? " Hazael could not think himself capable of such crimes ; and yet he no sooner had the opportunity than he fell into the evil up to the very neck. He was dog enough to be cruel, for he was dog enough to fawn upon himself. You do not believe, young man, that you will ever be dishonest ; and yet that little gambling speculation of yours will lead to it. You cannot think that you will ever be godless ; and yet you are even now departing from the good old ways of your home, and making a jest of sacred things when in certain company. They that trust in themselves are storing up the fuel for a great fire of sin. The pride which lifts itself up will throw itself down. Because the fine young fellow does not know how blind he is, we therefore lament his blindness, and are the more earnest in bringing him to Jesus, that he may receive his sight. " Lord, open his eyes, that he may see ! "

Next, we pray this prayer because we have reason to fear that you are surrounded by those who will mislead you. We know the young man well. He has come to London from that sober, orderly, country home, and he has no notion of the snares which will be laid for him by the fowlers, male and female. Oh, you who have no experience, and little discretion, hear the voice of warning! Satan has cunning servants about him, that hunt for the precious life with double diligence. Our Lord Jesus has about Him servants who too often slumber; but the devil's servants are not slothful in their dreadful business. You will find them waylay you in the streets without, and press around you in the haunts of pleasure within. They are everywhere, and they leave no stone unturned that they may entrap the unwary. And what if this blind young man is put down in the midst of all these blood-suckers? They will devour him if they can. What if he is left to be their victim? It is like turning out a sheep among a pack of wolves. "Lord, open the eyes of the young man, that he may see!

We pray this prayer for some of you, because you are going away from those who have hitherto watched over you, and this is a dangerous change for you. Your mother—ah! we can never tell what a blessing a godly mother is to a young man—your mother parts from you with great anxiety. Will you ever forget her tender words? Our fathers are all very well—God bless them!—and a father's godly influence and earnest prayers are of untold value to his children; but the mothers are worth two of them, mostly, as to the moral training and religious bent of their sons and daughters. Well, I say, you are going right away from your mother's holy influence, and from your father's restraining admonitions. You will now have nobody to encourage you in the right way. You will miss your sister's holy kiss, and your grandmother's loving persuasions. You are going out of

the hot-house into a night's frost : well may we pray
concerning you, that you may carry with you well-
opened eyes, to see your way, and look before you
leap. The young man is now to walk alone : " Lord,
open his eyes, that he may see ! " If he does not
look before he leaps, he will soon be in the ditch ; and
who shall pull him out ?

Again, we pray this prayer with the more pleasure,
because you will do so much good if your eyes are
opened. A blind man in the midst of such a world
as this, what can he do ? He cannot help other
travellers, for he has to seek aid for himself. You
wish to give rather than to take, do you not ? Some
have great abilities, and I want them to use them
aright. I am persuaded that I am speaking to young
people whom God has ordained to be of great service
to their age. That youth yonder does not as yet
know what is in him. He is playing with himself ;
he is making a fool of himself ; he is throwing his
pearls before swine ; he is wasting his strength. If
the Lord should open his eyes, he would see what he
is doing. What a man he would make if he were
but right with God ! Think of Saul of Tarsus, how
he harassed the Church of Christ ; but when the
scales fell from his eyes, the Lord had no better
servant under heaven than that once-furious perse-
cutor. With both hands diligently he built up the
Church which once he laboured to cast down. " The
thing which has been is the thing which shall be."
Pray, therefore, for our young men, who have sinned,
that they may be restored ; and for those who are as
yet ignorant, that they may be enlightened ; for the
cause of God has need of these, and in these the

Church shall find her champions! Little know we the wealth of comfort for the faithful which may lie in one young life. Surely, we ought to pile on our prayers, and make our intercession flame like some great beacon-light for the rising youth of our time.

There is yet another reason, fetched from the other side of the case. We should pray for the blinded one, since he may terribly sin if not soon made to see. How capable of doing mischief is a man blinded by ignorance, by passion, by ambition, or by any other form of sin! Who knows the capacities for evil that lie within a single soul? That once bright spirit, Satan, when he first thought of raising revolt against the God of Heaven; it was, perhaps, a single momentary flash of rebellious thought; but before long he had become proudly antagonistic to his Maker, and the dragon had drawn down with his tail a third part of the stars of heaven to quench them in the eternal night of endless wickedness. Then he came to this earth, and polluted Paradise, and seduced our first parents from their happy innocence, so that they became the progenitors of an unhappy race, steeped up to their lips in sin. That one first thought of ill, oh, how pregnant was it with innumerable evils! So, too, among ourselves. A boy, his mother's pride, to whom she looks forward as the honour of the family, may for a while appear to be everything that love can hope; but he falls into the hands of one of those tempters to unbelief who are so abundant in this great city. He is taught to pour ridicule upon his mother's piety, and soon he casts off the bands of his father's God. He forgets the sanctity of God's holy day, and forsakes the house of prayer; and then he learns the way to the houses of strange women, and to the palace of strong drink ; and he plunges into one sin after another, till he is himself the leader of others down to the abyss. That boy, who used to kneel at his mother's knee, and say his childish prayer, and then stand up, and sing of Jesus and His love, was fondly regarded as one who would honour Jesus in his life ; but see him now : he staggers home after midnight, vomiting oaths ! He is foul both in soul and in body, and those who love him best are saddest at the sight of him. If we would not see children or friends running to this excess of riot, and sinking in this superfluity of naughtiness, let us in agony of spirit plead with God at once on their behalf. Oh, for an immediate entrance of the light into their souls ! Lord, open their eyes, that they may see ! Lord, cause them to start back from the beginnings of sin, which are as the breaking out of the water-floods ! O Saviour, quench in them the spark of evil ere it grows into a fire, and rages to a conflagration !

We want men's eyes to be opened, that they may know, first, that spiritual forces really exist. The things which we see are not the only real things, nor even the most real things. The things that are seen are temporal ; they are, in truth, but shadows of the unseen. The substantial realities are not seen by these poor eyes : the substance is only perceived by our true selves. All that is visible is the mere shadow : the very image of the things is out of sight. Faith teaches us to believe in the existence of the most glorious of all spirits, the great God, in whom we live, and move, and have our being. Faith reveals

to the heart the existence of that divine and ever-
adorable Person, the Lord Jesus Christ, who is at this
hour with His Church, and will abide with her to the
end of the world. Faith also makes us know the
existence, and power, and presence of the Holy
Ghost, who dwelleth with believers, and is in them,
working out the eternal purpose of God in their
sanctification. No knowledge is more sublime than
to know the Trinity in Unity ; Father, Son, and
Holy Ghost, one Jehovah. When we come to realize
that the Lord God is the source of all things ; that
God hath made us, and not we ourselves, and that all
things come into being by His sovereign will and
power ; then we come to recognize His presence, to
consult His will, and to lean upon His might. God
becomes real in our thought and apprehension. Since
He whom we cannot see nevertheless supporteth all
things that are, we feel that the invisible is the basis
of all things. Oh, that we could get men's minds out
of these time-worn ruts of things seen, these narrow
bounds of space, and time, and seeing, and handling !
Oh, that they could rise into the region where the
dim faculties, which are bounded by so small a circle,
would give place to perceptions which know the
infinite, the eternal, the true, the divine ! Oh, that
the human mind, which was made in the image of
God, could find itself at home with God, whose child
it may become, by a second birth, of the living and
incorruptible seed, by the Word of God, which liveth
and abideth for ever !

THE SWIFTNESS OF LIFE.

LET me speak to you of the frailty of human
life, the fleeting nature of time, how swiftly it
passes away, how soon we shall all fade as the leaf,
and how speedily the place which knows us now shall
know us no more for ever. The Apostle James says,
" What is your life ? " and, thanks to inspiration, we
are at no great difficulty to give the reply ; for Scripture being the best interpreter of Scripture, supplies
us with many very excellent answers. I shall attempt
to give you some of them.

It is a great fact that though life to the young
man, when viewed in the prospect, appears to be long,
to the old man it is ever short ; and to all men life is
really but a brief period. Human life is not long.
Compare it with the existence of some animals and
trees, and how short is human life ! Compare it with
the ages of the universe, and it becomes a span ; and
especially measure it by eternity, and how little does
life appear ! It sinks like one small drop into the
ocean, and becomes as insignificant as one tiny grain
of sand upon the sea-shore. Life is swift. If you
would picture life you must turn to the Bible, and we
will walk through the Bible-gallery of old paintings.

You will find its swiftness spoken of in the Book
of Job, where we are furnished with three illustrations.
In the ninth chapter, and at the twenty-fifth verse, we
find, " Now my days are swifter than *a post.*" We

are most of us acquainted with the swiftness of post-conveyance. I have sometimes, on emergency, taken post-horses where there has been no railway, and have been amused and pleased with the rapidity of my journey. But since, in this ancient book, there can be no allusion to modern posts, we must turn to the manners and customs of the East, and in so doing we find that the ancient monarchs astonished their subjects by the amazing rapidity with which they received intelligence. By well-ordered arrangements, swift horses, and constant relays, they were able to attain a speed which, although trifling in these days, was, in those slower ages, a marvel of marvels; so that to an Eastern one of the greatest ideas of swiftness was that of a post. Well doth Job say our life is like a post. We ride one year until it is worn out, but there comes another just as swift, and we are borne by it, and it is gone, and another year serves us for a steed; post-house after post-house we pass, as birthdays successively arrive; we loiter not, but vault at a leap from one year to another, and still we hurry onward, onward, onward still. Our life is like a post; not like the slow waggon that drags along the road with tiresome wheels, but, like a post, it attains the greatest speed.

Job further says, "My days are passed away as the *swift ships.*" He increases, you see, the intensity of the metaphor; for if in the Eastern's idea anything could excel the swiftness of a post, it was the swift ship. Some translate this passage the "ships of desire;" that is, the ships hurrying home, anxious for the haven, and therefore crowding all sail. You may well conceive how swiftly the mariner flies from a threatening storm, or seeks the port where he will find his home. You have sometimes seen how the ship cuts through the billows, leaving a white furrow behind her, and causing the sea to boil around her. Such is life, says Job, like the " swift ships," when the sails are filled by the wind, and the vessel dashes on, dividing a passage through the crowding water. Swift are the ships, but swifter far is life. The wind of time bears me along. I cannot stop its motion ; I may direct it with the rudder of God's Holy Spirit ; I may, it is true, take in some small sails of sin, which might hurry my days on faster than otherwise they would go ; but, nevertheless, like a swift ship, my life must speed on its way until it reaches its haven. Where is that haven to be? Shall it be found in the land of bitterness and barrenness, that dreary region of the lost? or shall it be that sweet haven of eternal peace, where not a troubling wave can ruffle the quiescent glory of my spirit ? Wherever the haven is to be, that truth is the same, we are like " the swift ships."

Again : Job says, it is "as *the eagle that hasteth to the prey.*" The eagle is a bird noted for its swiftness. I remember reading an account of an eagle attacking a fish-hawk, which had obtained some booty from the deep, and was bearing it aloft. The hawk dropped the fish, which fell towards the water ; but before the fish had reached the ocean, the eagle had flown more swiftly than the fish could fall, and catching it in its beak, it flew away with it. The swiftness of the eagle is almost incalculable—you see it, and it is gone ; you see a dark speck in the sky yonder ; it is an eagle soaring. Let the fowler imagine that by-and-bye he shall overtake it on some mountain's craggy peak—it shall be gone long before he reaches it. Such is our life. It is like an eagle hasting to its prey; not merely an eagle flying in its ordinary course, but an eagle hasting to its prey. Life appears to be hasting to its prey—the prey is the body; life is ever flying from insatiate death; but death is too swift to be outrun, and as an eagle overtakes his prey, so shall death.

If we require a further illustration of the swiftness of life, we must turn again to Job, upon which I shall not dwell. It will be found in the seventh chapter, at the sixth verse; he says, it is " swifter than *a weaver's shuttle*," which the weaver throws so quickly that the eye can hardly discern it. But he gives us yet a more excellent metaphor in the seventh verse of the same chapter, where he says, " O remember that *my life is wind.*" Now, this excels in velocity all the other figures we have examined. Who can outstride the winds? Proverbially, the winds are rapid; even in their gentlest motion they appear to be swift. But when they rush in the tornado, or when they dash madly on in the hurricane—when the tempest blows, and rends down everything—how swift then is the wind! Perhaps some of us may have a gentle gale of wind, and we may not seem to move so swiftly; but with others, who are only born, then snatched away to Heaven, the swiftness of it may be compared to the hurricane, that soon snaps the ties of life, and leaves the infant dead. Surely our life is like the wind.

Oh! if you could but catch these ideas! You know we are all really in motion. This world is turning round on its axis once in four-and-twenty hours ; and besides that, it is moving round the sun in the 365 days of the year. So that we are all moving ; we are all flitting along through space. And as we are travelling through space, so we are moving through time, at an incalculable rate. Oh ! what an idea it is, could we grasp it ! We are all being carried along, as if by a giant angel, with broad outstretched wings, which he flaps to the blast, and flying before the lightning makes us ride on the winds. The whole multitude of us are hurrying along—whither remains to be decided by the test of our faith and the grace of God ; but certain it is, we are travelling. Do not think that you are stable things ; fancy not that you are standing still ; you are not. Your pulses each moment beat the funeral marches to the tomb. You are chained to the chariot of rolling time—there is no bridling the steeds, or leaping from the chariot ; you must be constantly in motion.

Concerning the uncertainty of life we have abundant illustrations. "For what is your life ? It is even *a vapour*, that appeareth for a little time, and then vanisheth away." If I were to ask for a child's explanation of this, I know what he would say. He would say, " Yes, it is even a vapour, like a bubble that is blown upward." Children sometimes blow bubbles, and amuse themselves thereby. Life is even as that bubble. You see it rising into the air ; the child delights itself by seeing it fly about, but it is all gone in one moment. "It is even a vapour, that appeareth for a little time, and then vanisheth away." But if you ask the poet to explain this, he would tell you that in the morning, sometimes at early dawn, the rivers send up a steamy offering to the sun. There is a vapour, a mist, an exhalation rising from the rivers and brooks, but in a very little while after the sun is risen all that mist is gone. Hence we read of the morning cloud and the early dew that passeth away. A more common observer, speaking of a vapour, would think of those thin clouds you sometimes see floating in the air, which are so light that they are soon carried away. Indeed, a poet uses them as the picture of feebleness—

> " Their hosts are scatter'd, like thin clouds
> Before a Biscay gale."

The winds move them, and they are gone. " What is your life? It is even a vapour, that appeareth for a little time, and then vanisheth away." So uncertain is life !

Again : if you read in the Book of Ecclesiastes, at the sixth chapter, and the twelfth verse, you will there find life compared to something else, even more fragile than a vapour. The wise man there says that it is even "as *a shadow.*" Now what can there be less substantial than a shadow ? What substance is there in a shadow ? Who can lay hold thereof? You may see it, but the moment the person passes away it is gone. Yea, and who can grasp his life ? Many men reckon upon a long existence, and think they are going to live for ever ; but who can calculate upon a shadow ? Go, thou man, who sayest to thy soul, " Eat, drink, and be merry ; I have much goods laid up for many years "—go thou, and store thy room with shadows ; go thou and pile shadows up, and say, " These are mine, and they shall never depart." But, sayest thou, " I cannot catch a shadow " ? No and thou canst not reckon on a year, for it is as a shadow, which soon melteth away and is gone.

The prophet Isaiah also furnishes us with a simile, where he says that life is as *a thread which is cut off.* You will find this in his thirty-eighth chapter, at the twelfth verse, " Mine age is departed, and is removed from me as a shepherd's tent : I have cut off like a weaver my life." The weaver cuts off his thread very easily, and so is life soon ended. I might continue my illustrations at pleasure concerning the uncertainty of life. We might find, perhaps, a score more figures in Scripture, if we could search. Take, for instance, the grass, the flowers of the field, etc., etc.

But though life is swift, and though it is to pass away so speedily, we are still generally very anxious to know what it is to be while we have it. For we say, if we are to lose it, still while we live let us live ; and whilst we are to be here, be it ever so short a time, let us know what we are to expect in it.

THE CHANGES OF LIFE.

IF you want pictures of the changes of life, turn to this wonderful book of poetry, the Sacred Scriptures, and there you will find metaphors piled on metaphors. And, first, you will find life compared to a *pilgrimage* by good old Jacob in the forty-seventh chapter of Genesis, and the ninth verse. That hoary-headed patriarch, when he was asked by Pharaoh what was his age, replied, "The days of the years of my *pilgrimage* are an hundred and thirty years : few and evil have the days of the years of my life been, and have not attained unto the days of the years of the life of my fathers in the days of their pilgrimage." He calls life a pilgrimage. A pilgrim sets out in the morning, and he has to journey many a day before he gets to the shrine which he seeks. What varied scenes the traveller will behold on his way ! Sometimes he will be on the mountains ; anon he will descend into the valleys ; here he will be where the brooks shine like silver, where the birds warble, where the air is balmy, and the trees are green, and luscious fruits hang down to gratify his taste ; anon he will find himself in the arid desert, where no life is found, and no sound is heard, except the screech of the wild eagle in the air, where he finds no rest for the sole of his foot—the burning sky above him and the hot sand beneath him—no roof-tree, and no house to rest himself ; at another time he finds himself in a sweet oasis, resting himself by the springs of water, and plucking fruit from palm trees. One moment he walks between the rocks, in some narrow gorge, where all is darkness ; at another time he ascends the hill, Miza ; now he descends into the valley of Baca ; anon he climbs the hill of Bashan, " a high hill is the hill of Bashan ; " and yet again going into a den of leopards, he suffers trial and affliction. Such is life— ever changing. Who can tell what may come next ? To-day it is fair, the next day there may be the thundering storm ; to-day I may want for nothing, to-morrow I may be like Jacob, with nothing but a stone for my pillow, and the heavens for my curtains. But what a happy thought it is, though we know not where the road winds, we know where it ends ! It is the straightest way to Heaven to go round about. Israel's forty years' wanderings were, after all, the nearest path to Canaan. We may have to go through trial and affliction ; the pilgrimage may be a tiresome one, but it is safe ; we cannot trace the river upon which we are sailing, but we know it ends in floods of bliss at last. We cannot track the roads, but we know that they all meet in the great metro- polis of Heaven, in the centre of God's universe. God help us to pursue the true pilgrimage of a pious life !

We have another picture of life in its changes, given us in the ninetieth Psalm, at the ninth verse, " We spend our years as a *tale that is told.*" Now David understood about tales that were told ; I dare- say he had been annoyed by them sometimes. There are in the East professed story-tellers, who amuse their hearers by inventing tales such as those in that foolish book, the "Arabian Nights." When I was foolish enough to read that book, I remember some- times you were with fairies, sometimes with genii, sometimes in palaces, anon you went down into caverns. All sorts of singular things are conglomerated into what they call a tale. Now, says David, "We spend our years as a tale that is told." You know there is nothing so wonderful as the history of the odds and ends of human life. Sometimes it is a merry rhyme, sometimes a prosy subject, sometimes you ascend to the sublime, soon you descend to the ridiculous. No man can write the whole of his own biography ; I suppose if the history of a man's thoughts and words could be written, scarce the world itself could contain the words that should be written, so wonderful is the tale that is told. Our lives are all singular, and must, to ourselves, seem strange, of which much might be said. Our life is " as a tale that is told."

Another idea we get from the thirty-eighth chapter of Isaiah, at the twelfth verse. " I am removed *as a shepherd's* tent." The shepherds in the East build temporary huts near the sheep, which are soon removed when the flock moves on ; when the hot season comes on they pitch their tents, and each season had its suitable position. My life is like a shepherd's tent. I have pitched my tent in a variety of places already, but where I shall pitch it by-and-by I do not know—I cannot tell. Present probabilities seem to say that—

> " Here shall I make my settled rest,
> And neither go nor come,—
> No more a stranger or a guest,
> But like a child at home."

But I cannot tell, and you cannot divine. You have been opening a new shop lately, and you are thinking

of settling down in trade, and managing a thriving
concern : now paint not the future too brightly ; don't
be too sure.   Another has for a long time been engaged in an old establishment ; your father always
carried on business there, and you have no thought of
moving.   Here you have no abiding city ; your life
is like a shepherd's tent ; you may be here, there, and
almost everywhere before you die.   It was once said
by Solon, " No man ought to be called a happy man
till he dies," because he does not know what his life is
to be ; but Christians may always call themselves
happy men here, because wherever their tent is carried,
they cannot pitch it where the cloud does not move,
and where they are not surrounded by a circle of fire.
" I will be a wall of fire round about them, and their
glory in the midst."   They cannot dwell where God
is not householder, warder, and bulwark of salvation.

> " All my ways shall ever be
> Ordered by His wise decree."

I know that my tent cannot be removed till God
says, " Go forward ; " and it cannot stand unless He
makes it firm.   If any who are God's people are going
to change their condition, are going to move out of
one situation into another, to take a new business, or
remove to another county, you need not fear ; God
was with you in the last place, and He will be with
you in this.   " Be not dismayed, for I am thy God."
That is an oft-told story of Cæsar in a storm.   The
sailors were all afraid, but he exclaimed, " Fear not !—
thou carriest Cæsar and all his fortunes."   So with
the poor Christian.   There is a storm coming on :
" Fear not !—thou art carrying Jesus, and you sink or
swim with Him."   Well may we say, Lord, if Thou

art with me, it matters not where my tent is, "Though I make my bed in hell, Thou art there;" all must be well, though my life is "removed like a shepherd's tent."

Again : our life is compared in the Psalms to *a dream.* Now, if a tale is singular, surely a dream is more so. If a tale is changing and shifting, what is a dream ? As for dreams, those flutterings of the benighted fancy, those revelries of the imagination, who can tell what they consist of ? We dream of everything in the world, and a few things more! If we were asked to tell our dreams, it would be impossible. You dream that you are at a feast ; lo, the viands change into a Pegasus, and you are riding through the air ; or, again, suddenly transformed into a morsel for a monster meal. Such is life. The changes occur as suddenly as they happen in a dream. Men have been rich one day ; they have been beggars the next. We have witnessed the exile of monarchs, and the flight of a potentate ; or, in another direction, we have seen a man, neither reputable in company, nor honourable in station, at a single stride, exalted to a throne ; and you who would have shunned him in the streets before, were foolish enough to throng your thoroughfares to stare at him. Ah! such is life. Leaves of the Sybil were not more easily moved by the winds, nor are dreams more variable : " Boast not thyself of to-morrow, for thou knowest not what a day may bring forth." How foolish are those men who wish to pry into futurity ; the telescope is ready, and they are looking through ; but they are so anxious to see that they breathe on their glass with their hot breath, and they dim it, so that they can discern nothing but clouds and darkness. Oh! ye who are always conjuring up black fiends from the deep unknown, and foolishly vexing your mind with fancies, turn your fancies out of doors, and begin to rest on never-failing promises. Promises are better than forebodings: " Trust in the Lord, and do good ; verily thou shalt be fed ; thou shalt inherit the land, and dwell therein for ever."

What is to be the end of this life? We read in Samuel, we are like " water that is spilt upon the ground, and cannot be gathered up again." Man is like a great icicle, which the sun of time is continually thawing, and which is soon to be water spilt upon the ground, that cannot be gathered up. Who can recall the departed spirit, or inflate the lungs with a new breath of life ? Who can put vitality into the heart, and restore the soul from Hades ? None. It cannot be gathered up. The place shall know it no more for ever.

But here a sweet thought charms us ! This water cannot be lost, but it shall descend into the soil to filter through the rock of ages, at last to spring up a pure fountain in Heaven, cleansed, purified, and made clear as crystal. How terrible if, on the other hand, it should percolate the black earth of sin, and hang in horrid drops in the dark caverns of destruction !

Such is life ! Then make the best use you can of it, because it is fleeting. Look for another life, because this life is not a very desirable one,—it is so changeable. Trust your life in God's hand, because you cannot control its movements ; rest in His arms, and rely on His might ; for He is able to do for you exceeding abundantly above all that you can ask or think !

ON BEING DILIGENT IN BUSINESS.

YOU know those venerable city gentlemen. I hope you reverence them as I do, since they are the embodiment of wisdom. One of these said to his son, " William, I am pleased to see you incline towards religion. But take my advice, and be reasonable. I have been in business now for forty years, and my advice is—stick to trade and make money, and then attend to religion." Now, the young man, as young men are apt to do, had begun to think for himself ; and, for a wonder, his thoughts ran in the right groove, and therefore he replied, " Father, I am always grateful to you for your good advice ; but this time you must excuse me if I differ from you, for the Scripture says, ' Seek ye first the kingdom of God, and His righteousness,' and therefore I cannot go in for making money first, but I must at once serve God, and yet I hope I may be none the less attentive to business." It is a good rule to begin as you mean to go on. That son was wiser than his counsellor. True godliness is as good for this life as for the next. If I had to die like a dog, I would still wish to be a Christian. Place religion first in the order of time. Begin each week by carefully consecrating the first day to rest and holy worship. Begin each day by giving the dew of the morning to communion with Heaven. Begin your married life by seeking the blessing of the great Father, and choosing for a partner one who will agree with you in the fear of God. In opening a new business, sanctify the venture with the supplications of godly friends, and in all fresh enterprises be guided of the Lord. If we begin, continue, and end with God, our way will be strewn with blessings.

Seek also the kingdom of God first in order of preference. If it should ever become a choice between God and mammon, never hesitate. If wealth and righteousness run counter to each other, let the gold perish, but hold thou fast to righteousness. Follow Christ, however dear it cost thee. Blessed is that man who never deliberates, because his mind is made up rather to "suffer affliction with the people of God than to enjoy the pleasures of sin for a season." Blessed is the man who knows no policy but that of thorough consecration to God and righteousness— who is not careful to answer in this matter, but has his mind decided once for all. This is his motto :—

> " 'Tis done ! The great transaction's done :
> I am my Lord's, and He is mine."

We have lifted our hand unto the Lord, and we cannot go back.

" Well," cries one, " but, you know, we must live." I am not sure about that. There are occasions when it would be better not to live. An old heraldic motto says, " Better death than false of faith." I am, however, quite clear about another necessity — we must die ; and we had better take that *must* into consideration, and not quite so often repeat the cant phrase, " We must live."

But we *shall* live ; we shall live without grinding

the poor, or stooping to questionable finance, or lying to the public by a false prospectus. We shall live without dishonour. Take your ground and keep it. Say, "I shall do what I feel it right to do, God helping me." Any little difficulties which now arise will soon come to an end if you are firmly conscientious. Never be a coward.

> " I had as lief not be, as live to be
> In awe of such a thing as I myself."

Let none of us ever raise a question about whether we shall please or displease by doing right, but let us " seek first the kingdom of God."

Let godliness be first *in intensity*. It is to be feared that many give their force to their worldly pursuits, and their feebleness to their religion. They are " all there " during banking hours ; but they are not " all there " at the hour of prayer. They remind me of one whose voice in our assemblies for prayer was exceedingly low, and well-nigh inaudible ; but in the shop he could be heard almost too well. Should it be so, that self should have our energies and Christ should have our lukewarmness ? If ever we grow ardent and enthusiastic, it should be in the noblest of all causes, in the service of the best of Masters. In that work we cannot be too earnest ; seldom enough do we meet with a person who verges upon excess of zeal in this matter. For Him who has redeemed us with His precious blood we cannot do too much ; our heart complains that we cannot do enough. Alas ! the comparative sizes of the Bible and the ledger are frequently symbolical : a neat little Bible is buried under a huge ledger. I claim for things Divine a

different place ; let that be first which is first ; throw
your whole soul into the love and service of the
Lord.

" Is your father a Christian ? " said a Sunday-school
teacher to a child. The girl answered, " Yes, I
believe that father is a Christian, but he has not
worked much at it lately." No doubt there are many
of that sort. Their religion has taken a holiday, and
they themselves have gone up to a sluggard's bed.
Let them be aroused, for it is high time to awake out
of sleep.

Seek the kingdom of God and His righteousness
first, by giving to true religion a sovereignty over
your lives. The helm by which life is steered should
be in the hand of God. To glorify God and promote
righteousness should be our master passion. This
Aaron's rod should swallow up all other rods. Be
first a man of God : after that a banker, or a merchant, or a working-man. I like to see our public
men first Christians, then Englishmen, then Conserva-
tives, or Liberals, or Radicals, as their convictions
sway them ; but in any case let a man be first a man
of God. I would to God that our politics, our
merchandise, our literature, our art, were all saturated
with this idea—first a Christian. Then the secondary
character would rise in excellence and nobility.
Science, social laws, trade usages, domestic life, would
all be the better for coming under the supremacy of
living religion. The fear of God should be the
foundation and the topstone of the social edifice.
" Christ first," and other things in their due order.
Over and above all, let consecration to God shine
forth even as the pillar of fire in the wilderness

covered and illuminated the entire camp of Israel.
Does anyone demand, "What will become of our
business if we place godliness first?" The answer is,
" All these things shall be added unto you." A young
man beginning life, resolving that he will do everything in the fear of God, and that as God helps him
he will do nothing that is contrary to the mind of
the Lord Jesus Christ—shall he prosper? He shall
get on so far as this : he shall have bread to eat, and
raiment to put on—all that is needful for this life
" shall be added to him."

" Alas!" sighs one, "I am out of place, and I know
not how to provide for myself." Are you sure that
this trial has come without your own fault? Then be
not of doubtful mind, for the Lord will provide for
you. He has said, "Trust in the Lord and do good ;
so shalt thou dwell in the land, and verily thou shalt
be fed." David's experience was, "I have been young
and now am old ; yet have I not seen the righteous
forsaken " The drunken, the vicious, the idle, the
dishonest may suffer hunger, and it will be well for
them if such discipline amends them ; but to the
upright there arises light in the darkness. They that
serve God shall not have to complain of His deserting
them. In the reign of Queen Elizabeth, a certain
merchant was desired by her Majesty to go abroad
for her upon affairs of state. He pleaded that his
own business would suffer ; whereupon her Majesty
replied, " Sir, if you will mind my business, I will
mind your business." Rest you assured that God will
care for you if you make His service your delight.
" All these things shall be added unto you "

The blessings of this life come to gracious men in

the best shape and form ; for they come by Divine promise. Suppose that it were now put into the power of each one of us to be rich, I suspect that the most of us would be eager to avail ourselves of the opportunity ; and yet it is a moot point whether it would be best for certain of us to have the burden of wealth. It is a question whether some people, who behave splendidly where they now are, would be half as good, or a tithe as happy, if they were lifted to higher positions. I have seen heroes drivel under the influence of luxury. Many are the creatures of circumstances, and make but poor creatures when their circumstances allow of self-indulgence. We do not know what is best for us. It is sometimes very much better for us to suffer loss and disappointment than to obtain gain and prosperity. When that eminent servant of God, Mr. Gilpin, was arrested to be brought up to London to be tried for preaching the gospel, his captors made mirth of his frequent remark, " Everything is for the best." When he fell from his horse and broke his leg, they were specially merry about it ; but the good man quietly remarked, " I have no doubt but that even this painful accident will prove to be a blessing." And so it was ; for, as he could not travel quickly, the journey was prolonged, and he arrived at London some days later than had been expected. When they reached as far as Highgate, they heard the bells ringing merrily in the city down below. They asked the meaning, and were told, " Queen Mary is dead, and there will be no more burnings of Protestants." " Ah ! " said Gilpin, " you see it is all for the best." It is a blessing to break a leg if thereby life is saved. How often our calamities are our pre-

servatives ! A less evil may ward off a greater. Many
a man might have soared into the clouds of folly if
his wings had not been clipped by adversity. Better
struggle and be honourable than become wealthy by
disgraceful deeds. Agur's prayer, " Give me neither
poverty nor riches," was a wise one ; but our Lord's
is still better, " Not as I will, but as Thou wilt."

" All these things shall be added unto you," and
the measure of the addition shall be arranged by in-
fallible wisdom. Temporal things shall come to you
in such proportion as you would yourself desire them,
if you were able to know all things, and to perform a
judgment according to infinite wisdom. Would you
not prefer a lot selected by the Lord to one chosen by
yourself? Do you not joyfully sing with the Psalmist,
" Thou shalt choose mine inheritance for me " ?

Does not the promise also imply that needful things
shall come to the believer without vexatious worry
and consuming labour ? While others are worrying,
you shall be singing. While others rise in the morning and cry, " How shall we live through the day?"
you shall wake to a secure provision, and you shall
have a happy enjoyment of it. Your place of defence
shall be the munitions of rocks ; your bread shall be
given you, and your waters shall be sure. Contentment with your lot, and confidence in God, will make
life peaceful and happy ; a dinner of herbs with content will yield a flavour of satisfaction unknown to
those who eat the stalled ox. It is better to be
happy than to be rich ; and happiness lies in the
heart rather than in the purse. Not what a man has,
but what a man is, will decide his bliss or woe in this
life and the next. Oh, yes, if God Himself adds to

you the things of this life, while you are serving Him, the lines will fall to you in pleasant places, and you will have a goodly heritage.

"All these things shall be added unto you," reminds me that the acquisition of property often decreases a man rather than adds to him. Have you not seen a man become visibly smaller as his riches grew greater? It is a wretched sight, which has often pained me. I have distinctly seen a man become "the architect of his own fortune" and the destroyer of himself. He has built up a palatial estate upon the ruins of his own manhood. It is a pity when a man bricks himself up with his growing gains. See you that hole in the wall? The man stands in it and greedily cries for bricks and mortar. Golden bricks and silver mortar he must have. They bring him the materials. He cries eagerly for more. He cannot be content unless he builds himself in. The wall which shuts him out from his fellow-men, and from the light of peace and true joy, rises higher and higher month by month, and year by year. His sympathies and character are bricked up. Still he pines for more metallic material. At last he is built in, buried beneath his own gatherings, lost to all manhood through his accumulations.

THE BUSINESS MAN'S GOOD SERVICE.

"SEEK first the kingdom of God and His righteousness," by which I understand the practical part of true religion. Seek to have the imputed righteousness of Christ by all means ; but seek also to exhibit the infused righteousness which comes of sanctification. Let us aspire after a high degree of holiness. We are called to be saints ; and saints are not miraculous beings to be set up in niches and admired ; but they are men and women who live, and trade, and do righteousness, and practise charity in the streets of a city, or the fields of a village. Those who are washed in the blood of the Lamb should not be satisfied with the common cleanliness of morality ; but the garment of their life should be whiter than any fuller can make it. Purity becomes the disciples of Jesus. In spirit, soul, and body we ought to be holiness to the Lord. Our righteousness must exceed that of the scribes and Pharisees ; it should be a reproduction of the character of our Lord.

By the phrase " His righteousness," I understand that power in the world which is always working, in some form or other, for that which is good, and true, and pure. Everything in this world which is holy, and honest, and of good repute, may count upon the Christian as its friend, for it is a part of God's righteousness. Does drunkenness eat out the very life of our nation ?   Do you want men of temperance to battle this evil ?   The Christian cries, " Write down my name."   When the slave had to be freed, the subjects of God's kingdom were to the front in that deed of righteousness ; and to-day, if oppression is to be put down, we dare not refuse our aid.   If the people are to be educated, and better housed, we hail the proposal with delight.   If the horrible sin of the period is to be denounced and punished, we may not shrink from the loathsome conflict.   Let each man in his own position labour after purity ; and, as God shall help us, we may yet sweep the streets of their infamies, and deliver our youth from pollution.   Every Christian man should say of every struggle for better things, " I am in it, cost what it may."   Hosts of your professors of religion forget to seek God's righteousness, and seem to suppose that their principal business is to save their own souls—poor little souls that they are !   Their religion is barely sufficient to fill up the vacuum within their own ribs, where their hearts should be.   This selfishness is not the religion of Jesus.   The religion of Jesus is unselfish : it enlists a man as a crusader against everything that is un-righteous.   We are knights of the red cross, and our bloodless battles are against all things that degrade our fellow-men, whether they be causes social, political, or religious.   We fight for everything that is good, true, and just.

True religion is diffusive and extensive in its opera-tions.   I see people drawing lines continually, and saying, " So far is religious, and so far is secular." What do you mean ?   The notion is one which suits with the exploded notions of sacred places, priests, shrines, and relics. I do not believe in it. Everything is holy to a holy man. To the pure all things are pure. To a man who seeks first the kingdom of God and His righteousness, his house is a temple, his meals are sacraments, his garments are vestments, every day is a holy day, and he himself is a priest and a king unto God. The sphere of Christianity is co-extensive with daily life. I am not to say, " I serve God when I stand in the pulpit"; for that might imply that I wished to serve the devil when my sermon was over. We are not only to be devout at church, and pious at prayer-meetings ; but to be devout and godly everywhere. Religion must not be like a fine piece of mediæval armour, to be hung upon the wall, or only worn on state occasions. No ; it is a garment for the house, the shop, the bank. Your ledgers and iron safes are to be made by grace "holiness unto the Lord." Godliness is for the parlour and the drawing-room, the counting-house and the exchange. It can neither be put off nor on. It is of the man and in the man if it be real. Righteousness is a quality of the heart, and abides in the nature of the saved man as a component part of his new self. He is not righteous who is not always righteous.

Undefiled religion is a vital matter ; it is in the life of the man. I am afraid that the religion of some people is like the shell of the hermit crab. At sea the dredge brings up creeping things innumerable, and among them creatures which have their own natural shells to live in ; but here comes a fellow who has annexed the shell of a whelk, and bears it about as if it were his own. He lives in it while it suits him, and he gives up the tenancy when it becomes inconvenient ;

the shell is not part of himself. Avoid such a religion. Beware of a Sunday shell, and a week-day without the shell. That religion which you *can* part with, you had better part with. If you can get rid of it, get rid of it. If it is not part and parcel of yourself, it is good for nothing. If it does not run right through you like a silver thread through a piece of embroidery, it will not avail for your eternal salvation.

I remember a remark of John Newton, once rector of St. Mary Woolnoth. He was a thoroughly Calvinistic preacher ; but when one asked him whether he believed in Calvinism, he replied, " I am a Calvinist, but I do not take it as children eat lumps of sugar ; I use it to flavour all my preaching, as men use sugar in tea or food." Hypocrites swallow religion in lumps, inviting all to admire the quantity ; but sincere seekers after righteousness quietly dissolve their godliness in their lives and sweeten all their common relationships therewith. The real saint flavours his ordinary life with grace, so that his wife and his children, his servants and his neighbours, are the better for it. Rowland Hill used to say that a man was not a true Christian if his dog and his cat were not the better off for it. That witness is true. A man's religion ought to be to him what perfume is to a rose, or light to the sun : it should be the necessary outcome of his existence. If his life is not fragrant with truth, and bright with love, the question arises whether he knows the religion of our Lord Jesus. The division between sacred and secular is most unhappy to both divisions of life : we want them united again. In the days of Queen Mary, a foolish spite dug up the bones of the wife of Bucer. Poor woman! she had done no ill, except that she had married a teacher of the gospel ; but she must needs be dragged from her grave to be buried in a dung-hill for that grave offence. When Elizabeth came to the throne, her bones were buried again ; but to make the body secure from any future malice of bigots, our prudent forefathers took the relics of a certain Popish saint, who was enshrined at Oxford, and mixed the remains of the two deceased persons past all chance of separation. Thus Mistress Bucer was secured from further disrespect by her unity with the body of one of the canonized. I want the secular to be thus secured by union with the sacred. If we could only feel that our common acts are parts of a saintly life, they would not so often be done carelessly. If we lay our poor daily life by itself, it will be disregarded ; but if we combine it with our holiest aspirations and exercises, it will be preserved. Our religion must be part and parcel of our daily life, and then the whole of our life will be preserved from the destroyer. Doth not the Scripture say, "Whether ye eat or drink, or whatsoever ye do, do all in the name of the Lord Jesus"?

"But," says one, "are we not to have amusements?" Yes, such amusements as you can take in the fear of God. Do whatever Jesus would have done. This is liberty enough for one who aspires to be like Jesus. There is happiness enough in things which are pure and right ; and if not, we will not do evil to find more. We find pleasure enough without hunting for it in the purlieus of sin. There are joys which are as far above the pleasures of folly as the feasts of

kings are above the husks of swine.   At times our
inner life flames up into a blaze of joy ; and if usually
it burns lower, there is at least a steady fire of peace
upon our hearth which makes our life such that we
envy none.   It is not slavery that I set before you
when I say that we are first of all to seek the kingdom
of God and His righteousness : there is a present
recompense which justifies the choice ; and as
for the eternal future, it pleads for it with voice of
thunder.

A far more desirable idea is for a man to
rise above his possessions, elevating life upon
stepping-stones of these dead gains ; building with
them a pedestal, above which the inner manhood
rises.

This is what God intends to do in providence to the
man who serves Him heartily : He will add to him
the things of this life.   These shall be thrown in as
supplements to the Divine heritage.   I incur certain
little outlays in connection with my study ; we need
a few matters which may be paid for out of petty
cash ; but I have never seen, as far as I recollect, a
single penny for string and brown paper ; because, as
a reader and writer, I buy books, and then the string
and brown paper are added to me.   My purchase is
the books, but the string and brown paper come to
me, added as a matter of course.   This is the idea :
you are to spend your strength on the high and noble
purpose of glorifying God, and then the minor matters
of "What shall we eat? and What shall we drink ? and
Wherewithal shall we be clothed ?" are thrown in as
supplements.   Earthly things are but the brown paper
and string ; and I pray you never think too much of

them. Some people get so much of this brown paper and string that they glory in them, and expect us to fall down and worship them. If we refuse this homage, they are foolish enough to adore themselves. It must not be so among the servants of God. To us the man is the man, and not the guinea's stamp. "All these things" are to us small matters ; the real life of the soul is all in all. Do not slice pieces out of your manhood, and then hope to fill up the vacancies with bank-notes. He who loses manliness or godliness to gain gold is a great cheater of himself. Keep yourselves entire for God and for His Christ, and let all other matters be additions, not subtractions. Live above the world. Its goods will come to you when you do not bid high for them. If you hunt the butterfly of wealth too eagerly you may spoil it by the stroke with which you secure it. When earthly things are sought for as the main object, they are degraded into rubbish, and the seeker of them has fallen to be a mere man with a muck-rake, turning over a dunghill to find nothing. Set your heart on nobler things than pelf! Cry with David, " I will lift up mine eyes to the hills, whence cometh my help." Let us so live that it will be safe for God to add to us the blessings of the life that now is ; but that can only be done with safety when we have learned to keep the world under our feet.

HOW GOD WOULD WIN THE HEART.

A Talk to City Men.

W HAT has God done to win our hearts? If a
father has lost the love of his child, our first
question would be, " Does he do anything to get it
back?" Our God is always doing much to gain man's
heart. He maketh His sun to rise upon the evil and
upon the good, and He gives the rain from heaven,
and fruitful seasons. We have much happiness, for
this world is not, after all, a prison, or a penal colony.
We have bright days, and elastic spirits ; we sometimes rejoice with great joy, and are never quite
hopeless. He who gives us our many mercies says,
as He gives them, " Wilt thou not love Me, My child,
because these things are given to thee? Wilt thou
not see My hand and believe in My love?" If God
has prospered thee in business, if God has spared
thee the wife of thy youth, if He has given thee
children to laugh upon thy knee, love Him for them.
These are His love-tokens wooing thee to love Him.
Yes, and when He changes His hand, and gives us
trouble, He has still the same end and aim. We
have our household idols, and He cannot bear these
rivals, for He is God alone, and must have our whole
heart, and therefore He removes the idols. From
some He takes away wealth ; for when crushed with
the fear of poverty the soul has often sought its

wealth in God, and God has been kinder in the taking away than in the giving. A dear child is taken home whose curly ringlets had entangled all our affections, and when it has gone among the angels we also send our hearts to Heaven. Just as a sheep that will not follow the shepherd is made to follow him when the shepherd takes its lamb and carries it in his bosom, so has it been with many a father's heart. Dear babes have been evangels— gospels in flesh and blood, little messengers of mercy to call us back to our great Father. Men are not without troubles, I am certain. There is not one among us but has had his wintry months and his long nights of darkness. To us, then, as in the visions of the night, God speaks, and He says, "Wilt thou not turn away from the broken cisterns which can hold no water, and drink of Me the everlasting fount of joy and love?" Thus with silvery words of gentleness and harsher syllables of trial He calls for our love.

And He has put in all of us a conscience which works to the same end. Some have tried to drug conscience, and, alas! it goes to be drugged till it is stupefied. Conscience will become silent by degrees, but yet there is a conscience in us which cries every now and then, "This is not right; this is not right. There is no peace in this course of life. There is no future bliss to be hoped for in this way." Conscience rings the alarm-bell, and knocks at our door, like the watchman at night when the house is on fire; conscience says to us, "Things will be wrong for ever, unless there is an amendment. Awake and seek thy God!" Do you hear a still small voice within you calling you to seek your God ?   Hearken to it at once, for it is your life.

But, best of all, to win our love, God has unveiled Himself in the book of inspiration, and in the person of His dear Son.   The face of God is so supremely beautiful that angels at the sight of it perpetually adore, and when men behold it, though it be but " in a glass darkly," love is inevitable.   Dr. Watts has well sung—

> " His worth if all the nations knew,
> Sure the whole world would love Him too."

" How did He unveil His face ? " say you.   It was in the person of His only begotten Son, who sooner than that we should die would die Himself, who out of pure disinterested love left the throne and the royalties of Heaven to descend to the manger and to be made like ourselves : here to live in poverty and at last to die.   Lo ! on Calvary, where God Himself bears the consequences of sin that we might escape from them ; where Jehovah-Jesus bows His head that was girt with a crown of thorns, and gives up the ghost in order that, without any violation of justice, God might extend boundless mercy—it was there He said, " Men, see what I am ! the God of love !   Just, but even in My stern justice anxious not to unsheathe the sword or to inflict the penalty upon you if you will but turn unto Me, and now give Me your hearts and accept My love in Jesus Christ, trusting My Son with your souls."   To-day the God of love publishes an act of amnesty and oblivion for all the past.   No matter how little ye may have loved, now may ye begin to love, for He will cast your transgressions into the depths of the sea.   No matter how far we have gone into the far-off country, He is willing to press us to His bosom, and to take us back again as if we had never wandered—yea, and to rejoice over us as the father in the parable rejoiced over the returning prodigal. He will say concerning our offences, if we believe in Jesus as the propitiation for sin, "I have cast all their sins behind My back. They shall not be remembered against them any more for ever."

And then to show His love He puts before us a very simple way of salvation. If you go into a dark room, and set before yourself the problem, "How can I get this darkness out?" you will be in a great difficulty. You may send round to all your philosophers and thinkers this puzzle—"How can we pump the darkness out of the room?" and they will not be able to solve the question. But a little child comes in, and opens the window, and the darkness is gone. Now all the sin and enmity that is in the human heart it would be impossible for us to remove ; but, lo! the gospel says, "Believe in the love of God as it is revealed in Jesus Christ, trust Him and all will be light." That opens a window, and the darkness flies at once ; the soul has light and peace, and begins to love God, not because it ought, but because it cannot help loving One who has forgiven so readily and so freely, and given His own Son for our redemption—yea, given that Son to death itself, in order that all the past might once for all be obliterated. It is wonderful what effects accompany a childlike faith in Jesus ; the transformations which it works are moral miracles. Many a man would like to be a child again, and stand at his mother's knee, where he learned his first prayer. He would like to be laid in the cradle again, to have the name of Jesus mingled with the hush of lullaby, and begin life anew with wiser purposes and nobler aims. But, oh ! those dark years which have come in between our childhood and to-day, those years of wandering and sin ! But, courage, you may begin again. Your dream may be in some sense realized. Behold, the Lord proposes to you that you should be born again —that you should be made new creatures in Jesus Christ ; and whosoever will come and trust Christ— for that is faith, simply coming and trusting God in Christ Jesus,—shall find himself reconciled to God by the death of His Son.

Nor fail to remember that the Lord has promised one other great gift which proves His love by a present boon : He has given us the promise of His Holy Spirit. Inasmuch as our spirit has become weak and wayward, He gives His own Divine Spirit to come and dwell within us. Young man, that Holy Spirit will dwell in you, and subdue all errant passion, and excite in you all holy desire, till you shall be unto God His living and loving servant so long as you live. Men of middle life, the Holy Ghost will deliver you from carking care and greed and worldliness, and give you sublimer objects of pursuit. Aged men, that Divine Spirit will dwell in you and ripen you for the great day of ingathering, and for the Heaven which is prepared for believers. To one and all the Holy Ghost is indispensable, but it is written, "If ye then, being evil, know how to give good gifts unto your children ; how much more shall your heavenly Father give the Holy Spirit to them that ask Him ?"

I hear one excuse made. Somebody says, " I know

these claims, and I mean to think of them by-and-by ;
but I have no time just now." Well, your excuse will
not avail, because God has given you time. When
He made you and appointed your place He gave you
time, and you have wasted it, or appropriated it to
lower ends. Recollect, your time is not yours ; you
are only a servant, and you are responsible to your
Master for every moment of it. If you happen to be
a clerk, and your employer says, " That book is not
posted up ; that account was never made out," you do
not say, " I could not spare the time." Why, your time
belongs to him whose servant you are. And our
time is not our time, but God's time, and the first
thing a man has to do is to see that it is rightly used.
Besides, this business does not take any time away
from needful avocations. A man shall have all his
time for other pursuits just as much, when his main
pursuit, which sanctifies all, is the glory of God. Do
not tell me you have no time. The most industrious
business men are also very frequently Christian men,
and I have seen men who have found time for the
Sunday-school, time for the deaconate in our churches
—ay, and time to preach, who nevertheless are among
the most diligent in business. If they did neglect
their business they would also be failing, I think, in
the service of their God, since there is no sharp line of
division to be made between business and religion :
when rightly viewed our religion becomes our business, and our business is a living part of our religion.
It is mischievous to make a gulf in life between one
set of actions and another, for life ought to be all of
a piece. "Whether ye eat or drink, do all to the glory
of God." Somebody found fault with us for praying

about politics. I know no politics that I shall not
pray about. I know nothing among men that does
not come under the broad heavens of my religion ;
even if it be something downright wrong, still may I
pray *against* it. Religion should sit as queen both
over politics and business. " Oh, but," they say,
" business is business." I know it is, but business has
no business to be such business as it often is. The
greatest business of a business man should be to
pay his debts to his God, and seek to live to His
praise. He can do that, and yet find time enough to
pay his debts to man.

Another replies as if he had given a conclusive
answer, " But you see my heart is wrong. I have a
heart which will not love God." Ah, that is the mischief of it, but it is your fault, not your excuse. Here
is a man brought before my Lord Mayor, charged
with theft, and the excuse he makes is that somehow
or other he never could be honest. He always found
his heart so much inclined to roguery. " I was going
to give you a month," says the Lord Mayor, " but I
shall give you two after that, because, by your own
confession, you are a rogue in grain. Your theft was
not a chance action ; it is evident that you are a bad
fellow, and had better be kept under lock and key."
And when a man says, " But my heart is so hard ; my
heart is set upon evil,"—well, that is a confession of a
still greater sin. Having made it, do not use it as an
excuse, but look upon it as a reason for humbling
yourself before your God, and saying, " Create in me
a clean heart, O God : renew a right spirit within me."
These excuses evidently do not hold water even now.
What shall we do when we have to give in our last

account? I was once told that the Stock Exchange was shut, for it was settling-day. I do not understand the mysteries of that institution, but I do know that there is a settling-day coming to us all. You may feast if you will, but you will have to pay the reckoning. You may rejoice in your youth and your manhood, and spend your time and substance as you please, but He cometh on the clouds of heaven who will judge us all. I wish each man would quietly sit down and say, " I will suppose this to be the place where I shall be found at the judgment-day," then look you up, and with a little imagination you can picture the great white throne, and hear the last assize proclaimed by the archangel's trumpet. What will you say in that day to this question, " Didst thou love God with all thy heart ? " If you have lived a stranger to the ever blessed God you will give no answer but your silence, and that silence will seal your doom. God grant that you may not be found a defaulter in that day, but may you now be led of the Holy Spirit to repentance of past shortcomings, and to a simple, earnest trust in Jesus, and then you will meet the last summons without a shade of fear !

THE NEED OF A CITY MAN.

A PHILOSOPHER has remarked that if a man knew that he had thirty years of life before him, it would not be an unwise thing to spend twenty of those years in mapping out a plan of living, and putting himself under rule; for he would do more with the ten well-arranged years than with the whole thirty if he spent them at random. There is much truth in that saying. A man will do little by firing off his gun if he has not learned to take aim.

Possibly I address some who have hitherto lived at hazard; and if so, I invite them to a more hopeful method of living. To have a great many aims and objects is much the same thing as having no aim at all; for if a man shoots at many things he will hit none, or none worth the hitting. It is a grand thing to know what we are living for, and to live for a worthy object with the undivided energy of our being. Shall we, when the end comes, have made a success of life? Has our object been a right one, and has it been rightly pursued? Are the results of our conduct such as we shall wish them to have been when the conflict of this mortal life is over? These questions deserve consideration at once.

Another question arises out of them — What position should religion occupy in reference to a man's life? That is a question which naturally arises in the arranging of life; for, whatever we choose to think of it, there is such a thing as religion in the

world, and there is within us some yearning after
spiritual things. We cannot help feeling that we
need somewhat more than this visible world can offer
us. Many of us find our greatest joy in the cultiva-
tion of that feeling, for it is to us the token of our
spiritual nature, and the prophecy of immortality.
To us this life is mainly worth the living because it
promises to be the introduction to a better life.

> " Alas for love, if thou wert all,
> And nought beyond, O earth ! "

Alas for life if this were all, and there were not a
higher and better state of existence ! No knell would
be more doleful than that which signified the death
of man's hope of immortality.

What position should religion occupy in your life
and mine ? The answer must depend very much
upon another question—What is religion, and what
does religion itself demand ? What are the requirements of the great God, and of the soul, and of
eternity ? " *Seek ye first the kingdom of God, and His
righteousness ; and all these things shall be added unto
you.*" Undue anxiety is very common among City
men, and it is not rare anywhere. Certain of us are
nervous, timid, doubtful, and prone to fear. There
are plenty of pessimists about, although they will
hardly recognize themselves by that title. To them
evil is always impending : we are about to take a
leap in the dark. All their birds are owls or ravens.
All their swans are black. If it rains to-day, it will
rain to-morrow, and the next day, and the next, and
in all probability there will be a deluge ; or if it be
fine to-day, it will be dry to-morrow, and so on for
months, and the earth and all the meadows that are

therein will perish with drought. As to the sun, they observe with pleasing despondency that he has spots. His light they hardly notice, but they dote upon his spots with amiable horror. Minds of this sort

> Find poisons in trees, deaths in the running brooks,
> Dirges in stones, and ill in everything.

I suppose they cannot help it ; yet Christian men *must* help it ; for the Lord's precept is plain and binding : " Be not therefore anxious."

Fretful anxiety is forbidden to the Christian. It is needless. " Behold the fowls of the air," said Christ : " they sow not, neither do they reap, nor gather into barns ; yet your heavenly Father feedeth them. Are ye not much better than they ? " If you have a Father in heaven to care for you, are you not put to shame by every little bird that sits upon the bough and sings, though it has not two grains of barley in all the world ? God takes charge of the fowls of the air, and thus they live exempt from care ; why do not we ?

Our Lord also taught that such anxiety is useless as well as needless ; for, with all our care, we cannot add a cubit to our stature. Can we do anything else by fretful care ? What if the farmer deplores that there is no rain ? Do his fears unstop the bottles of heaven ? Or if the merchant sighs because the wind detains his laden ship, will his complainings turn the gale to another quarter ? We do not better ourselves a bit by all our fret and fume. It were infinitely wiser to do our best, and then cast our care upon our God. Prudence is wisdom, for it adapts means to ends ; but anxiety is folly, for it groans and worries, and accomplishes nothing.

Besides, according to our Saviour, anxiety about carnal things is heathenish : "After all these things do the Gentiles seek." They have no God and no providence, and therefore they try to be a providence to themselves. As for the man of God who can say, "God's providence is mine inheritance," why should he pine away with trouble ? Let the heir of heaven act a nobler part than the mere man of the world, who has his portion in this life, and lives without God and without hope. Our distrust of our God is childish and dishonouring. I was going through the streets one day, driven by a friend in a four-wheeled chaise, and he, being a good driver, must needs drive into narrow places, where it seemed to me that we should be crushed by the vans and omnibuses. I shrank back, in my timidity, and expressed my unwise alarms so freely, that with a smile he laid the reins in my hand, and said, " If you cannot trust me, would you like to drive yourself ? " From that ambition I was wholly free, and I assured him that he might drive as he liked, rather than make me the charioteer. Surely, the great God might well put the same proposal to those who are complaining of His providence. If we cannot trust *Him*, could we manage better ourselves ? If we are men in Christ, let us believe in our God, and leave the governance of the great world outdoors, and of the little world within our own gates, to the Lord God, our heavenly Father, who will surely cause all things to work together for good to them that love Him.

It is plain that within us there is a propensity to be anxious. Can we not utilize it ? Can we not turn it to account ? I think so. Some are naturally thoughtful and careful ; can they not transform this tendency into a benefit ? We have a tendency to be anxious. Very well, let us be anxious ; but let our anxiety run in the right direction. Here is a mental heat ; let us apply it to some useful purpose. " Seek ye first the kingdom of God, and His righteousness." Seek *that* with all your care ; seek *that* with all your energy. Be anxious about *that*. Let your whole mind run in that direction with eagerness and thought. You cannot be too careful or too energetic when God and righteousness are concerned.

True religion ; what is it ? " *The kingdom of God.*" Without using a single superfluous theological term. I may say that the great God has always had a kingdom in this world. In the olden times He set up a kingdom amongst His people Israel, to whom He gave laws and statutes ; but now the Lord is King over all the world : "The God of the whole earth shall He be called." "The earth is the Lord's, and the fulness thereof ; the world, and they that dwell therein." God has a kingdom in this world, but it is too much neglected and forgotten of men. The first thing to be done by us is to enter that kingdom. Blessed is that man who has the Lord God to be his King, and has learned to order his life according to divine law. The highest liberty comes from wearing the yoke of God. The servant of men who dares not call his soul his own is a serf to be pitied ; but the servant of God, who fears nothing but sin, is a man of princely mould. We must stoop before God, that we may conquer among men. If we determine to yield ourselves wholly unto the Lord, we shall become influential among our fellow-men.

We can only enter into this kingdom of God by being born again of His Spirit ; for " except a man be born again, he cannot see the kingdom of God."   In that new birth we learn to submit ourselves to the Lord Jesus Christ, and to find in Him eternal life.   God has appointed the Lord Jesus heir of all things ; by Him also He made the worlds.   He says of Him, " Kiss the Son, lest He be angry, and ye perish from the way, when His wrath is kindled but a little." Faith in Christ casts our sins at His cross foot, and brings us an inward life unto holiness.   We must believe in Jesus, and trust in His great atonement for sin, for apart from His full atonement there is no salvation, and no true service of God.   This faith puts us into the kingdom of God ; for to " as many as received Him, to them gave He power to become the sons of God, even to them that believe on His name." The first anxiety of every man should be to be a loyal subject of the kingdom of God.

And when we feel that we are reconciled to God, and are under His supreme sway, our next object should be to continue there, and to become more and more completely obedient to divine rule, so that we may more fully enjoy every privilege of the kingdom. In the kingdom of God every man is a king and a priest.   He that serves God reigns.   He that serves God is the possessor of all things.   All things are ours when we are Christ's.

> " This world is ours, and worlds to come :
>   Earth is our lodge, and heaven our home."

Let the Christian seek to know to the full what is the heritage of the saints in Christ Jesus.

Our next business should be to spread that kingdom—to try to bring others under the dominion of Christ. It should be the lifework of each man to bring others to own to the sovereignty of the Lord Jesus. What opportunities most of you possess! Your station, your education, your wealth, all give you advantages for serving the Lord. Are you using them ? It is a great joy to the Christian minister to have about him a people who are missionaries in their daily lives. With great joy have I listened to some poor girl who has confessed her faith in Christ, and then has added very timidly, " There is another girl waiting outside who would like to speak to you. She works with me in a warehouse in the City, and I spoke to her, and she sought Jesus, and I believe she is converted." I fear that many men of position are less diligent in winning souls than the poor workers they employ. Should it be so ? He lives most and lives best who is the means of imparting spiritual life to others. May not some of you at the last come to a lonely end from lack of usefulness ? We heard, not long ago, of the shipwreck from which a mother was washed on shore, but found all her children drowned. She telegraphed to her husband two words. The first was very pleasing to his eye : " *Saved.*" The next was full of misery : " Saved *alone.*" Ah me ! would you or I like to have it so—" Saved alone "? God forbid. When we reach heaven-gate may we be able to say, " Here am I, and the children that Thou hast given me."

This is the meaning of that word—" Seek the kingdom of God." The reign of our Lord is to be our main object if we would lead a well-ordered, useful, happy, and honoured life.

BLESS THE LADS.

JOSEPH was one by himself. In Jacob's family he was like a swan in a duck's nest ; he seemed to be of a different race from the rest, even from his childhood. He was the son of old age, the son of the elders—that is, a child who was old when he was young, in thoughtfulness and devotion. He reached an early ripeness, which did not end in early decay. In consequence of this, Joseph was one by himself in the peculiarity of his trials. Through his brothers' hatred of him he was made to suffer greatly, and at last was sold into slavery, and underwent trials in Egypt of the severest kind. "The archers have sorely grieved him, and shot at him, and hated him." But, see the recompense ; for he had blessings which were altogether his own. "His bow abode in strength, and the arms of his hands were made strong by the hands of the mighty God of Jacob." He was as distinguished by the favour of God as by the disfavour of his brethren. When Jacob is old and about to die, Joseph gave him a blessing all to himself, in addition to that which he received with his brothers. In the forty-ninth chapter of Genesis we read, "Gather yourselves together, and hear, ye sons of Jacob ; and hearken unto Israel your father." And they did so, and received as a family such blessings as their father's prophetic eye foresaw ; but before this, "by faith Jacob blessed the two sons of Joseph" at a private interview specially granted to

them. Had not his tribulations abounded, his con-
solations would not have so abounded. Do you seem
yourself to be marked out for peculiar sorrows? Do
the arrows of affliction make your life their target,
and are you chastened above all other men? Do not
be regretful, for the arrows are winged by covenant
love, which designs by their wounds to prepare you
for a special work which will lead up to a special
benediction from your Father who is in Heaven.

Jacob blessed Joseph, and we perceive that he
blessed him through blessing his children. Joseph
is doubly blessed by seeing Ephraim and Mannaseh
blessed. Dear young people, your fathers can
say, "We have no greater joy than this, that our
children walk in the truth." If any of you who are
unconverted knew the deep searching of heart of
your parents about you, I think you would not long
be careless and indifferent about Divine things; and
if you could conceive the flashes of heavenly joy that
would light up your parents' hearts if they saw you
saved in the Lord, it would be an inducement to you
to consider your ways, and turn unto the Lord with
full purpose of heart. God Himself, next to giving
to His chosen the covenant of grace, can do them no
greater earthly kindness than to call their children by
His grace into the same covenant. Will you not
think of this?

Young men and women usually feel great interest
in their father's life-story—if it be a worthy one—and
what they hear from them of their personal experience
of the goodness of God will abide with them. We
all read biographies, and we value the results of
experience which we find there, but the biographies of

our own relatives are peculiarly treasured ; and when these biographies are not read, but spoken, what wonderful force they have ! I recollect in my younger days hearing a minister, blind with age, speak at the communion table, and bear witness to us young people, who had just joined the church, that it was well for us that we had come to put our trust in a faithful God ; and as the good man, with great feebleness and yet with great earnestness, said to us that he had never regretted that he had given his heart to Christ as a boy, I felt my heart leap within me with delight that I had such a God to be my God. His testimony was such as a younger man could not have borne : he might have spoken more fluently, but the weight of those eighty years at the back of it made the old man eloquent to my young heart. We who are growing grey in our Master's service ought not to be backward to speak well of His name. You will not be able to do so much good in Heaven as you can on earth, for they all know about it up there ; but men here need our witness to the God whom we have tried and proved. Let us make occasions in which we may speak well of the Lord, even the God who has fed us all our life long, and redeemed us from all evil. This is one of the best ways in which to bless the lads. The benediction of Jacob was intertwisted with his biography ; the blessing which he had himself enjoyed he wished for them, and as he invoked it he helped to secure it by his personal testimony.

One thing further : I want you to note that *Jacob, in desiring to bless his grandsons, introduced them to God.* He speaks of " God, before whom my fathers

did walk: God who blessed me all my life long."
This is the great distinction between man and man:
there are two races—he that feareth God, and he that
feareth Him not. The religion of this present age,
such as it is, has a wrong direction in its course. It
seeks after what is called " the enthusiasm of
humanity," but what we want far more is enthusiasm
for God. We shall never go right unless God is first,
midst, and last. I despair for benevolence when it is
not based upon devotion. We shall not long have
love to man if we do not first and chiefly cultivate
love to God. What boys need in starting in life is
God; if we have nothing else to give them, they
have enough if they have God. What girls want
in quitting the nurture of home, is God's love in their
hearts, and whether they have fortunes or not, is a
small matter. In fellowship with God lies the essence
of true human life: life in God, life by the knowledge
of the Most High, life through the Redeeming Angel
—this is life indeed.

Jacob died as one who had been delivered from all
evil—ay, even the evil of old age. His eyes were dim;
but that did not matter, for his faith was clear. I
love to think that we are going where our vision of
God will not be through the eye, but through the
spiritual perceptions. These were brighter in Jacob
in his old age than ever before; his faith and love,
which are the earthly forms of those perceptions, were
apprehending God in a more forcible manner than ever,
and it therefore signified little that the eyes which
he would need no longer were failing him. We cannot say that he was in decay, after all; for he was
losing what he only needed in this world of shadows,

and was gaining fitness for the higher state. His
gracious faculties grew as his bodily faculties declined;
and therefore he felt that his life was ending in a
fulness of blessing such as he wished for the children
of his dearest son. How ardently do I wish the like
blessing for all young people! The Lord God
Almighty bless you! When your earthborn faculties
fail, may heavenly graces more than supply their
place!

"God, before whom my fathers Abraham and Isaac
did walk." As with a pencil he sketches the lives of
Abraham and Isaac. He does not fill in with
colouring, but the outline is perfect; you see the two
men in their whole career in those few words. They
were men who recognized God and worshipped Him
beyond all others of their age. God was to them a
real existence; they spake with God, and God spake
with them; they were friends of God, and enjoyed
familiar acquaintance with Him. No agnosticism
blinded their understandings, and deadened their
hearts. They were worshippers of the one living and
true God. Happy children who have such fathers!
Happier children who are like such fathers!

They not only recognized God, but *they owned Him
in daily life.* I take the expression, "God, before
whom my fathers Abraham and Isaac did *walk*," to
mean that He was their God in common life. They
not only knelt before God when they prayed, but they
walked before Him in everything. When they went
forth from their tents, and when they returned from
their flocks, they walked before God. They were
never away from His service, or without His presence.
He was their dwelling-place. Whether they sojourned

under an oak or dwelt by a well, whether they enter-
tained strangers or walked in the field to meditate,
they lived and moved in God. This is the kind of
life for you and for me : whether we live in a great
house or in a poor cottage, if we walk before God we
shall lead a happy and a noble life, whether that life
be public, or obscure. Oh, that our young people
would firmly believe this !

They walked before God ; that is, *they obeyed His
commands*. His call they heard, His bidding they
followed. Abraham quitted country and kindred to
go to an unknown land which God would show him ;
yea, more, he took his son, whom he greatly loved, and
stood prepared to sacrifice him at God's command.
Isaac also yielded himself up to be slain, if so
Jehovah willed. To them the will of the Lord was
paramount : He was law and life to them, for they
loved and feared Him. They were prompt to hear
the behests of God, and rose up early to fulfil them.
They acted as in the immediate presence of the
All-seeing.

To the full they trusted Him. In this sense they
always saw Him. *We* sometimes talk about *tracing*
Him. We cannot trace Him, except as we trust
Him ; and because they trusted, they traced Him.
Notwithstanding all the danger and difficulty of their
pilgrim state, they dwelt in perfect security in an
enemy's land, for the Lord had said, "Touch not Mine
anointed, and do My prophets no harm." They were
serene and tranquil because they walked before God,
knowing Him to be their friend, and that He was
their shield and their exceeding great reward. For
temporal things they had no anxiety, for they lived

upon the All-sufficient God. Therefore these two men, Abraham and Isaac, though much tried, led peaceful lives: they conversed with Heaven, while they sojourned on earth.

They enjoyed the favour of God, for this also is intended by walking before Him. His face was towards them : they sunned themselves in His smile. God's love was their true treasure. We read that God had blessed Abraham in all things, and of Isaac we hear even the Philistines say, "We saw certainly that the Lord was with thee." God was their wealth, their strength, their exceeding joy. I say again, happy sons who have such ancestors! Happier still if they follow in their track!

So Jacob spoke of Abraham and Isaac, and so can some of us speak of those who went before us. Those of us who can look back upon godly ancestors now in Heaven must feel that many ties bind us to follow the same course of life. Had they transgressed against the Lord our duty would have caused us to quit the ways of the family, even as Abraham left his kindred who dwelt on the other side of the flood ; but as their way was right, we are doubly called to follow it, because it is the good old way, and the way our godly fathers trod. There is a charm about that which was prized by our fathers. Heirlooms are treasured, and the best heirloom in a family is the knowledge of God. When I spoke, the other day, with a Christian brother, he seemed right happy to tell me that he sprang of a family which came from Holland during the persecution of the Duke of Alva, and I felt a brotherhood with him in claiming a like descent. I daresay our fathers were poor weavers, but

I had far rather be descended from one who suffered for the faith than bear the blood of all the emperors within my veins. There should be a sacredness to young people in the faith for which their ancestors suffered. Choose not the society of Egypt, and its wealth and honours, but keep to the stock of Israel, and claim the inheritance of Jacob, as Ephraim and Manasseh did. Let it not be said that as your family increased in riches it departed from the living God. Shall the goodness of God be perverted into a reason for apostasy?

The way of holiness in which your fathers went is a fitting way for you, and it is seemly that you maintain the godly traditions of your house. In the old times they expected sons to follow the secular calling of their fathers; and although that may be regarded as an old-world mistake, yet it is well when sons and daughters receive the same spiritual call as their parents. Grace is not tied to families, but yet the Lord delights to bless to a thousand generations. Very far are we from believing that the new birth is of blood, or of the will of the flesh, or of the will of man. The will of God reigns here supreme and absolute; but yet there is a sweet fitness in the passing on of holy loyalty from grandsire to father, and from father to son. I like to feel that I serve God " from my fathers." If our fathers were wrong we ought boldly to dissent from them, and obey God rather than man; but where they are right we are bound to follow them. I stood in a sort of dream as I gazed upon my much-beloved grandfather's place of sepulture. I was encouraged by seeing the record of his fifty-four years of service in the midst of one

church and people, and I rejoiced that, could he
rise from the dead, he would find his grandson
preaching that self-same old-fashioned and much-
despised Calvinistic doctrine of the grace of God,
which was his joy in life and his comfort in
death.

A godly ancestry casts responsibility upon young
people. These Ephraims and Manassehs perceive
that their fathers knew the Lord, and the question
arises, Why should they not know Him? Beloved
young friends, the God of your fathers will be found
of you and be your God. The prayers of your
fathers have gone before you ; let them be followed
by your own. Be hopeful of being heard at that
mercy-seat where they found grace to help in every
time of need. They died in the hope that you would
fill their places ; shall not their hopes become facts?
Do I speak to some who have godly parents in
Heaven, and yet they are themselves pursuing the
ways of sin or of worldliness? Registered upon that
file are your mother's prayers. I trust they will yet
be heard. Even now they stand like a hedge about
you, making it hard work for you to go to hell. Will
you force your way to perdition over a father's grave?
Will you, by a desperate effort, push aside your
pleading mother's form, and pursue your dreadful
road to ruin? If so, you will involve yourselves
in tremendous guilt. I beseech you hear the
tender voice of love which now invites you to
be blest !

A godly ancestry should invest a man's case with
great hopefulness. May he not argue, " If God
blessed my ancestors, why should He not bless me?

If they sought mercy, and found it, why should not I?
My father and my mother were not perfect, any more
than I am ; but they had faith in God, and He
accepted them and helped them. If I have faith in
God He will accept me, and be faithful to me.
They were saved as sinners trusting in the blood of
Jesus, and why should not I ? " I beseech you put
this argument to the test, and you will find it hold
good.

JACOB, A YOUNG WORKING MAN.

JACOB had been a shepherd, and therefore he knew what shepherding included : the figure is full of meaning. There had been a good deal of Jacob about Jacob, and he had tried to shepherd himself. Poor sheep that he was, while under his own guidance he had been caught in many thorns, and had wandered in many wildernesses. Because he would be so much a shepherd to himself, he had been hard put to it. But over all, despite his wilfulness, the shepherding of the covenant God had been exercised towards him, and he acknowledged it.

Our Version rightly says that the Lord had *fed* Jacob all his life long. Take that sense of it, and you who have a daily struggle for subsistence will see much beauty in it. Jacob had a large family, and yet they were fed. Some of you say, " It is all very well of you to talk of Providence who have few to provide for." I answer, it is better still to talk of Providence where a large household requires large provision. Remember Jacob had thirteen children, yet his God provided them bread to eat and raiment to put on. None of that large company were left to starve. You think, perhaps, that Jacob was a man of large estate. He was not so when he began life. He was only a working man, a shepherd. When he left his father's house he had no attendants with camels and tents. I suppose he carried his little

21

bit of provision in a handkerchief, and when he laid down that night to sleep, with a stone for his pillow, the hedges for curtains, the heavens for his canopy, and the earth for his bed, he had no fear of being robbed. God was with him ; apart from this, he had nothing to begin life with but his own hands. Whatever he received from his father Isaac afterwards, he had at first to fight his own way ; but he knew no lack either at the beginning or at the end, for he could speak of the great Elohim as "the God which fed me all my life long." Hundreds of us can say the same. I remember one who came to be wealthy who used to show me with great pleasure the axle-tree of the truck in which he used to wheel his goods through the streets when he began in business : I liked to see him mindful of his original. Mind you do not go and say, "See how I have got on by my own talents and industry!" Talk not so proudly, but say, "God hath fed me." Mercies are all the sweeter when seen to come from the hand of God.

But besides being fed Jacob had been *led*, even as sheep are guided by the shepherd who goes before them. His journeys, for that period, had been unusually long, perilous, and frequent. He had fled from home to Padan-aram ; after long years he had come back again to Canaan, and had met his brother Esau ; and after that, in his old age, he had journeyed into Egypt. To go to California or New Zealand in these times is nothing at all compared to those journeys in Jacob's day. But he says, "God has shepherded me all my life long" ; and he means that the great changes of life had been wisely ordered. At home and in exile, in Canaan and in Goshen, God had been a shepherd to him. He sees the good hand of God upon him in all his wanderings, until he now finds himself sitting up on his bed and blessing Joseph through his sons. I am glad that he went into detail with these young men, for they needed to be confirmed in their fidelity to God. They were in a perilous condition, for they had the *entrée* of the rank and fashion of Egypt, and were tempted to forsake the poor family of the Hebrews. Some young fellows begin where their fathers left off, and having the means of self-indulgence, are apt to follow the fashions and frivolities of the period. Oh that the Holy Spirit may make you feel that you want God with wealth as much as your fathers needed God without wealth! You may come to beggary yet with all your inheritance, if you cast off the fear of the Lord and fall into sin. You who begin life with nothing but your own brains and hands, trusting in your father's God, shall yet have to sing as your fathers sang, "the God which fed me all my life long." Young men and young women beginning life, I charge you seek first the kingdom of God and His righteousness! It is not life to live without God : you miss the kernel, the cream, the crown of life if you miss the presence of God. Life is but a bubble, blown up of toil and trouble, without God. Life ends in blighted hope if you have not hope in God. But with God you are as a sheep with a shepherd—cared for, guided, guarded, fed, and led, and your end shall be peace without end.

Bear with me while I follow Jacob in his word upon redeeming mercies. "The Angel which redeemed me from all evil." There was a mysterious Personage who was God, and yet the Angel or messenger of God. He puts this Angel in apposition with the Elohim : for this Angel was God. Yet was He his Redeemer. He saw Him doing the office of the next-of-kin : though God He was his *goel,* and as His kinsman, effected redemption for him. Jacob's faith enabled him, like Job, to know that his Redeemer liveth. He saw that this covenant messenger had redeemed him from all evil, and he magnified the name of the Lord who revealed Himself in this Angel. When he was in his sorest straits, this redeeming Angel always interposed. He fell into an evil state through the influence of his mother, and he did Esau serious wrong. He fled for his life, and at that time there was a great gulf between him and God. Then that Angel came in, and bridged the gulf with a ladder by which he might rise to God. The kinsman, God, came in, and showed him how the abyss might be crossed, so that he might return to his God. When he was away in Padan-aram he began to sink very low, while chaffering with churlish Laban. Then again the Angel came and said, " Get thee out from this land, and return unto the land of thy kindred." The Redeeming Angel held back wrathful Laban, and when Esau came to meet him in hot anger the Angel specially appeared to Jacob. The Angel wrestled, as a Man, with Jacob to get Jacob out of Jacob, and raise him into Israel. How marvellous was the redemption which was wrought for him that night at Jabbok ! Jacob came forth from the conflict halting, but he walked before the Lord far better than before. That same mysterious Person had bidden him go down into Egypt with the promise that He would go down with him. It was the Angel of God's presence who held His shield over Jacob, and preserved him from all evil.

Jacob has spoken of ancestral mercies, personal mercies and redeeming mercies, and now he deals with future mercies, as he cries, "*Bless the lads.*" He began with blessing Joseph, and he finishes with blessing his lads. O dear friends, if God has blessed you, I know you will want Him to bless others. There is the stream of mercy, deep, broad, and clear ; you have drunk of it, and are refreshed, but it is as full as ever. It will flow on, will it not? You do not suppose that you and I have dammed up the stream so as to keep it to ourselves ? No, it is too strong, too full a stream for that. It will flow on from age to age. God will bless others as He has blessed us. Unbelief whispers that the true church will die out. Do not believe it. Christ will live, and His church will live with Him till the heavens be no more. Hath He not said, "Because I live, ye shall live also "? "Oh," you say, "but we shall not see such holy men in the next generation as in past ages." Why not? I hope the next age will see far better men than any of those who are with us at this time. Pray that it may be so. Instead of the fathers, may there be the children, and may these be princes before the Lord !

The stream of Divine grace will flow on. Oh, that it may take sons and daughters in its course ! "*Bless the lads.*" Sunday-school teachers, is not that a good prayer for you? Pray the Lord to bless the lads and the lasses, because He hath blessed you.

We need not say in what precise form or way the blessing shall come : let us leave it in all its breadth

of inconceivable benediction.   May the Lord bless
our youth as only He can do it; and if He causes
them to fear and trust Him, He will be blessing all of
us, and blessing ages to come.   Upon these Ephraims
and Manassehs will depend the work of the Lord in
the years to come !   Therefore, with emphasis we pray,
" Bless the lads "   As for us, we are content to work
on, saying, " Let Thy work appear unto Thy servants " ; but our anxious desire is that our children
may reap the result of our labours, and therefore we
add, " and Thy glory unto their children."

In Essex, I took the opportunity to visit the place
where my grandfather preached so long, and where I
spent my earliest days.   I walked like a man in a
dream.   Everybody seemed bound to recall some
event or other of my childhood.   What a story of
Divine love and mercy did it bring before my mind !
Among other things, I sat down in a place that must
ever be sacred to me.   There stood in my grandfather's manse garden two arbours made of yew trees,
cut into sugar-loaf fashion.   Though the old manse
has given way to a new one, and the old chapel has
gone also, yet the yew trees flourish as aforetime.   I sat
down in the right-hand arbour and bethought me of
what had happened there many years ago.   When I was
staying with my grandfather, there came to preach in
the village Mr. Knill, who had been a missionary at
St. Petersburg, and a mighty preacher of the gospel.
He came to preach for the London Missionary
Society, and arrived on the Saturday at the manse.
He was a great soul-winner, and he soon spied out
the boy.   He said to me, " Where do you sleep ? for
I want to call you up in the morning."   I showed him

my little room. At six o'clock he called me up, and we went into that arbour. There, in the sweetest way, he told me of the love of Jesus, and of the blessedness of trusting in Him and loving Him in our childhood. With many a story he preached Christ to me, and told me how good God had been to him, and then he prayed that I might know the Lord and serve Him. He knelt down in that arbour and prayed for me with his arms about my neck. He did not seem content unless I kept with him in the interval between the services, and he heard my childish talk with patient love. On Monday morning he did as on the Sabbath, and again on Tuesday. Three times he taught me and prayed with me, and before he had to leave, my grandfather had come back from the place where he had gone to preach, and all the family were gathered to morning prayer. Then, in the presence of them all, Mr. Knill took me on his knee, and said, " This child will one day preach the gospel, and he will preach it to great multitudes. I am persuaded that he will preach in the chapel of Rowland Hill, where (I think he said) I am now the minister." He spoke very solemnly, and called upon all present to witness what he said. Then he gave me sixpence as a reward if I would learn the hymn—

> " God moves in a mysterious way
> His wonders to perform."

I was made to promise that when I preached in Rowland Hill's Chapel that hymn should be sung. Think of that as a promise from a child! Would it ever be other than an idle dream? Years flew by. After I had begun for some little time to preach in

London, Dr. Alexander Fletcher had to give the
annual sermon to children in Surrey Chapel, but as
he was taken ill, I was asked in a hurry to preach to
the children. " Yes," I said, " I will, if the children
will sing ' God moves in a mysterious way.' I have
made a promise long ago that so that should be sung."
And so it was : I preached in Rowland Hill's Chapel,
and the hymn was sung. My emotions on that
occasion I cannot describe. Still, that was not the
chapel which Mr. Knill intended. All unsought by
me, the minister at Wotton-under-Edge, which was
Mr. Hill's summer residence, invited me to preach
there. I went on the condition that the congregation
should sing, " God moves in a mysterious way "—
which was also done. After that I went to preach
for Mr. Knill himself, who was then at Chester.
What a meeting we had ! Mark this ! he was
preaching in a theatre ! His preaching in a theatre
took away from me all fear about preaching in secular
buildings, and set me free for the campaigns in Exeter
Hall and the Surrey Music Hall. How much this
had to do with other theatre services you know.

> " God moves in a mysterious way
> His wonders to perform."

After more than forty years of the Lord's loving-
kindness, I sat again in that arbour ! No doubt it is
a mere trifle for outsiders to hear, but to me it was an
overwhelming moment. The present minister of
Stambourne Meeting-house, and the members of his
family, including his son and his grandchildren, were
in the garden, and I could not help calling them
together around that arbour, while I praised the Lord

for His goodness. One irresistible impulse was upon me : it was to pray God to bless those lads who stood around me. Do you not see how the memory begat the prayer? I wanted them to remember when they grew up my testimony of God's goodness to me ; and for that same reason I tell it to young people. God has blessed me all my life long, and redeemed me from all evil, and I pray that He may be your God ! You who have godly parents, I would specially address. I beseech you to follow in their footsteps, that you may one day speak of the Lord as they were able to do in their day. Remember that special promise, " I love them that love Me ; and those that seek Me early shall find Me." May the Holy Spirit lead you to seek Him ; and you shall live to praise His name as Jacob did !